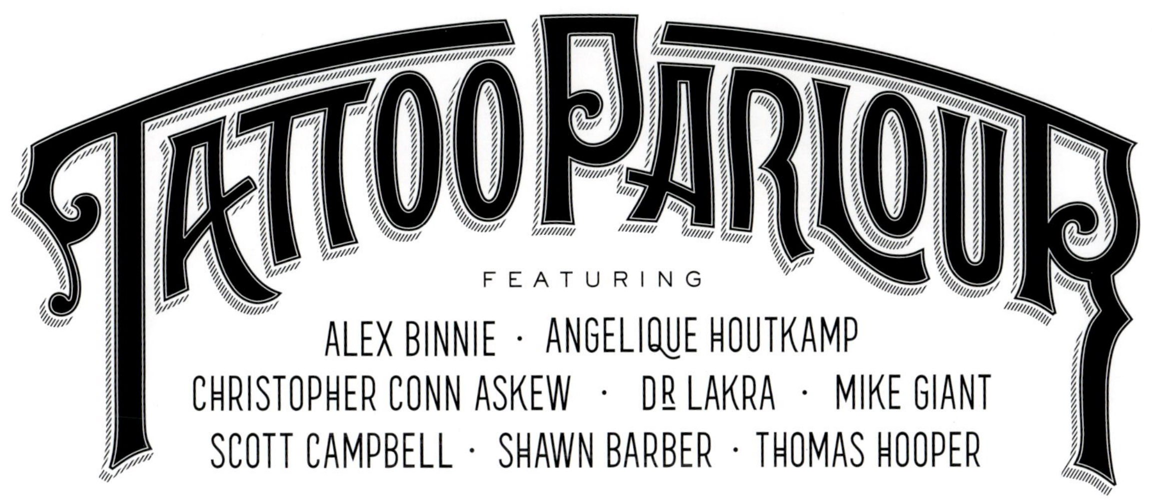

Tattoo Parlour

FEATURING

ALEX BINNIE · ANGELIQUE HOUTKAMP
CHRISTOPHER CONN ASKEW · DR LAKRA · MIKE GIANT
SCOTT CAMPBELL · SHAWN BARBER · THOMAS HOOPER

Artists from the World of Tattoo

EDITED BY
MARTIN McINTOSH AND GEMMA JONES

FOREWORD BY
CARLO McCORMICK

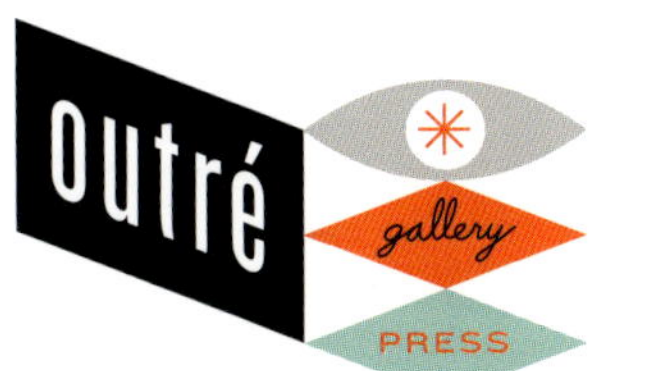

"Tattoo Parlour: Artists from the World of Tattoo"

Alex Binnie – www.alexbinnie.com
Angelique Houtkamp – www.salonserpent.com
Christopher Conn Askew – www.sekretcity.com
Dr Lakra – www.kurimanzutto.com
Mike Giant – www.mikegiant.com
Scott Campbell – www.scottcampbelltattoo.com
Shawn Barber – www.sdbarber.com
Thomas Hooper – www.meditationsinatrament.com

ISBN 978-0-9577684-3-7 – softcover – 2nd printing – August, 2012
ISBN 978-0-9577684-5-1 – numbered limited edition hardcover

Editors: Martin McIntosh and Gemma Jones
Foreword: Carlo McCormick
Artist texts: Gemma Jones
Layout and typesetting: Trevor Slabak
Cover design: Corey Simons – www.thefold.com.au

Photography credits:
Alex Binnie artwork photography by Cliff Trail – www.clifftrail.co.uk
Alex Binnie studio photography by Alex Wilson – www.awilsonphotographic.com
Angelique Houtkamp portrait/studio photography by fotofloor – Mike & Floor – www.fotofloor.com
Christopher Conn Askew portrait by Jon Dragonette – www.dragonettephotography.com
Dr Lakra studio/outdoor photography by Christel Rachinger
Mike Giant, Scott Campbell, & Shawn Barber portrait/studio photography by Stephen Doan & An Pham
Thomas Hooper portrait/studio photography by Seldon Hunt – www.seldonhunt.com

Thank you to:
All the artists, Greg Escalante, Mindy Liu, Amelia Hinojosa, Carlo McCormick, Trevor Slabak, Kristine Anstine, Colin Turner, everyone at Last Gasp, Claire Thompson, Saraid Banahan, Jessie Jean Steger, Matthew Gordon, Nick Edwards, CHR James, An Pham, Christel Crumpet, Anita Rivera, Pip Lincolne, Sass Cocker, Edward Janssen, Tom Supple, Shannon Michael Cane, and Louise McIntosh

Outré Gallery Staff
Jessica Steger, Erik Hecht, Gordon Doan, Megan van der Heyden, Holly Lander, Corey Simons, Leroi Waddington, Nate Day, Apple Bagios

Printed by Prolong Press, China

Outré Gallery Press titles are distributed in the US by
Last Gasp
777 Florida St, San Francisco, CA 94110, USA
www.lastgasp.com

Distributed in the UK and Europe by Turnaround Publisher Services
Tel: 020 8829 3002 / email: orders@turnaround-uk.com

Distributed in Australia by Thames & Hudson Australia

Published by Outré Gallery Press
G.P.O. Box 5442
Melbourne
VIC 3001
AUSTRALIA
www.outregallery.com

CONTENTS

TATTOO ART AND THE BODY POLITIC

BY CARLO McCORMICK

It is hard to imagine any medium that is at once so ancient and contemporary as tattooing. With the oldest known example, Ozli The Iceman discovered in the Alps between Austria and Italy at over five thousand years old, tattoos span the world and the centuries as recorded in ancient cultures ranging from the Egyptian, Greek and Roman to the Persian, Celt and Viking. The relatively recent resurgence of tattoos as a coded language of youth culture is now so prevalent that it is almost easy to lose track of how remarkable such a historical translation this actually is. So exceptional is this post-primitive recontextualization, the equivalent we might presume would be as if kids suddenly began doing cave paintings.

As the revival of tattoo art began in the last decades of the 20th century, it rapidly went from the underground to mainstream recognition. It is worth bearing in mind here that its contemporary genesis is one very much born in the moment of post-modernism. That is, tattoos are emblematic of a wider condition in which meaning is appropriated and mediated out of preexisting forms. This sense that one's own self-expression could be cobbled together from a lineage of images already out there has made this art inherently malleable and hybrid. The history of imagery, styles and meanings now processed by contemporary tattoos is situational and relative. Iconography now is a matter of pastiche, both ironic in its appropriation and yet utterly sincere in its recontextualization.

Within a milieu where the composite of one's self is conjured from multiple sources rather than some emblematic generational definition, absolute signification has been lost, or at least temporarily misplaced. So to sport a classic pin-up image rendered in circa 1930s lines, any number of religious talismanic tropes from the Virgin of Guadalupe to the Rock of Ages, or even for that matter to opt instead for some manner of pop culture reference, is not necessarily to ascribe wholly to its original meaning. Rather it is more a matter of adopting and adapting its highly redolent references as a manifestation of a more personal construction of one's own idiosyncratic identity. Whatever people may now wear on their skin, for us to read it properly we must accept that these decisions are done as much with hand on heart as tongue in cheek. This is not to imply that anyone has become overly casual about selecting what he or she will have on their body for the rest of their natural days (poor decisions may still be made in misguided spontaneity, but proportionally hardly more so than when tattoos were the province of drunken sailors and servicemen) but it is to acknowledge that this pictorial language is far more riddled with ambiguity and multiplicity than ever before.

In this fractured deviation and derivation of signs we are not talking about an outright abandonment or abnegation of meaning so much as a flexibility and fluidity to how iconography is read in an age of surfeit images. What is significant in this, is that where relativist subjectivity takes precedence over absolutist objectivity, and where emotions and ideas are allowed the vaguer dimensions of ambivalence, we enter a more complex realm of aesthetic interpretation, or simulation, that is best suited to artists. If you want to produce an icon of inevitable consequence you give the job to a skilled craftsman, but if you prefer instead a more diffusive iconography of open-ended and variable implication, well, you best ask an artist for that. This it would seem is the commonality that binds the work collected here in *Tattoo Parlour*. It's not to say that as a kind of genre there is no room left for the literal in tattoos, only to suggest that within this larger specie of creative expression there is a strain of poetics that defies the specifics of a singular reading.

Tattoos almost invariably offer a narrative, a story that is anecdotally entertaining but rarely complete. The problem is that, though it is a collaborative process between the client who has some idea of what they want and the artist they commission who often makes myriad and far more significant decisions regarding the rendering of this image, it is typically the wearer rather than the creator who speaks for the work. Most dedicated aficionados will be able to tell you who actually made their tattoo, but still the tale of the ink will be about where and when they got it, and why – what it means to them. Nothing terribly wrong with that, such is the vanity of the patron, but what about the hand and vision that brings this work to life? To allow our understanding of this medium to be defined by those who sweat and squirm half-naked under the gun as a canvas to the creation of others is the dubious equivalent of asking the owners of art to speak for the artists. And if you've never had the pleasure of listening to art collectors talk about what they have, trust us on this one, there is absolutely nothing more trivializing to the meaning and magic of creative process. This book thankfully tells the other side of this story from some of the very best out there. Compelling as it may be to think about why some individuals choose to illustrate their bodies, the sum of their reasons collectively do not add up to the curious alchemy by which any one artist chooses apply themselves to so culturally marginalized a medium.

It is certainly problematic, if not outright perilous, to describe or define any number of artists by some single commonality. The outstanding are unique enough that they defy such generalization, and benefitting from their own explanations as to the how and why of their work as we do here, there is not all that much more to add. Because however this is not simply a collection of tattoo art like the many that have already seen print, but is rather a more involved document about the other kinds of work that is done in the studio – distinct from, yet symbiotically connected to their practice as tattoo artists – it does beg consideration of some fundamental comparisons. To state the obvious, not everyone who does tattoos rises to the level of what we would call an artist. This is not merely conditional on the usual terms by which we make such distinctions – the quality of craft or the virtue of the vision – but is more dependent on the even more elusive terms of intent. The eight artists included here are trying to do more than make tattoos, they are trying to innovate, and in doing so have conjoined the imagery, skills and vernacular of tattooing to the particular language and lineage of fine art.

What is notable in the broader oeuvre of Shawn Barber, Alex Binnie, Scott Campbell, Christopher Conn Askew, Mike Giant, Thomas Hooper, Angelique Houtkamp and Dr Lakra is, going both ways, how much the fine art informs the tattoo work and conversely how much their studio practice is similarly informed by their tenure as tattoo artists. Mostly we find they are artists first, compelled to make images from an early age and ultimately arriving at their work in tattoos by some combination of fiscal day-job practicality and their own fascination with the medium and its history. This is significant not only because, unlike typical tradesmen who end up in some form of commercial image making with the uninspired ethic of wage earners, these are creative spirits who have quite deliberately sought out the challenges of working on flesh, but also because artists are by nature migratory in their pursuits, rarely committing solely to a single mode of expression – as evidenced here by the wide array of visual media they have explored outside the tattoo parlour. It is to this latter aspect of their work, the wealth of material from drawings and paintings to all manner of print techniques and even sculptural objects that we must pay some final attention. Not only does such work situate them as artists who do more than toil over the bodies of others and subject themselves to demanding clients, but quite uncannily they are consistently and unmistakably the works of tattoo artists.

The hybridity of this art as something that could as easily be placed in a gallery as on a body is its most appealing quality. It is also endemic to what it means to be a tattoo artist today. Much like other subcultural niches that have similarly spawned a generation of fine artists, such as comics and graffiti, what these figures bring to the art world is a remarkable capacity to convey the immediacy and urgency of a youth-driven vernacular within the more contemplative and nuanced rarified experience of what it means to look at a picture on the wall. Yes, these artists speak to both their formal training in the craft of tattooing (along with its historical redolence in the criminal, carnie, and outsider undergrounds) and the strategies of contemporary art (in many cases acquired in art school), but they also address a fuller scope of experiences and references, including not merely the aforementioned comics underground and graffiti movements but so much else ranging from skateboarding, street culture, burlesque, body modification and fantasy to the music they listen to. This mélange of meanings and associations is not particular to these artists nor even tattoo art but, more importantly to the times in which we live. What they express – perhaps far better than most – is the way in which their patrons and most of us in general have had our attitudes, styles, politics and aesthetic sensibilities deeply impacted by an unruly assortment of cultural tendencies. In this way tattoo art has come to work on something more than the human form itself – wholly inscribing the body politic of our age.

Carlo McCormick is a New York based pop culture critic, curator and Senior Editor of Paper magazine.

ALEX BINNIE

Born – 1959
Hometown – Oxford, England
Study / Apprenticeship – Fine Art degree. Self taught tattooer
Lives and Works – London and Brighton, UK
Years as a tattooist – 23 years
Favourite medium – tattooing and printmaking

Alex Binnie is an artist and a craftsman with an overarching fascination with the body, and as such it makes logical sense that he has carved his professional life as a tattooist and printmaker.

From the get go, Alex was magnetically attracted to the few tattooed people that crossed his path as a youngster.

"I was fascinated by tattoos from my early teens, there were very few in my family though, my mother's cousin had one. Remember this was in the 70's in rural England, there wasn't much to be seen. I remember seeing them on the "tough" boys that worked the funfair that came through our small town, I was hooked."

And at 17 he got his first tattoo, a small rose on his forearm.

With the dream of being a tattooist always in his mind, Binnie detoured via art school where he was involved in body oriented performance art (for all the radical and messy associations tied to it); and then via a job as a medical illustrator.

This broad experience in understanding the body, in drawing and in thinking as an artist have informed his long career as a tattooist and printmaker. Binnie has immersed himself in the processes of tattoos and printmaking as a way to drive and direct his work.

"Tattooing being essentially a craft has taught me to be able to get my head down and work! A big tattoo is a lot of hard, focused work, and that has helped me to be able to get down for a whole day and make these woodcuts, which require a similar level of concentration and hours."

For Binnie the closeness of printmaking and the craft of tattooing makes perfect sense. The use of ink. The finite commitment of mark making. The hand-madeness. As he says, "The wood, or skin, is cut, and the ink makes it absolute."

His large monochrome woodcut portraits on delicate paper are tributes to his heroes – fellow tattoo artists and colleagues, "These prints then work on two primary levels – they are a social document of some of the people surrounding me; and a contemporary exploration of a somewhat neglected medium."

These portraits are best seen in context as part of their place in the larger set of 32 prints, and in person, to appreciate their fine detail and inimitable handmade quality.

At home, Binnie can be found sitting Japanese-style at a low desk surrounded by his well tamed collection of tattoo books, 18th and 19th century prints of tattooed people (mostly from the Pacific), tribal art, medical curiosities and more art.

Since that first rose tattoo, Binnie's body has become a walking salon of international practitioners (and non-tattooers too), with work by over 50 different people including Horiyoshi 3, Bob Roberts, Leo Zulueta and even his own kids.

"I regard my self as an artist who enjoys to to work in different mediums, tattooing is still my bread and butter however, and my first 'real love' and I'm fine with that."

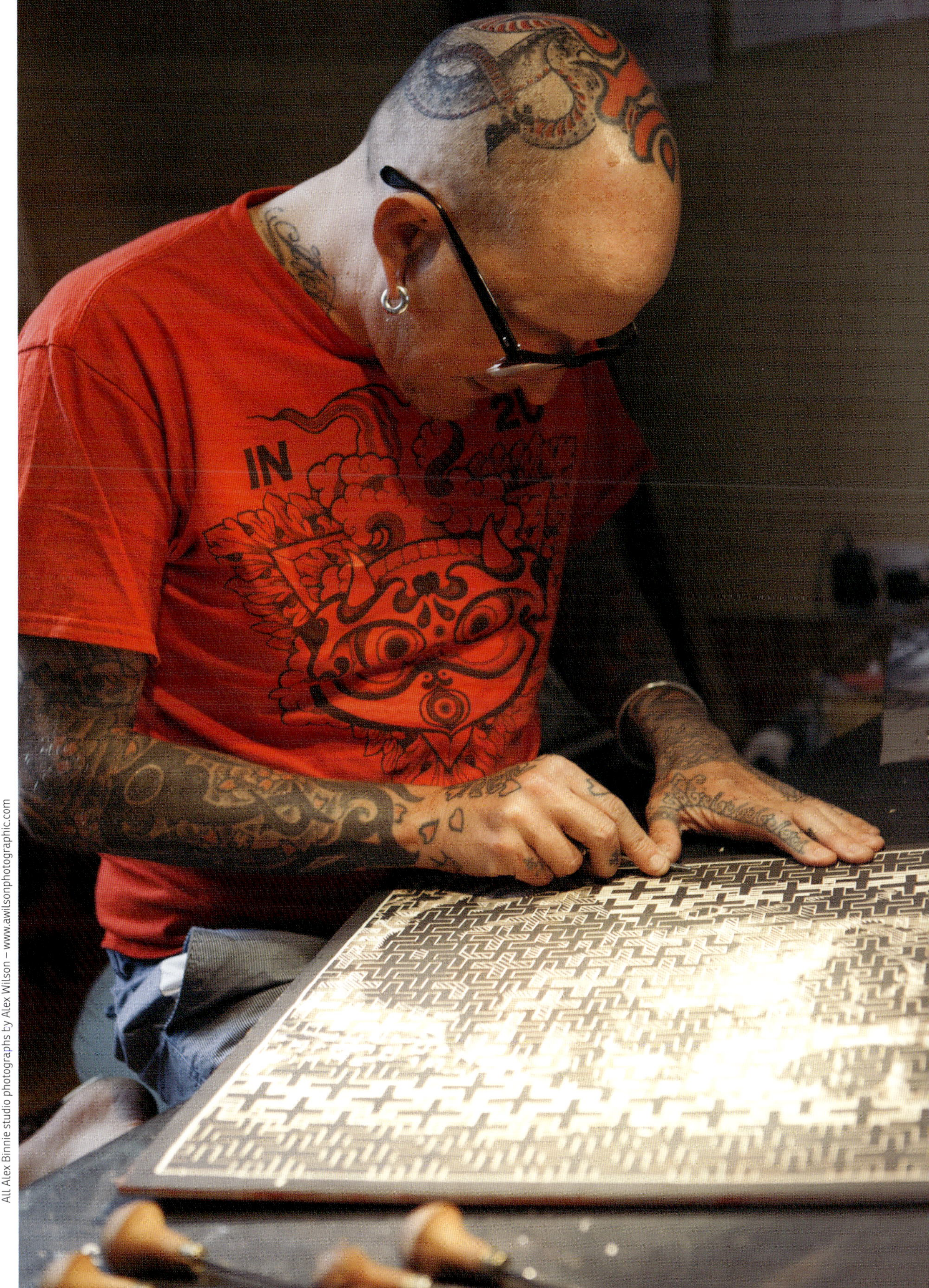

All Alex Binnie studio photographs by Alex Wilson – www.awilsonphotographic.com

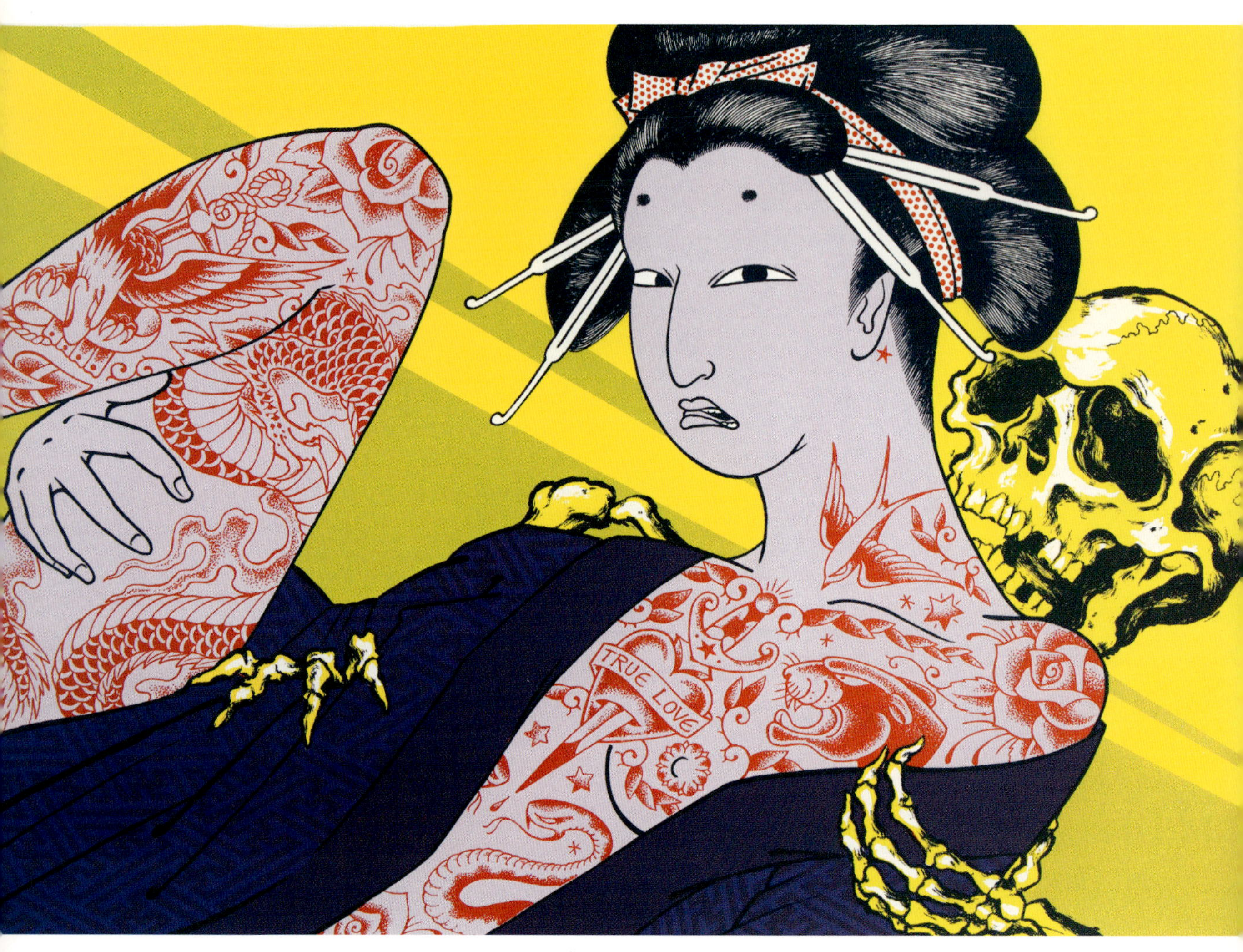

Alex Binnie, True Love, 2007, screen print, 45 x 65cm

(opposite)
(top left) **Alex Binnie**, An I for an Eye, 2009, screen print, 65 x 45cm
(top right) **Alex Binnie**, Madonna and Child, 2008, screen print, 65 x 45cm
(bottom left) **Alex Binnie**, Ground Zero, 2008, screen print, 65 x 45cm
(bottom right) **Alex Binnie**, Lady Grinning Soul, 2009, pencil and coloured pencil, 75 x 55cm

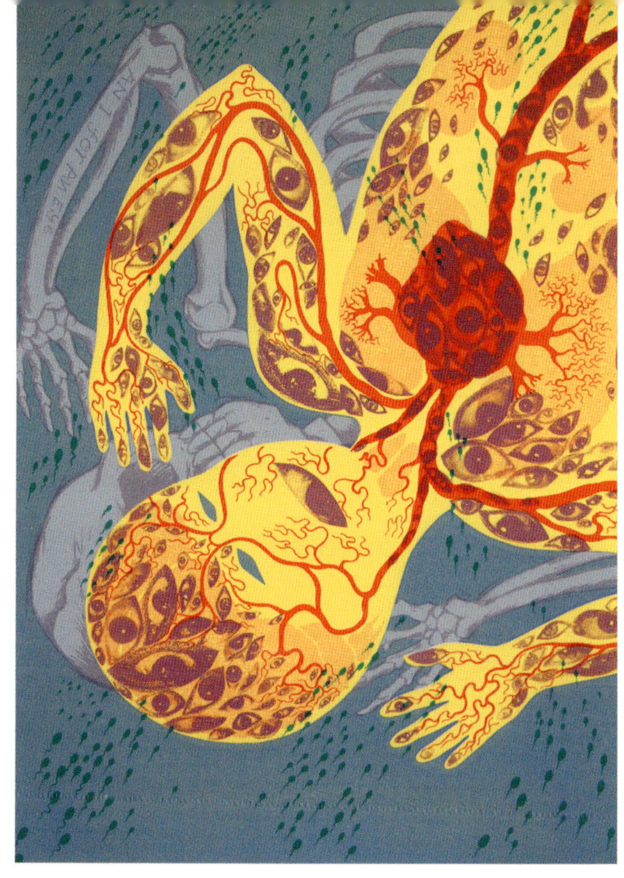
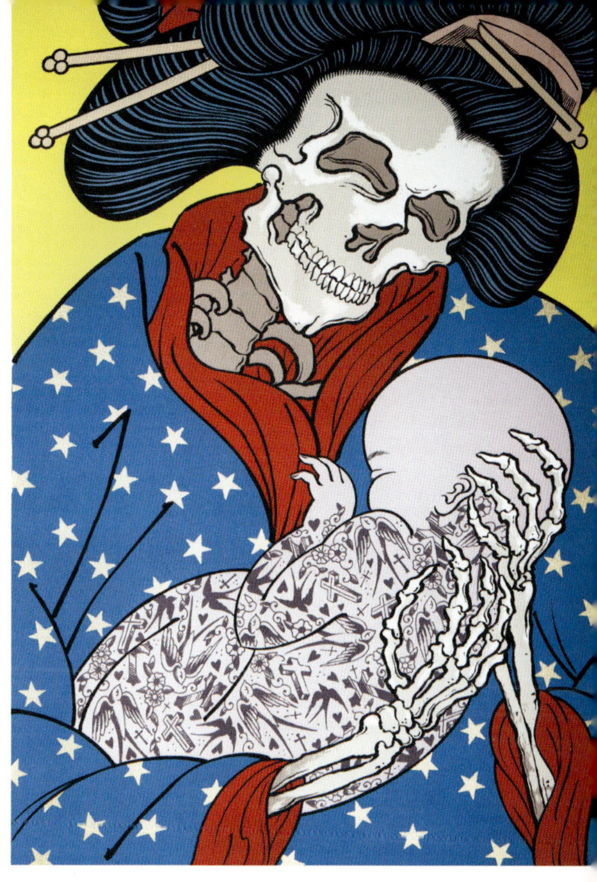
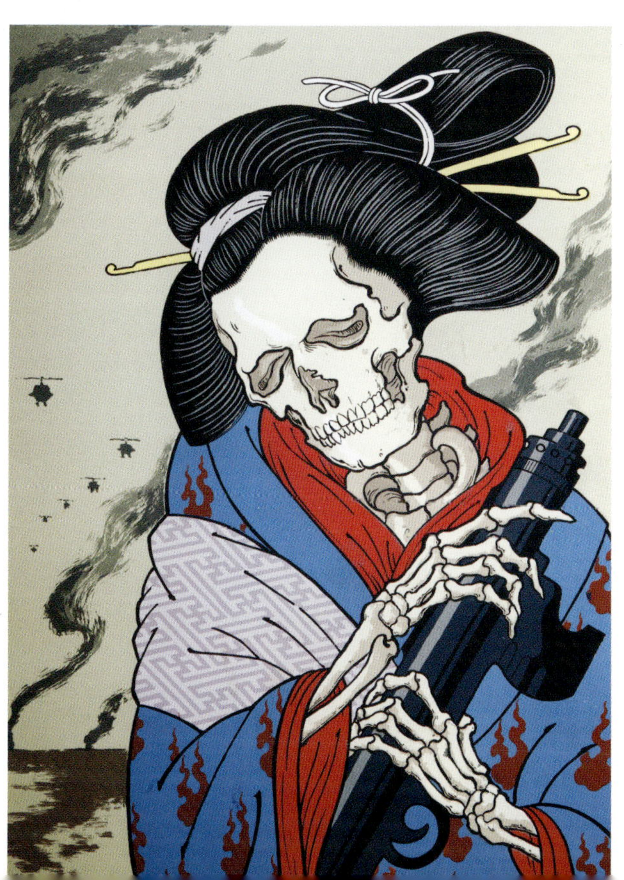
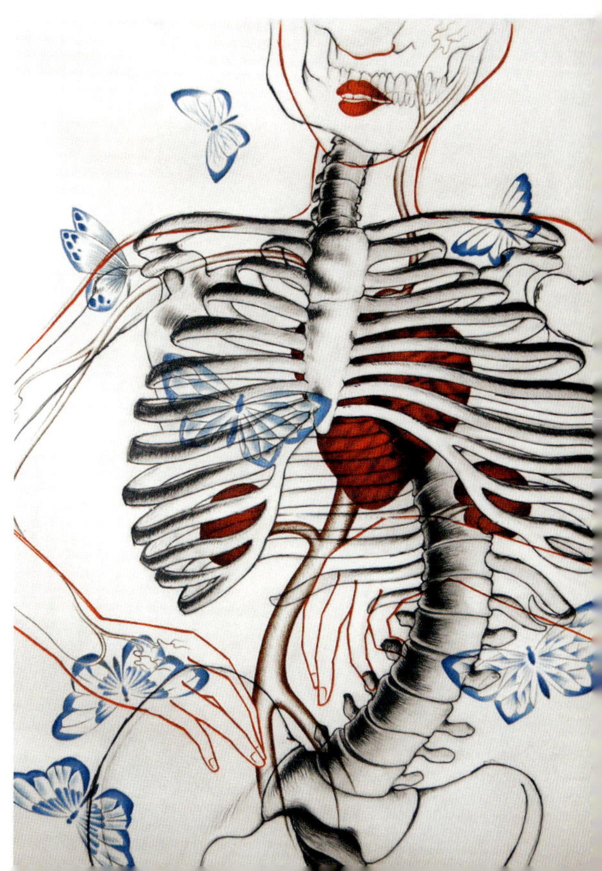

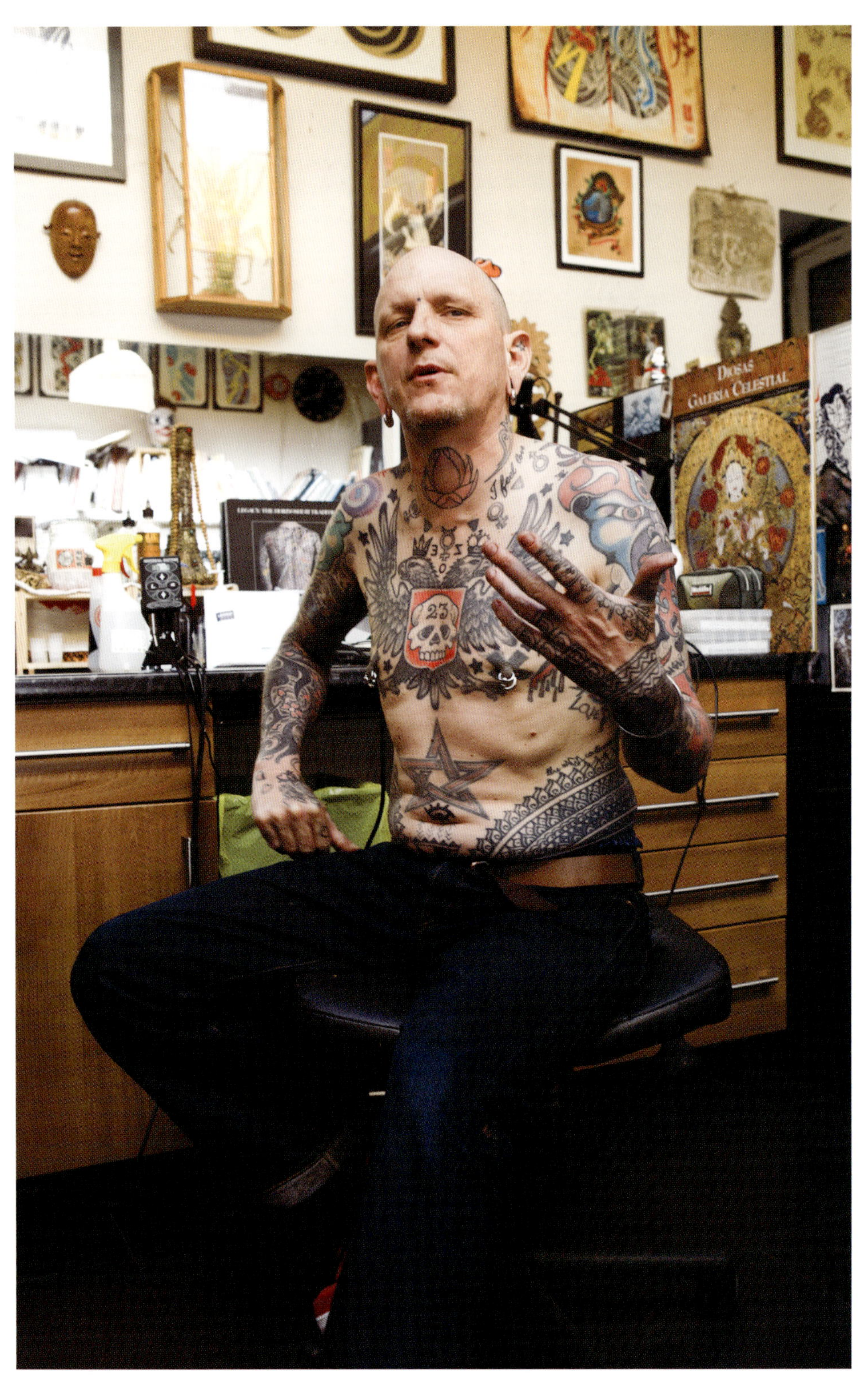

(opposite)
Alex Binnie, Me,
2010, woodcut,
60 x 45cm

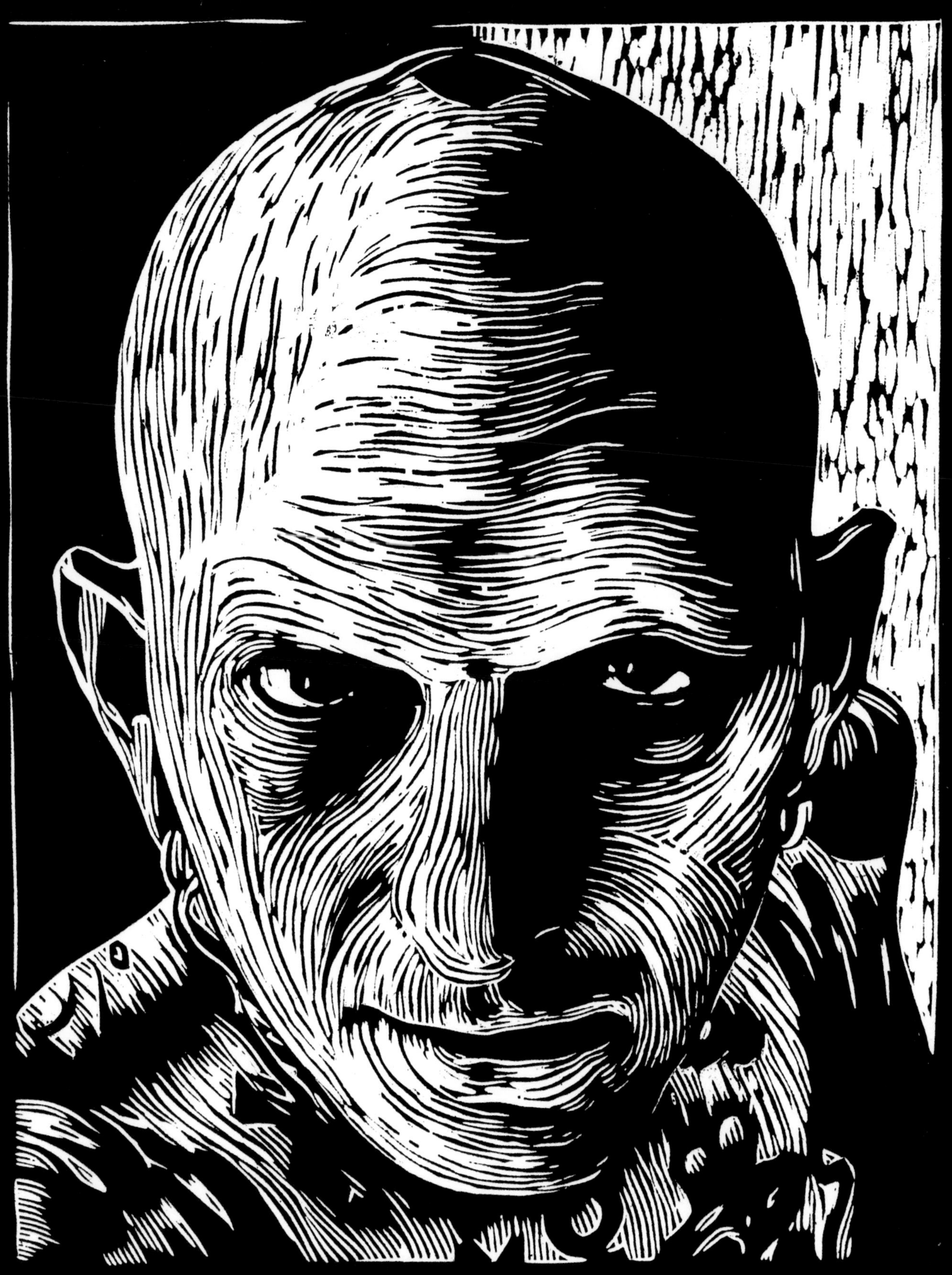

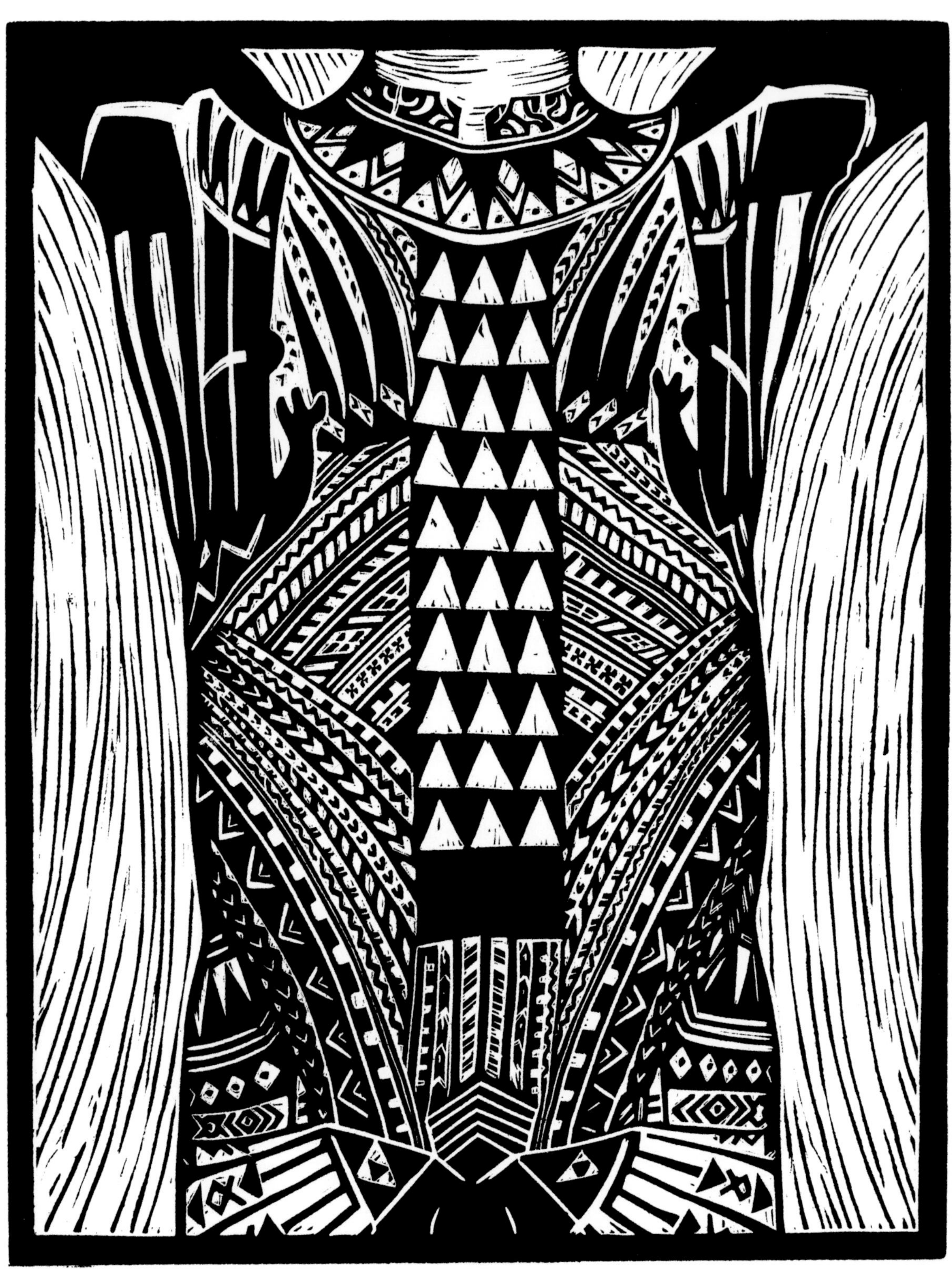

Alex Binnie, Croc, 2010, woodcut, 60 x 45cm

(opposite) **Alex Binnie**, Duncan, 2010, woodcut, 60 x 45cm

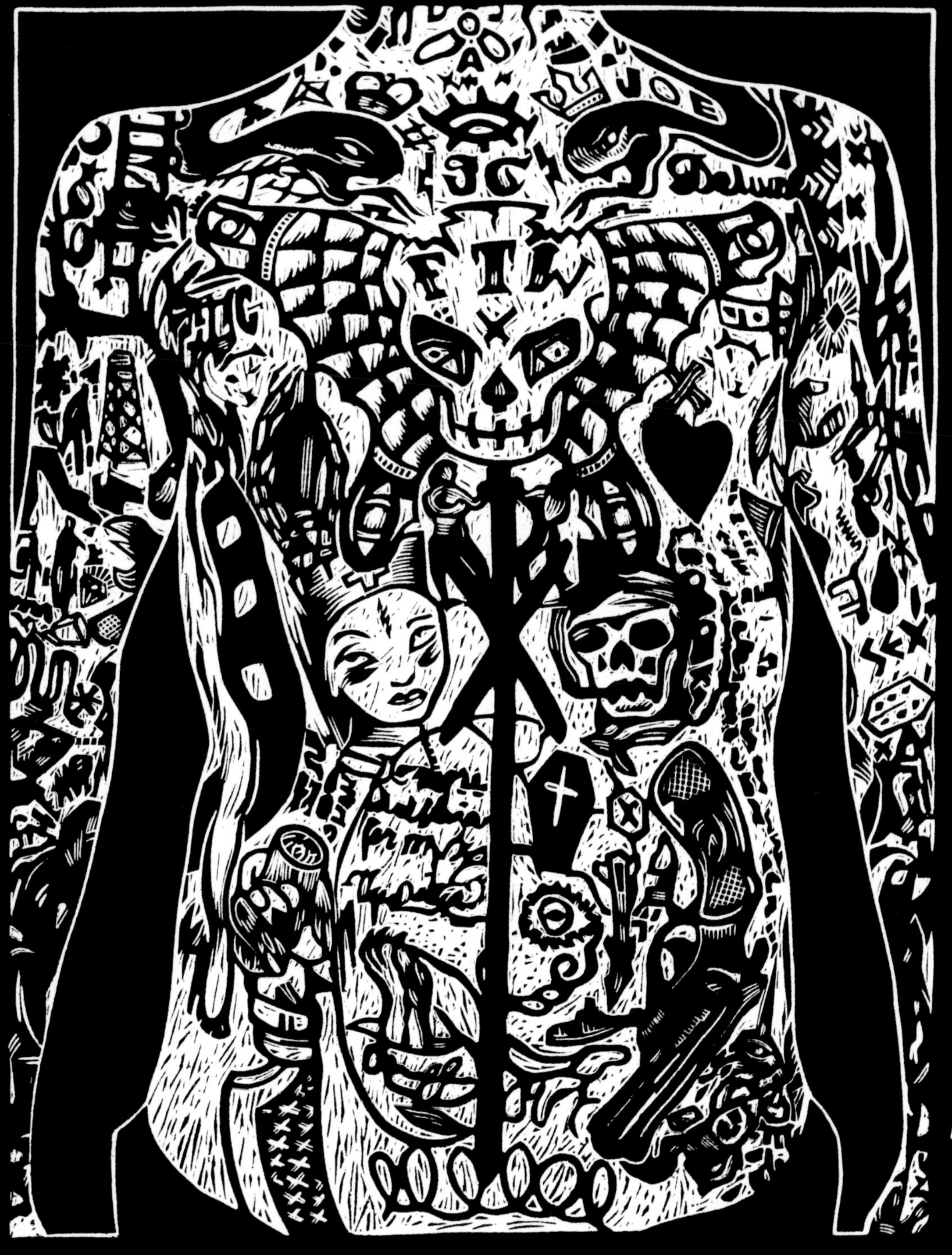

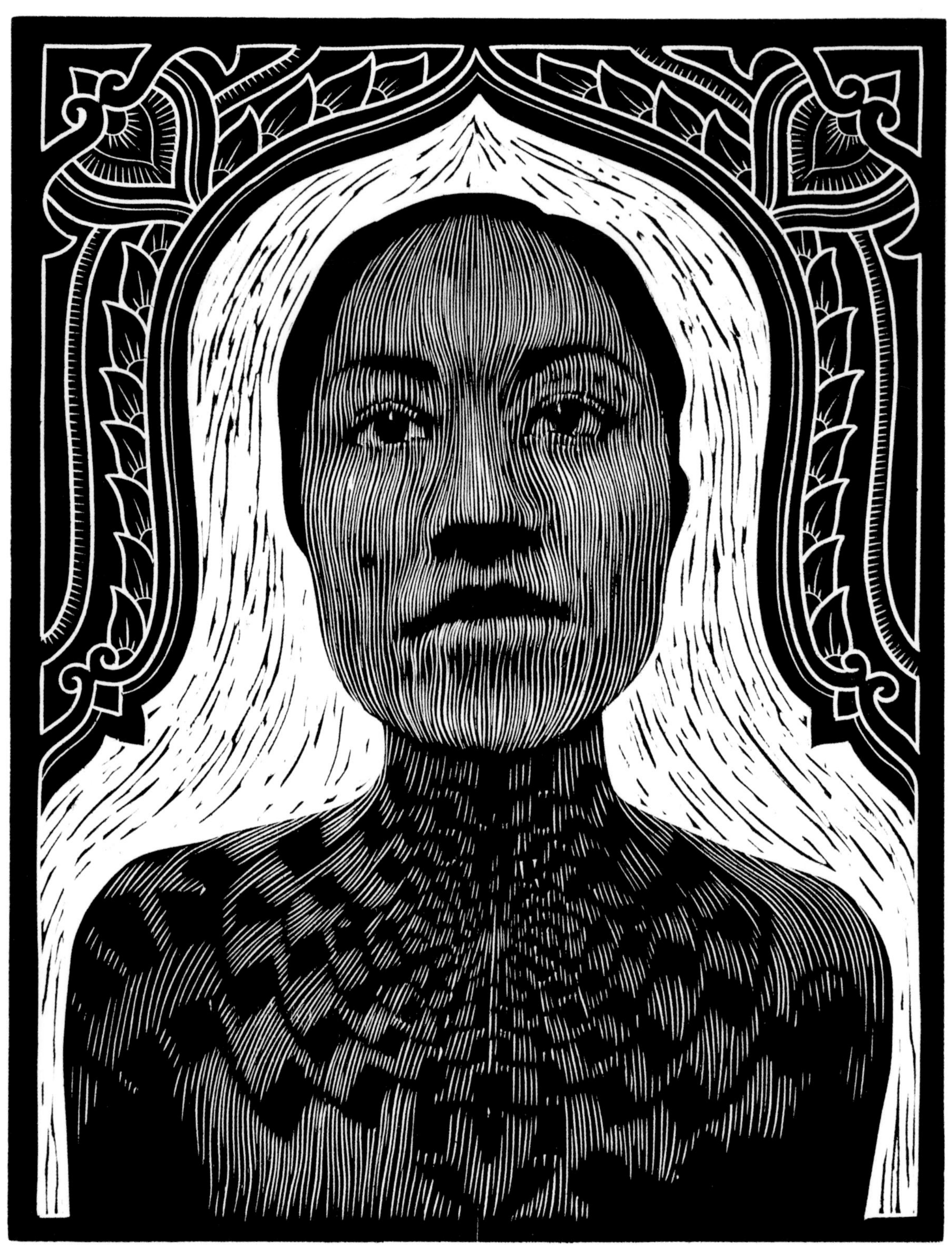

Alex Binnie, Alex, 2011, woodcut, 60 x 45cm

(opposite) **Alex Binnie**, Khan, 2010, woodcut, 60 x 45cm

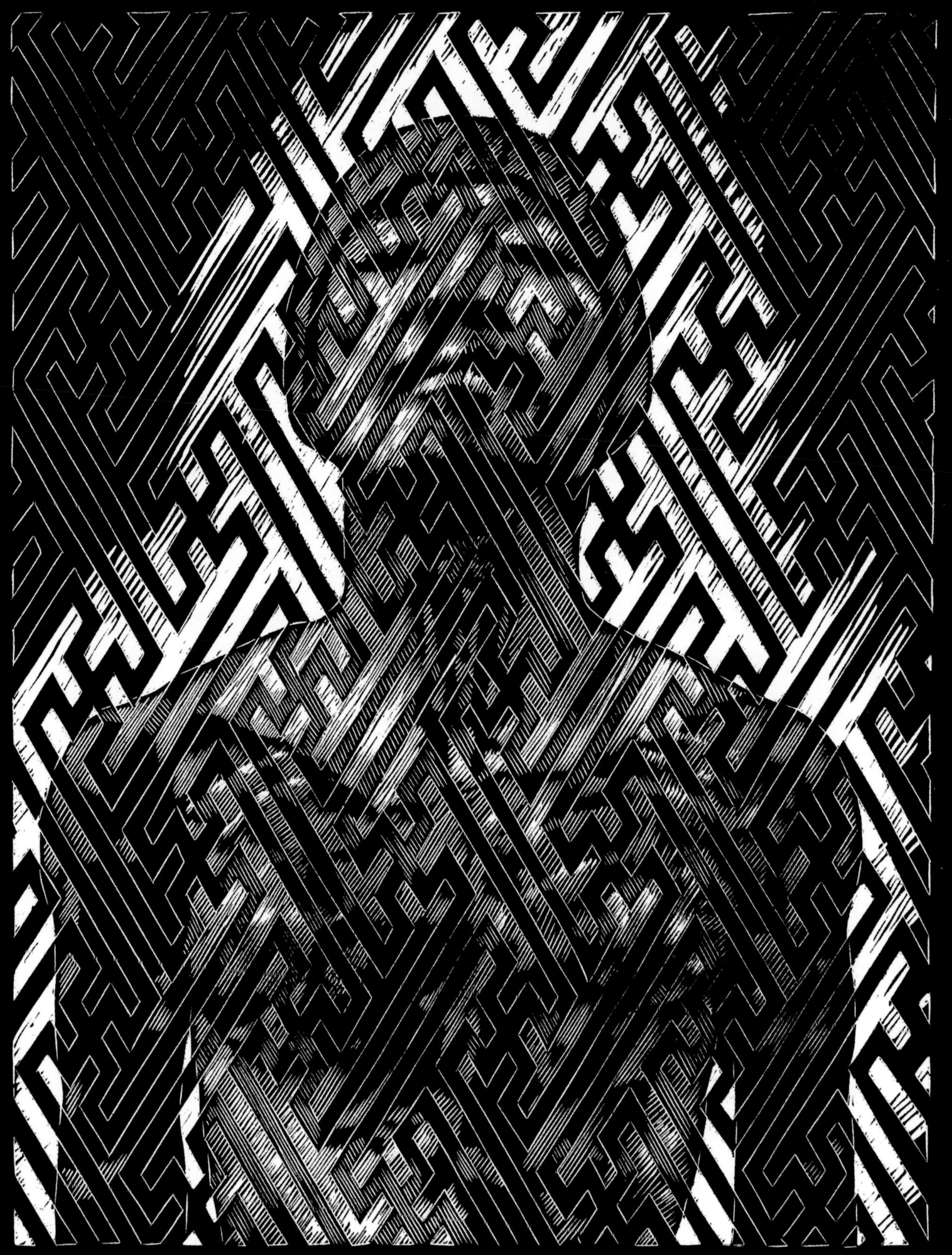

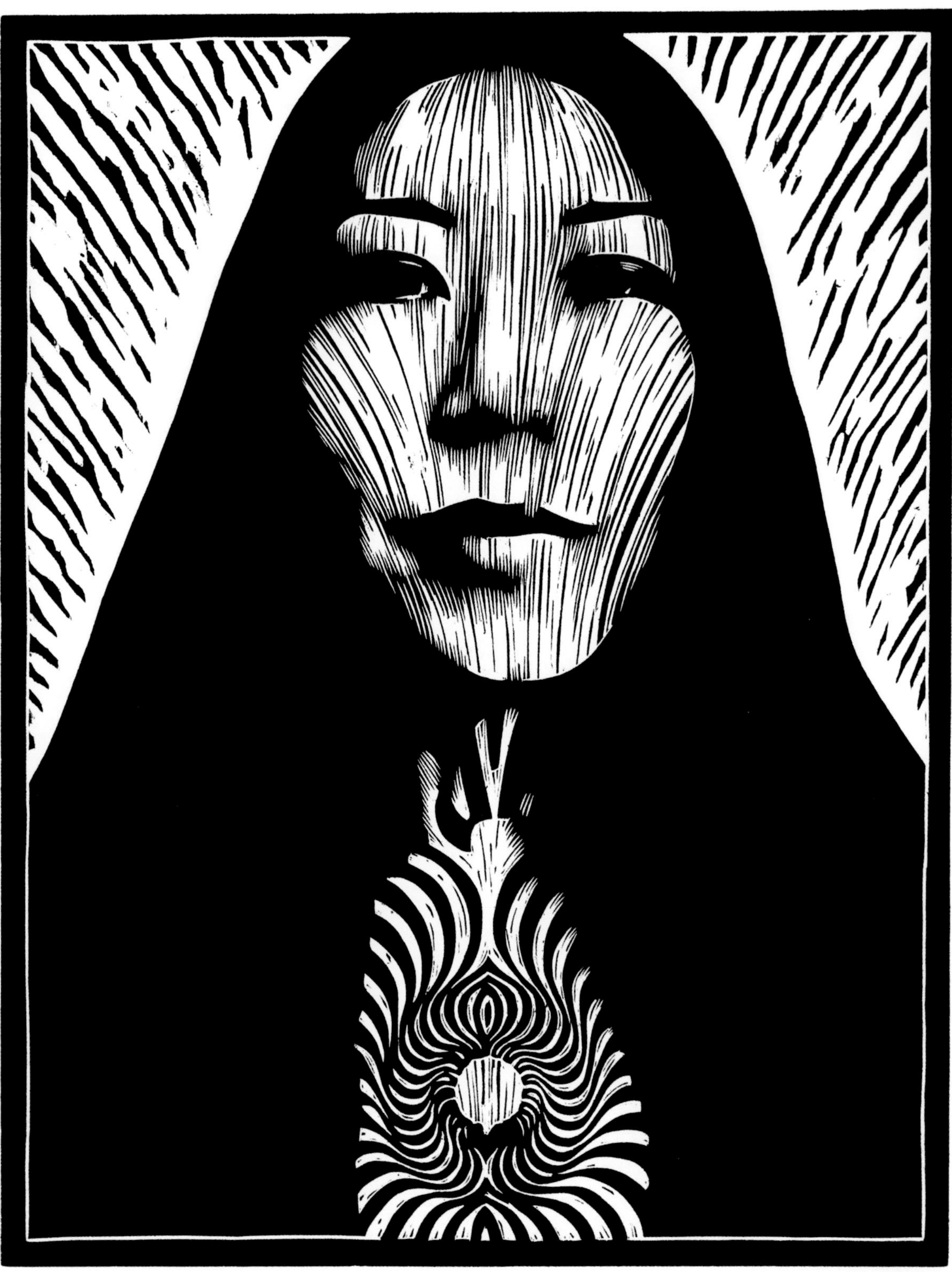

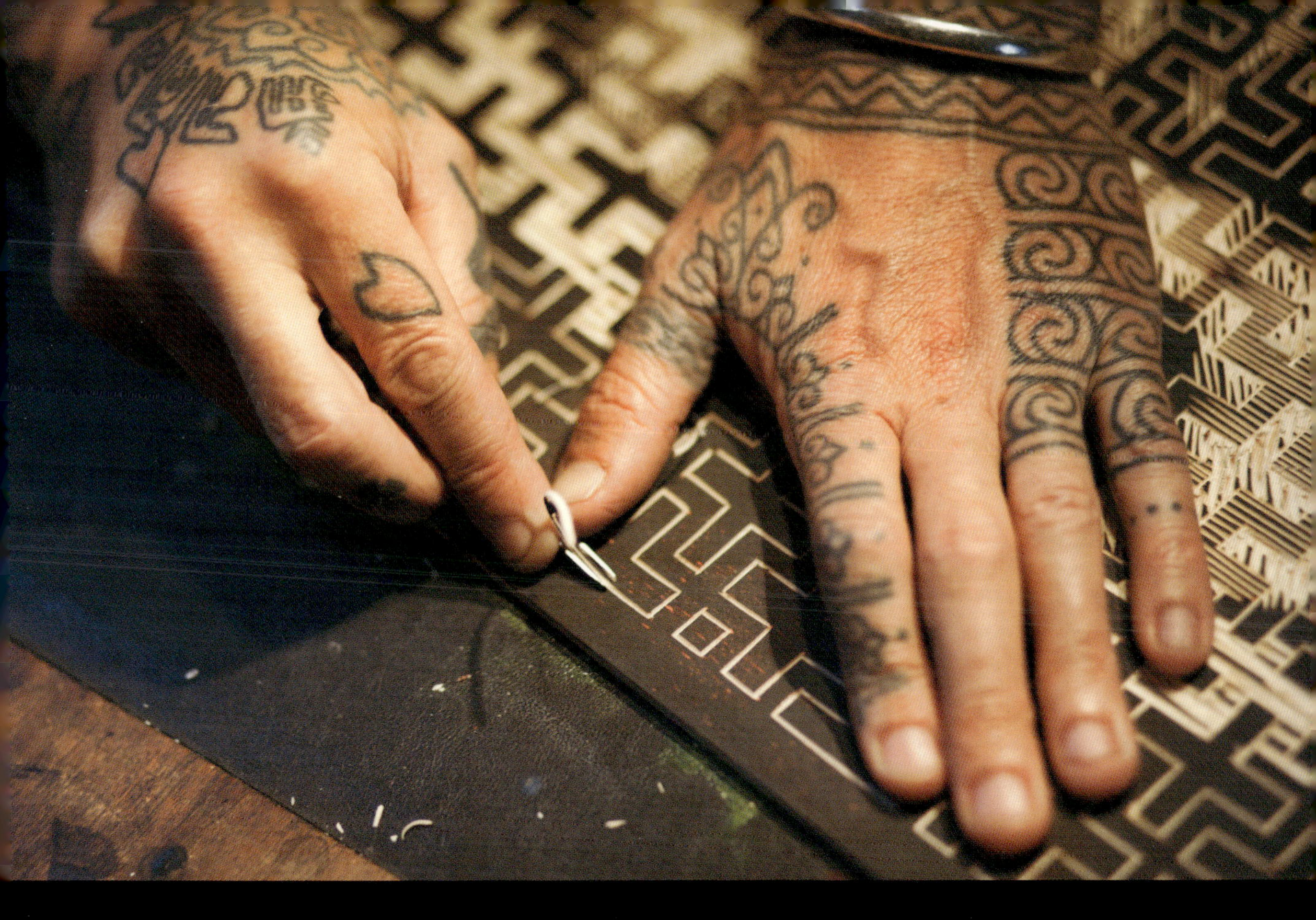

(opposite) **Alex Binnie**, Chisaki, 2011, woodcut, 60 x 45cm

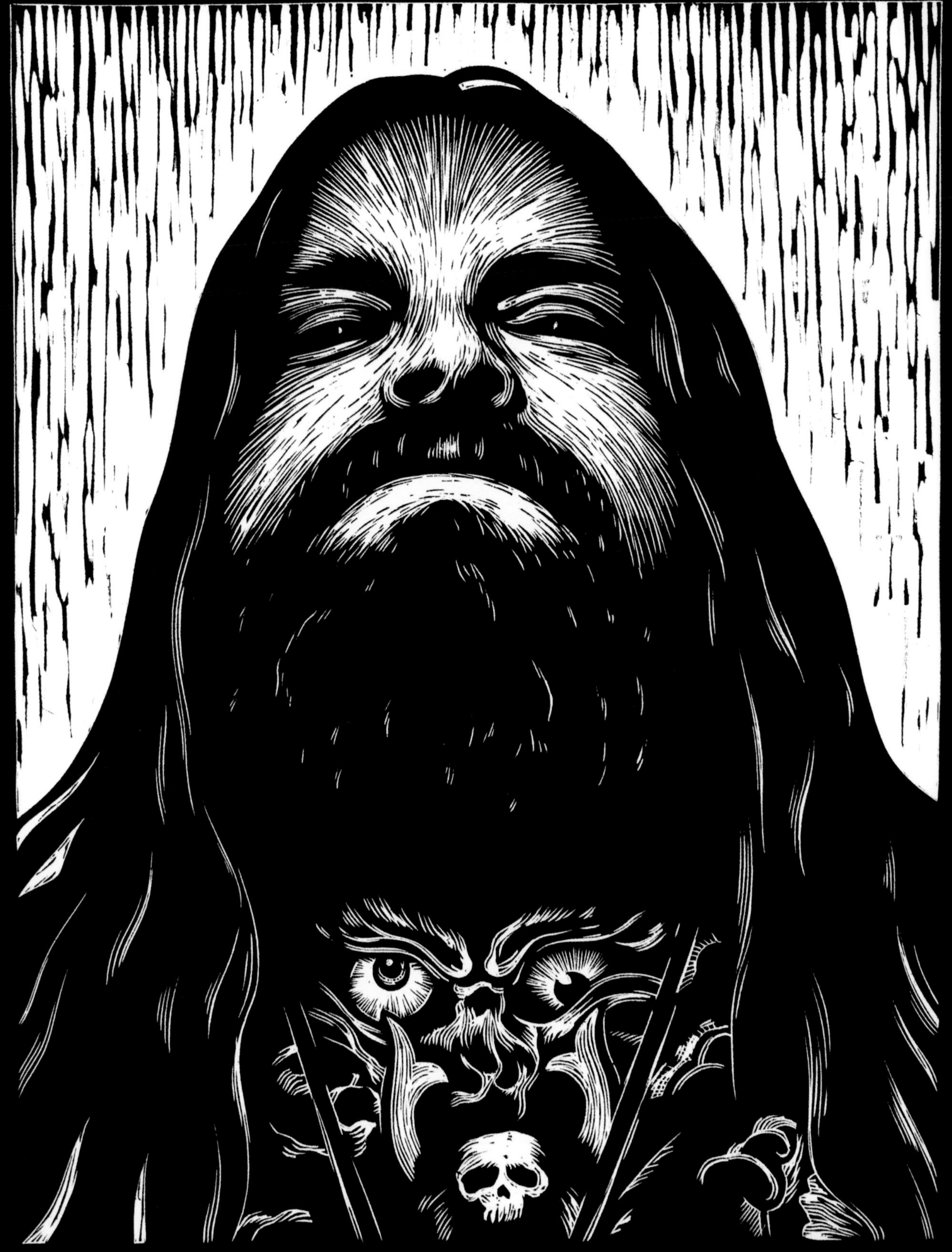

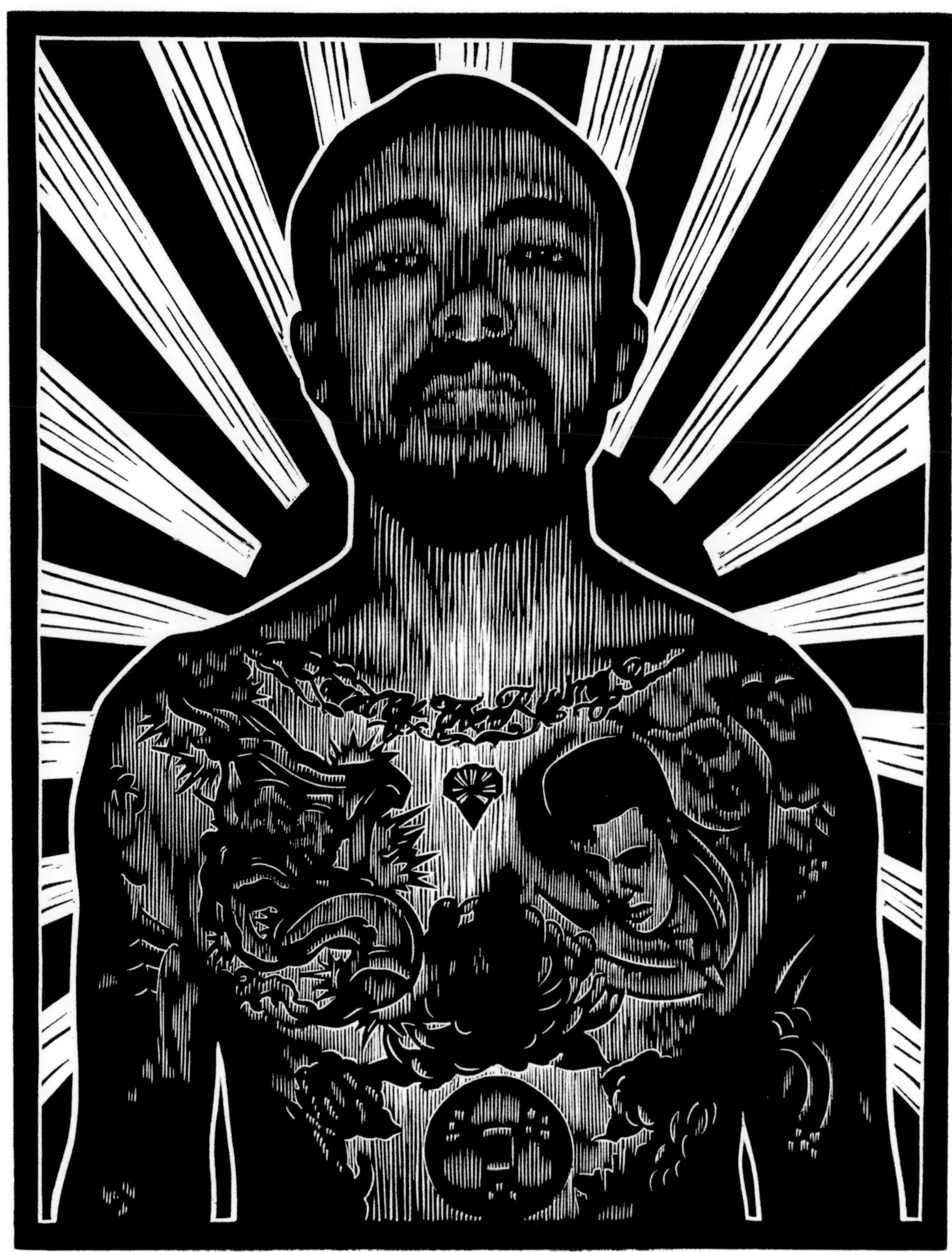

Alex Binnie, Shinji, 2011, woodcut, 60 x 45cm

(opposite) **Alex Binnie**, Tim, 2010, woodcut, 60 x 45cm

ANGELIQUE HOUTKAMP

Born – 1968
Hometown – Uithoorn, The Netherlands
Study / Apprenticeship – Life
Lives and Works – Parlour du Salon Serpent, Amsterdam, The Netherlands
Years as a tattooist – 12 years
Favourite medium – watercolours

Angelique Houtkamp is an artist and tattooist with an eager cult following of fans who love her as much as her work. Her personality and positivity have become part of the package that makes her art so collectible.

She is a coffee drinking perfectionist who is moving into a brand new phase since recently opening her own parlour in Amsterdam, bringing together tattooing and art.

"When I decided I wanted a space of my own about six months back, I knew I wanted to be able to do everything I do in the one place. Meaning painting, tattooing, sending out print orders, having a shop area and a place to invite people to come by... I've got someone else tattooing with me here as well, which is super 'gezellig'."

To enter her new parlour is to step back in time to a kind of Victorian salon. Her wood panelled walls are completely covered in artworks and ephemera in a way that gives the illusion of chaos.

"I am pretty organised and behind my table are lots of small cabinets and drawers, sort of like an apothecary drawer. So I've got everything at hand. I actually don't have to get up at all during the day."

For Houtkamp tattooing and art making are very close. Her art bloomed when she started tattooing, giving her painting direction and substance.

"In general they blend very well together, as I do like to paint in the same way and style as I design tattoos. With paintings though, I do sometimes take more liberties with detail that perhaps would not translate into a tattoo as time would take its toll on it."

Her love of watercolours is directly linked to its similarity to the execution, look and feel of tattooing. She is able to translate the same black lines, shading and luminous colours from her tattoo work to her works on paper.

"Yes, tattooing has everything to do with me working with watercolours."

As well as mirroring her mediums in this way, Houtkamp carries across her obsession with traditional tattoo symbolism into her artwork.

"Tattoo loves symbolism. Maybe even as much now as in the superstitious days. Maybe this is also why I love tattooing and my artwork is so linked to my tattoo work. It all easily flows together. Even something as simple as a heart shape, which I think is one of the strongest symbols in the world, has been tattooed for as long as western tattooing exists."

The aesthetic, the symbolism and also the history of tattooing are all wrapped up in Houtkamp's total vision of what she does.

"I have a very romantic, not necessarily accurate, view on tattoo history. Sailors going from port to port, getting drunk and getting sweethearts' names tattooed on them. But also the adventure and rogue aspect of it. It was not done by respectable people. The circus and carnival was involved, all totally appealing to me."

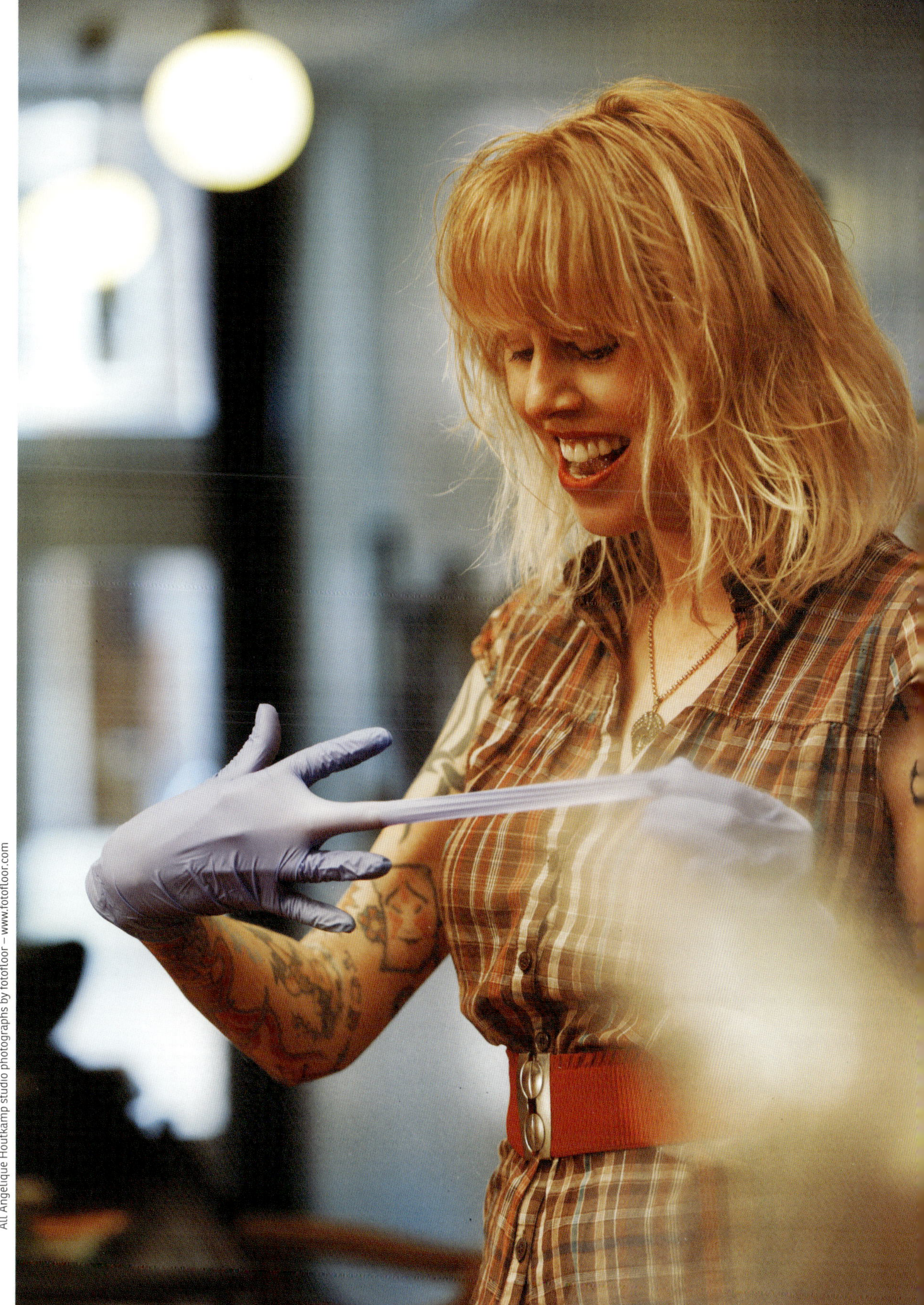

All Angelique Houtkamp studio photographs by fotofloor – www.fotofloor.com

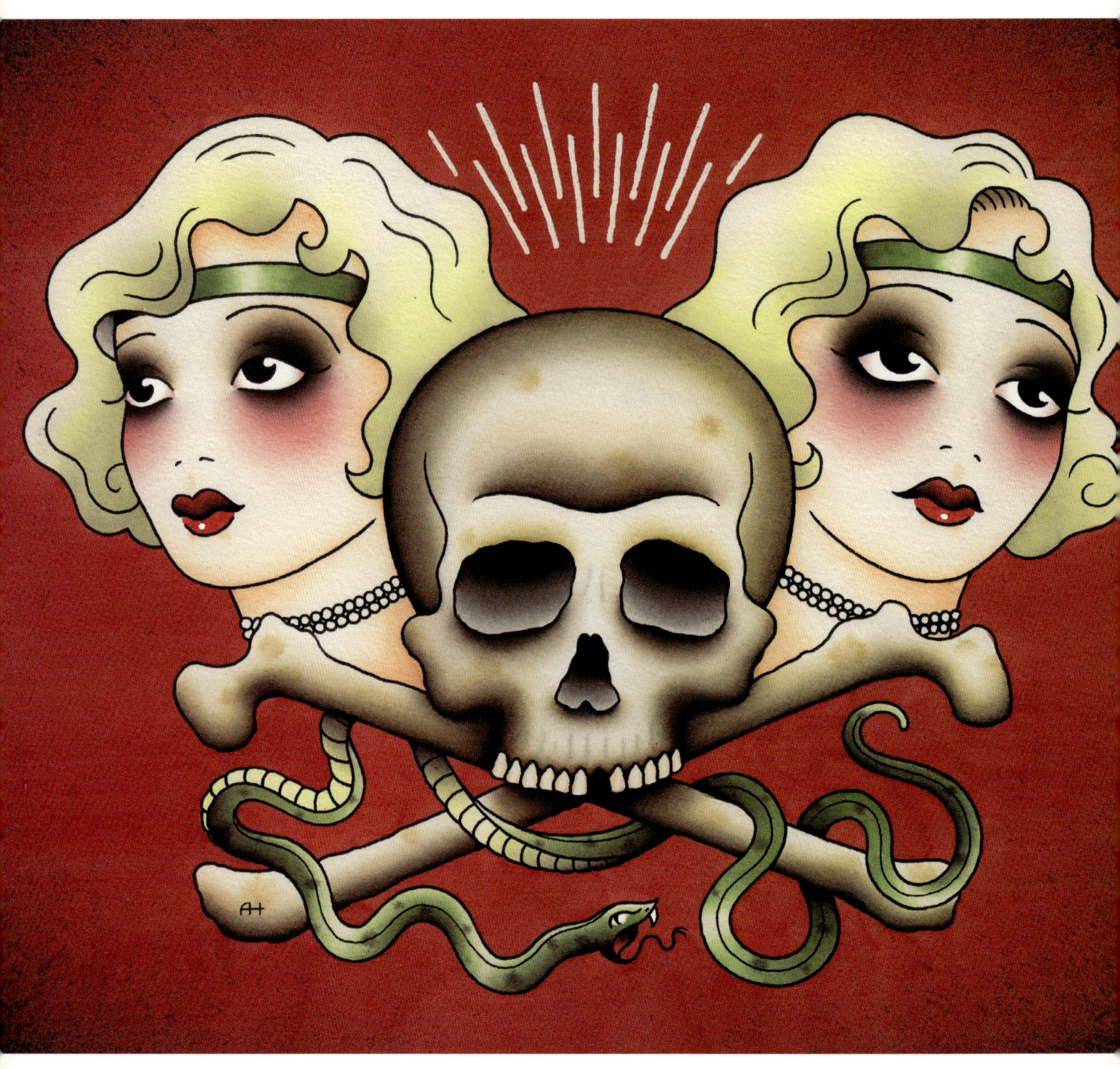

Angelique Houtkamp, Death and the Maidens, 2010, pen, Indian ink and watercolour on paper, 29 x 34cm
(opposite) **Angelique Houtkamp**, Accessorise, 2010, pen, Indian ink and watercolour on paper, 29 x 20cm

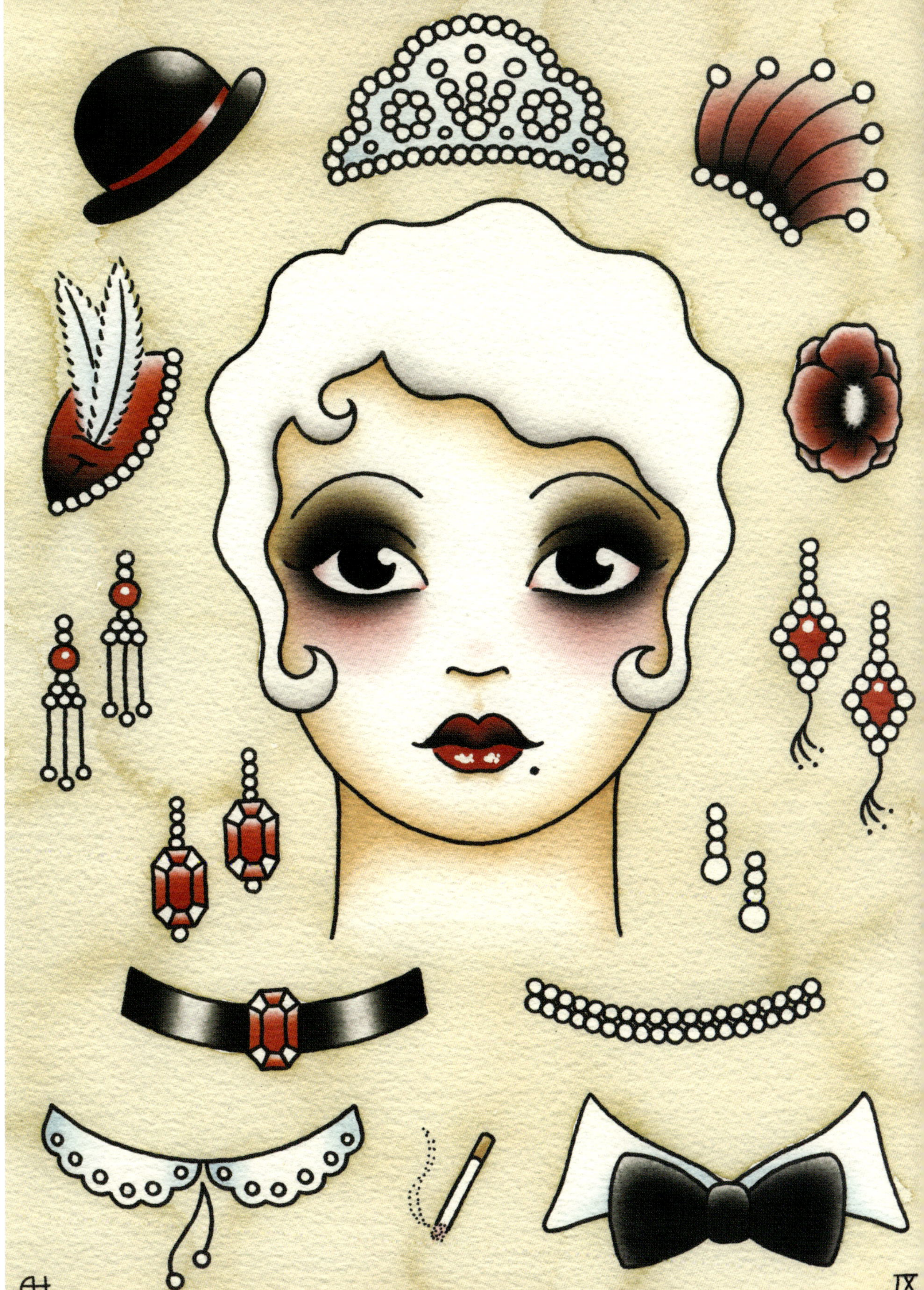
AH
IX

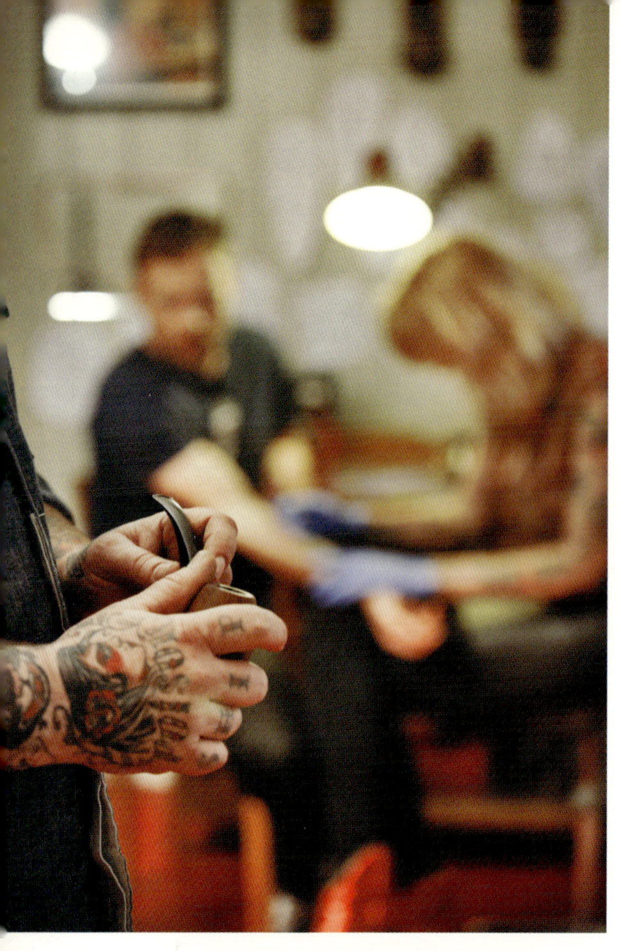

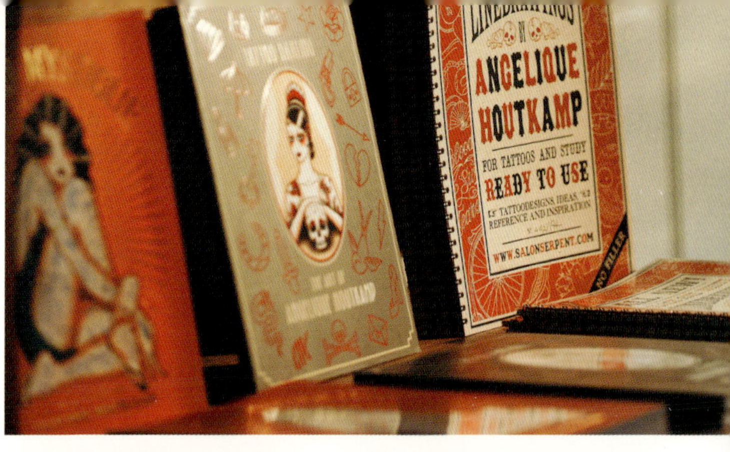
ANGELIQUE
HOUTKAMP
FOR TATTOOS AND STUDY
READY TO USE
WWW.SALONSERPENT.COM

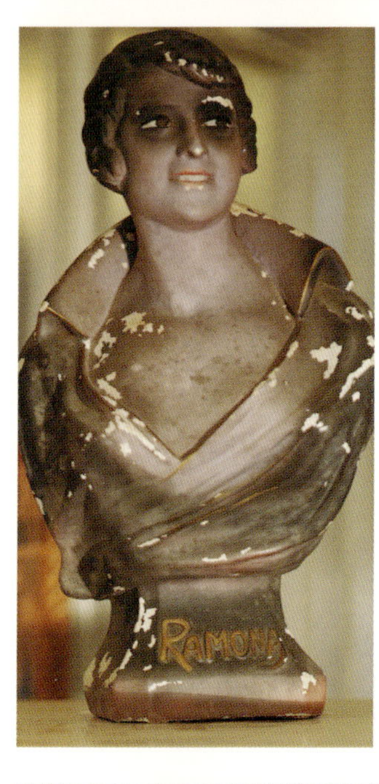
RAMONA

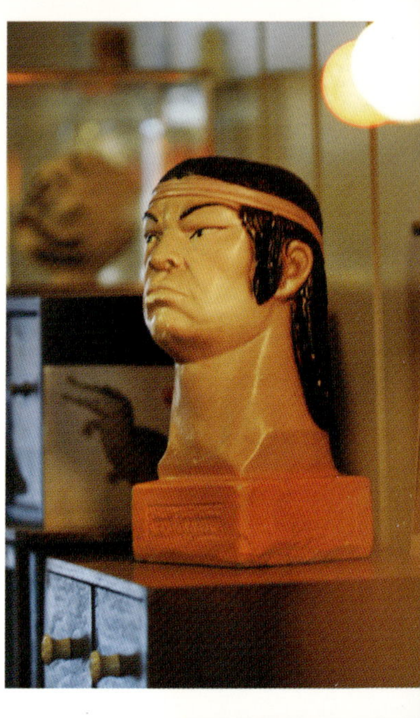

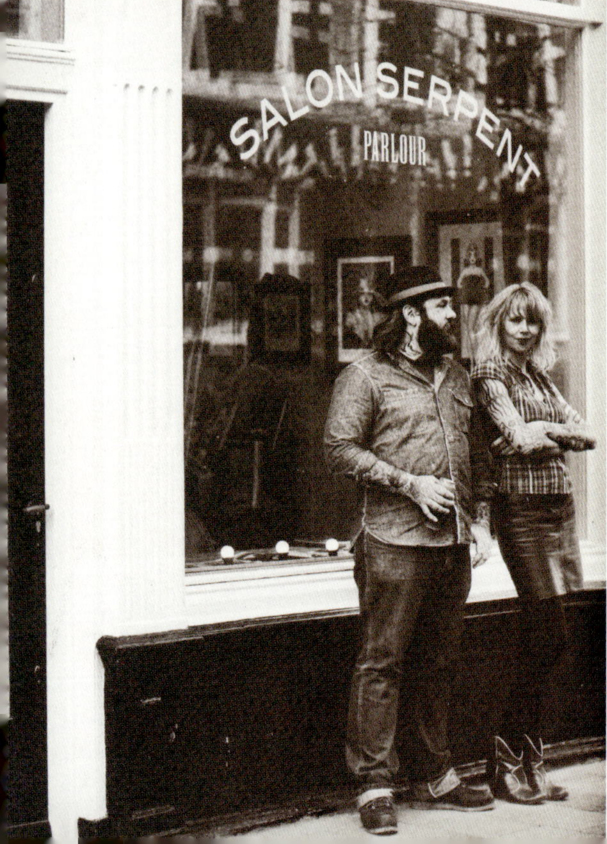
SALON SERPENT
PARLOUR

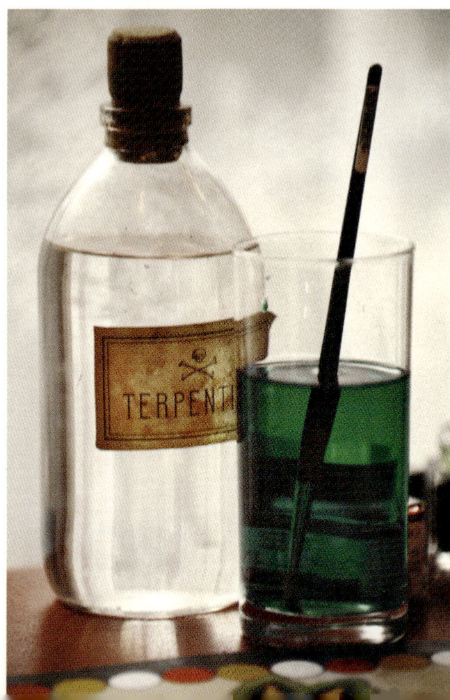
TERPENTI

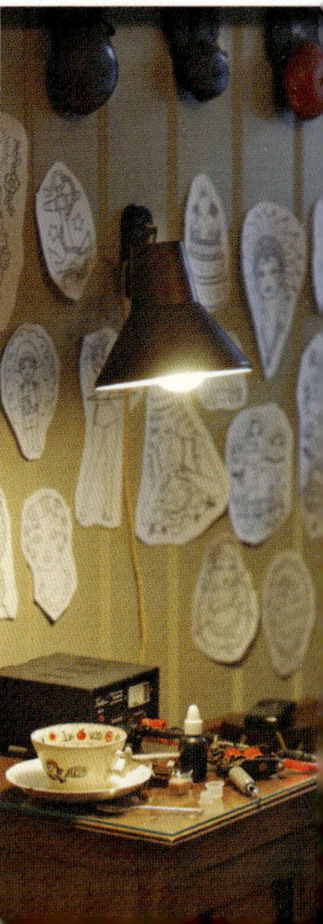

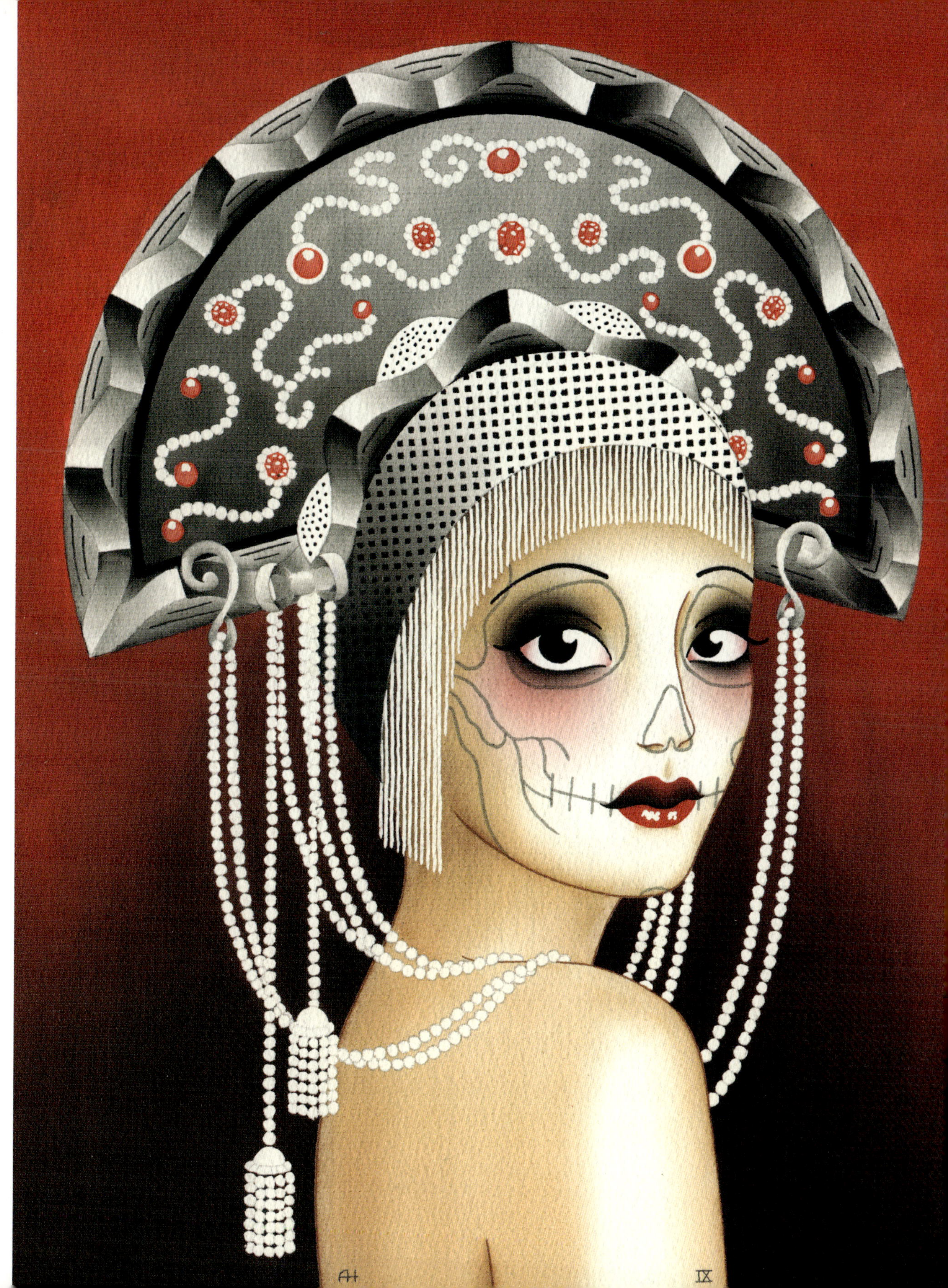
IX

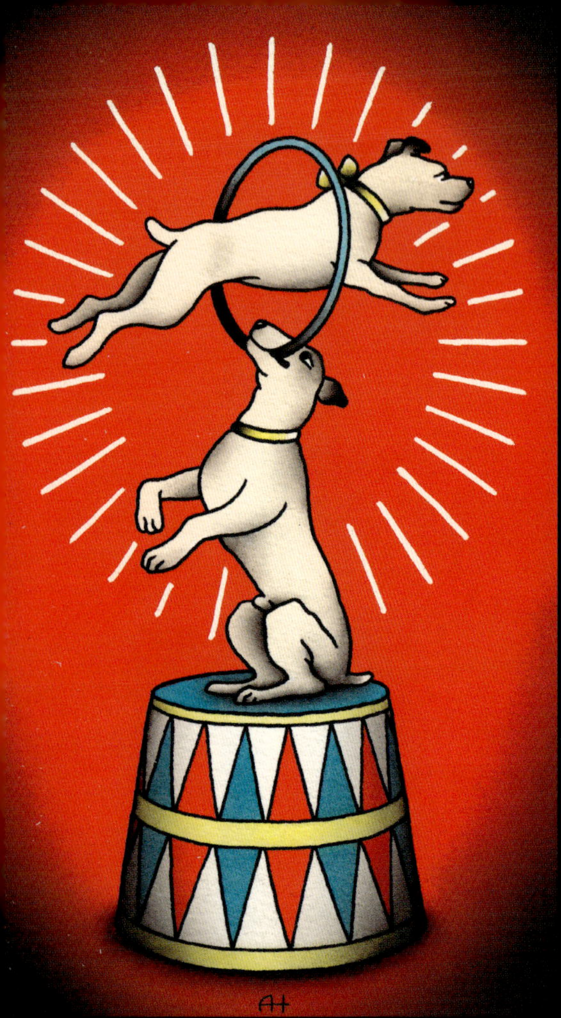

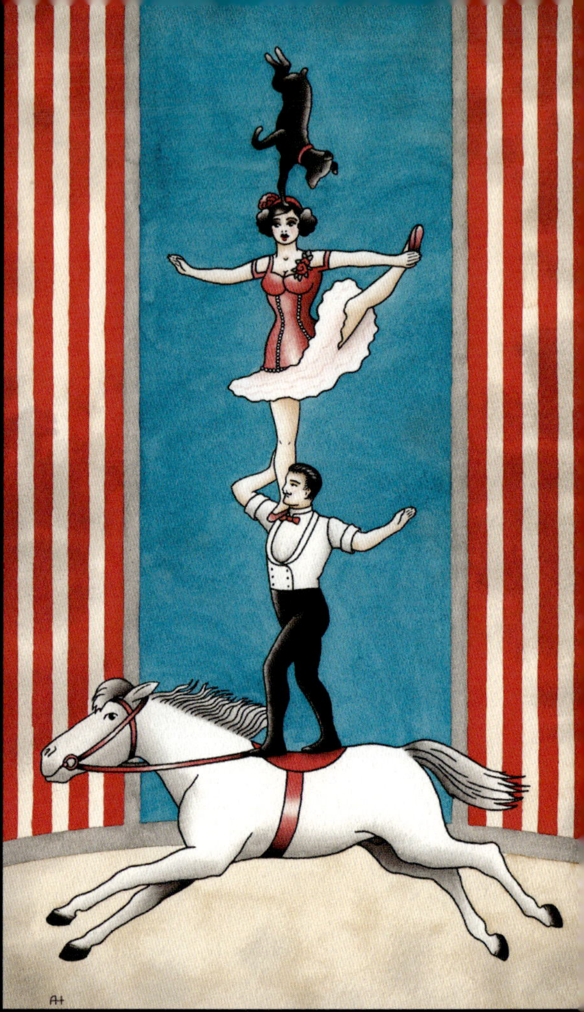

(previous page) **Angelique Houtkamp**, Orlova, 2010, pen, Indian ink and watercolour on paper, 40 x 29cm

(left) **Angelique Houtkamp**, Trevor & Tandie, 2010, pen, Indian ink and watercolour on paper, 23 x 13cm
(right) **Angelique Houtkamp**, Troupe le Monceau, 2010, pen, Indian ink and watercolour on paper, 44 x 25cm

(opposite) **Angelique Houtkamp**, Drifting Heart, 2010, pen, Indian ink and watercolour on paper, 28 x 13cm

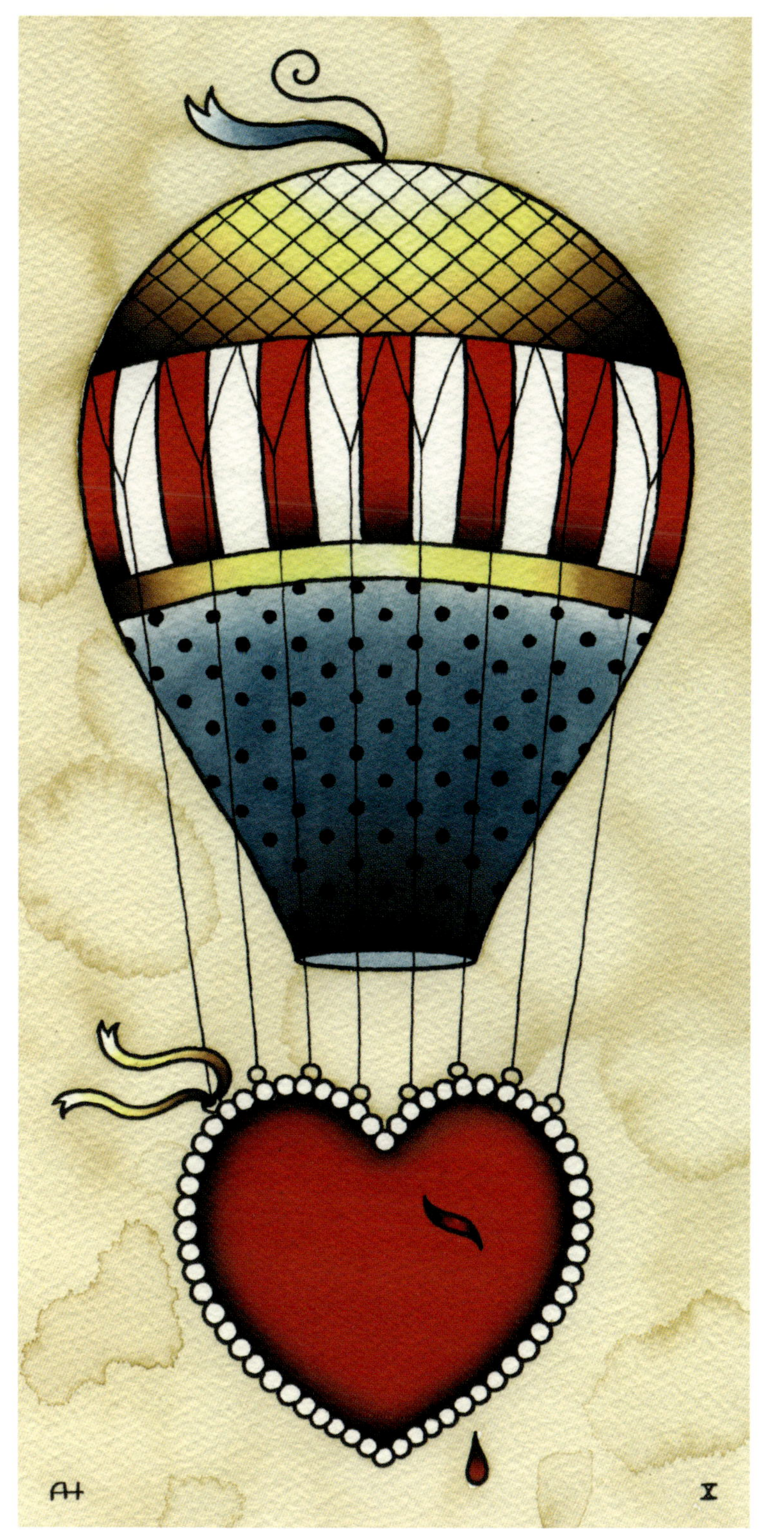

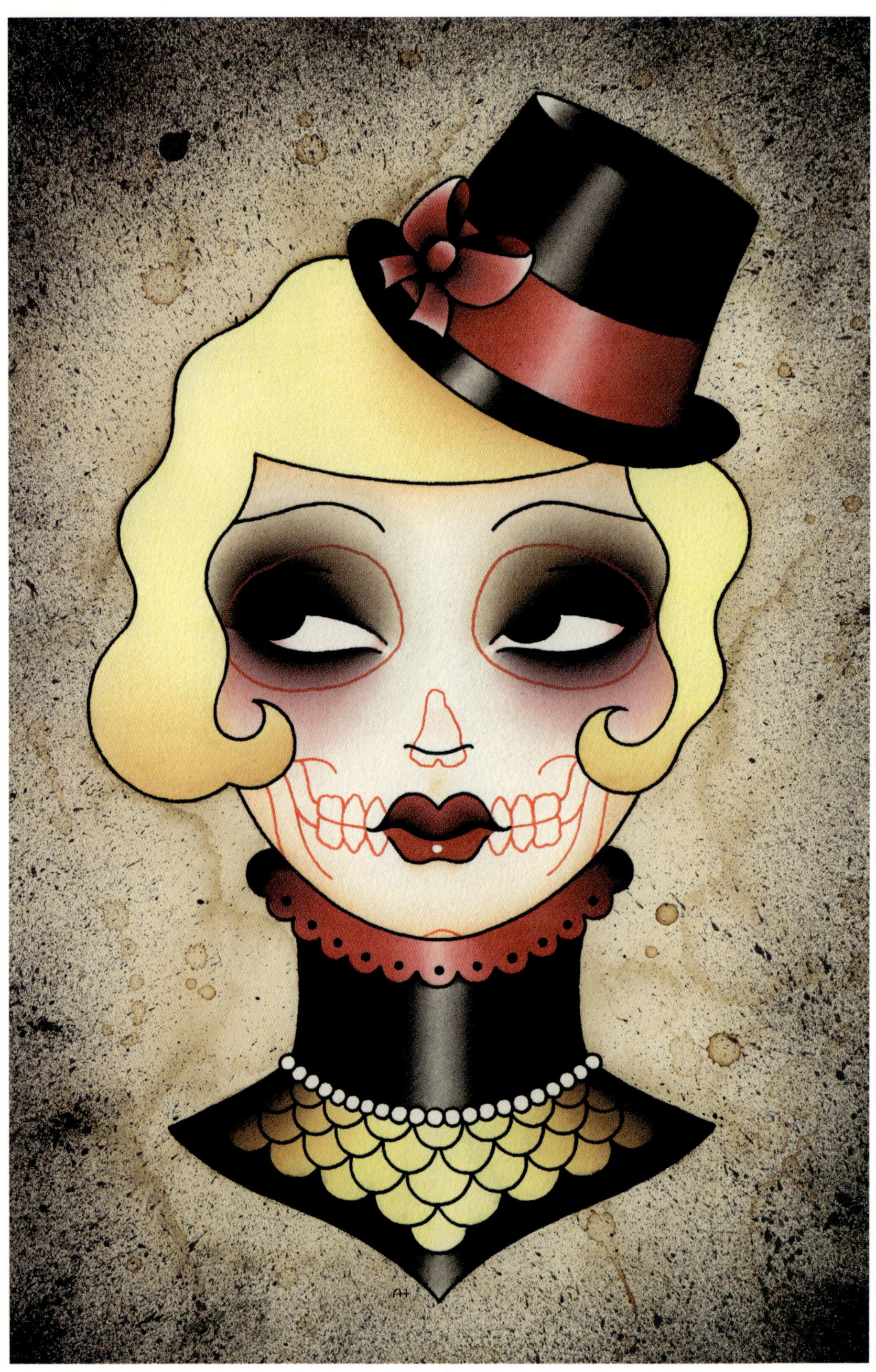

Angelique Houtkamp, Sisco, 2011,
pen, Indian ink and watercolour on paper, 37 x 24cm

(opposite) **Angelique Houtkamp**, Stella, 2010,
pen, Indian ink and watercolour on paper, 28 x 23cm

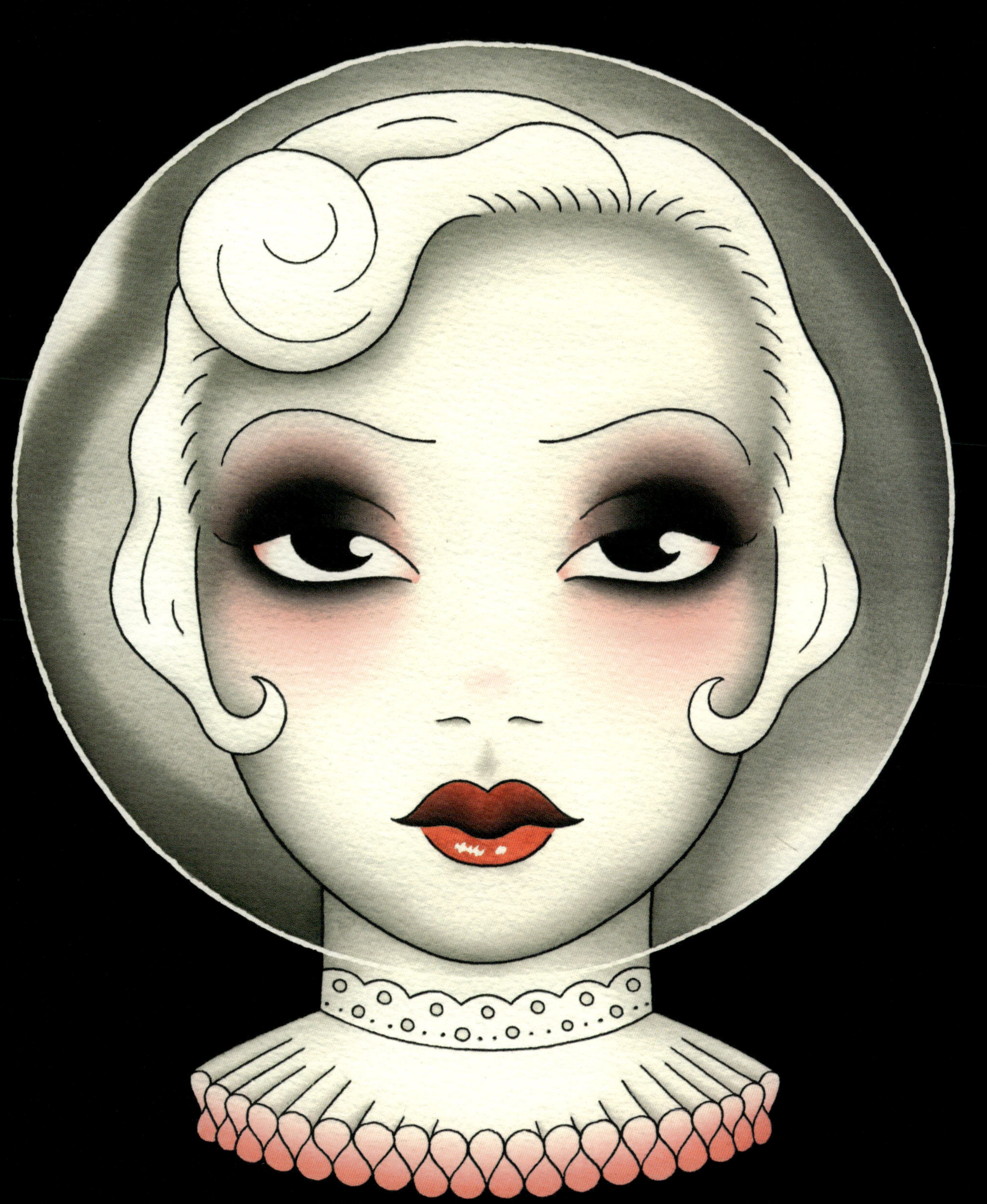

IX

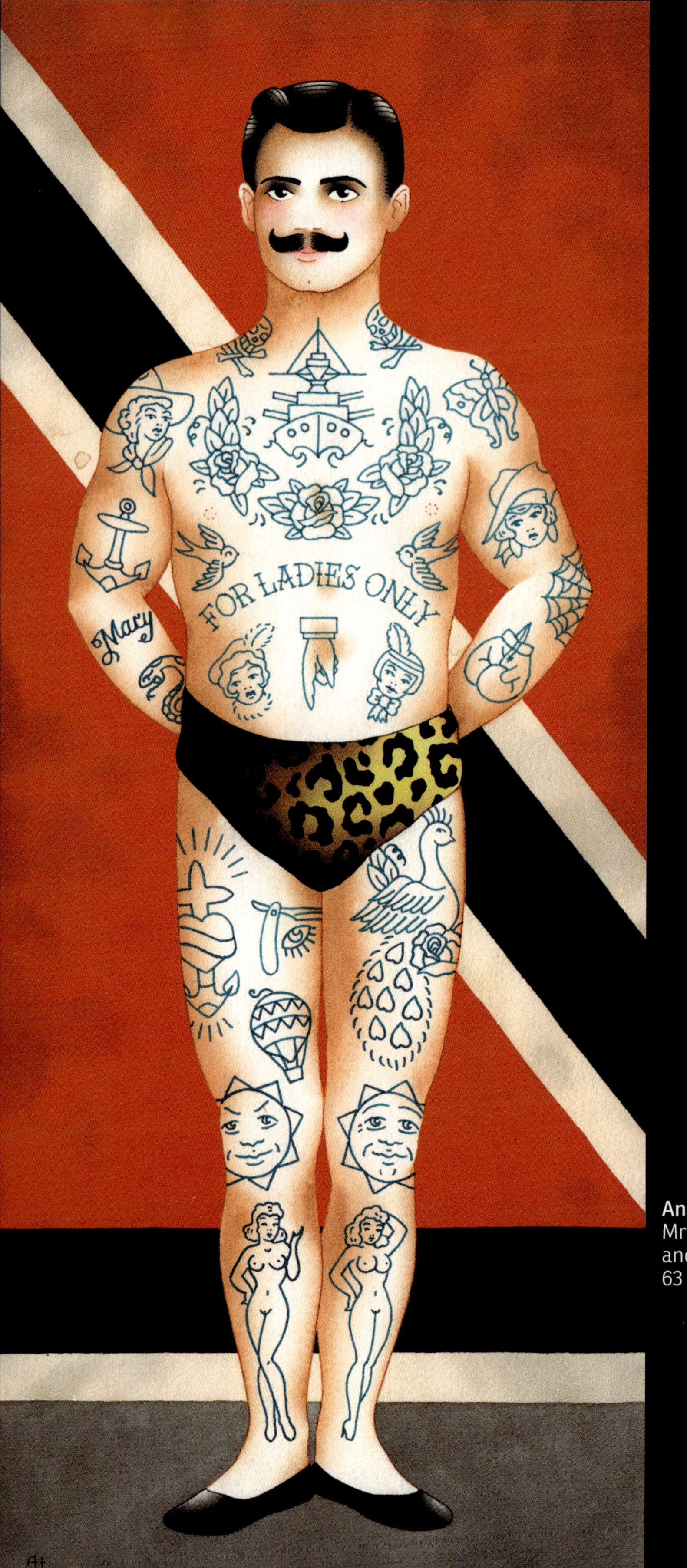

Angelique Houtkamp,
Mr Rigby, 2010, pen, Indian ink and watercolour on paper, 63 x 26cm

(opposite)
Angelique Houtkamp,
Victoria, 2010, pen, Indian ink and watercolour on paper, 40 x 19cm

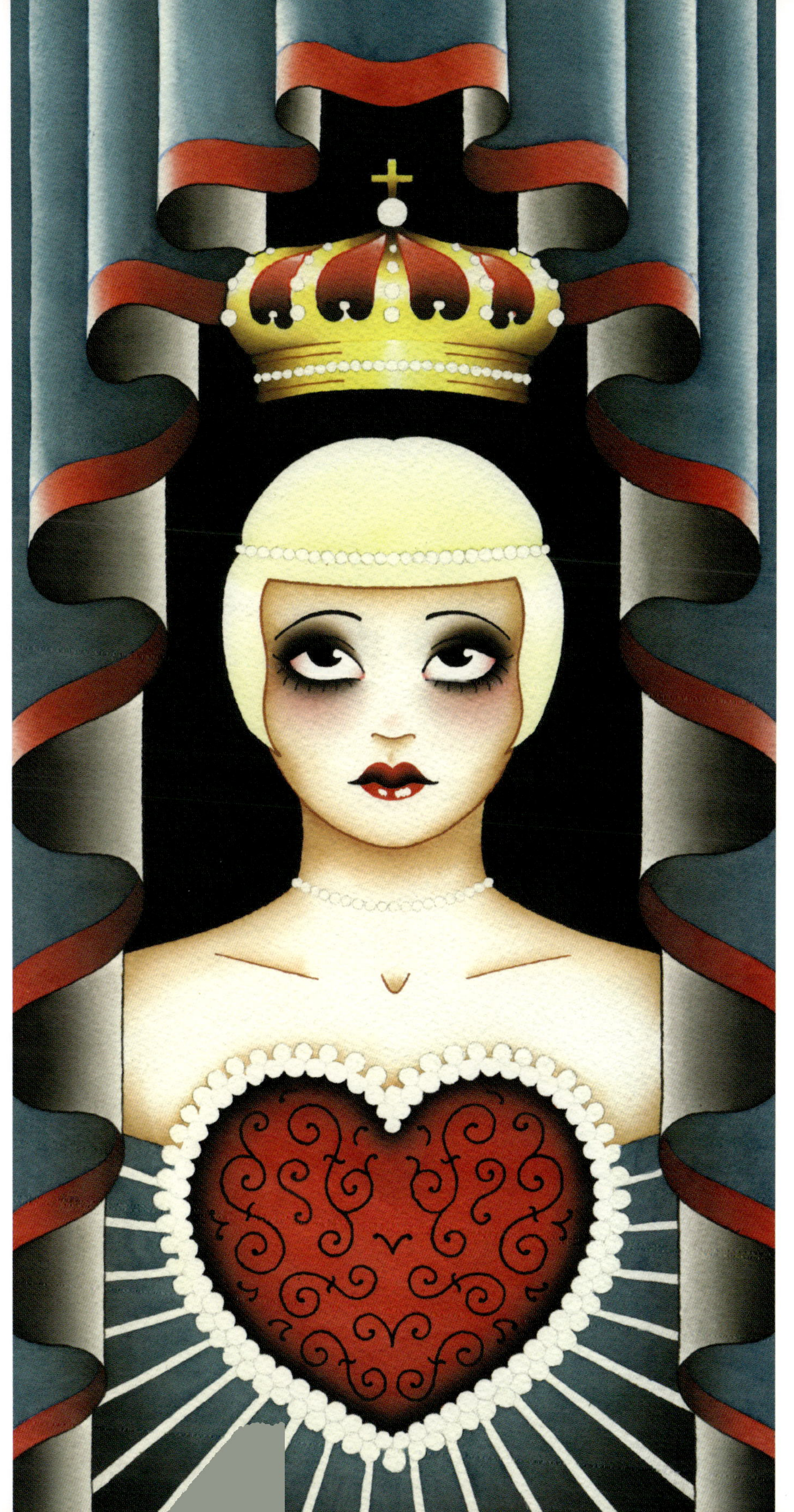

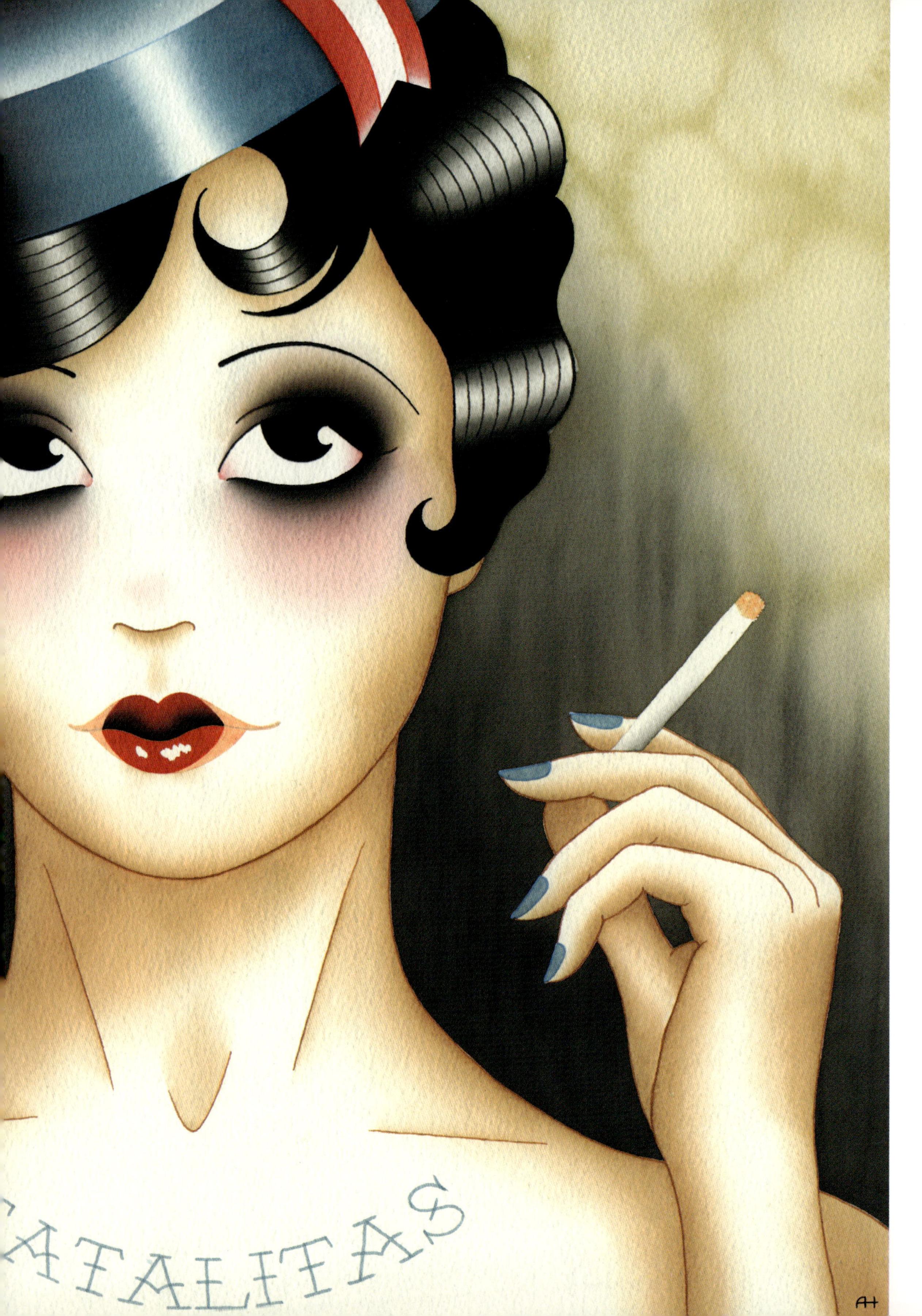
ATALITAS

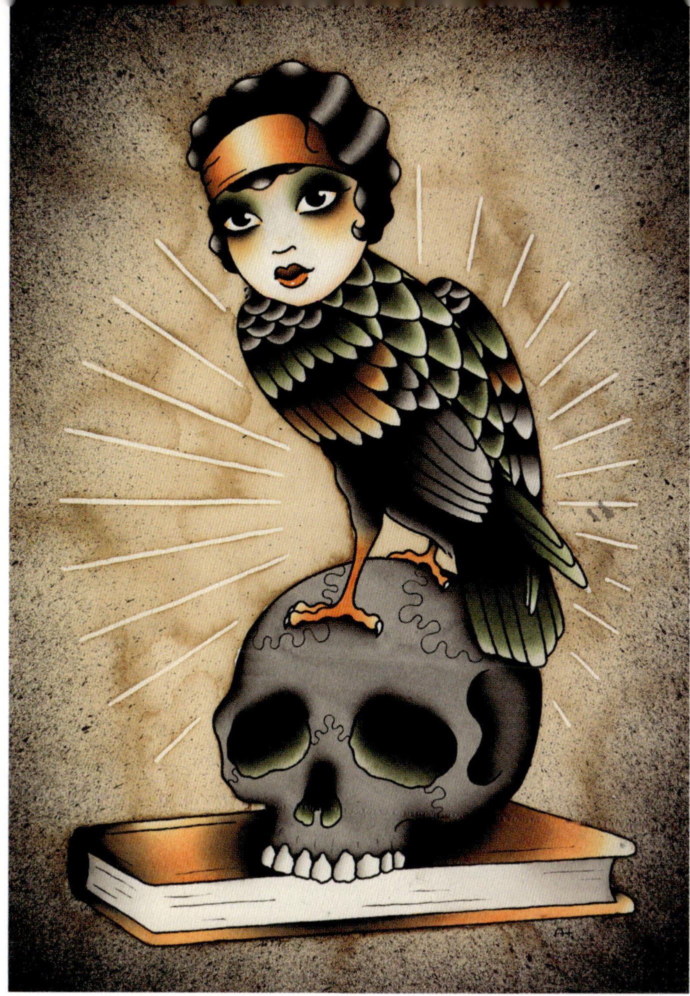

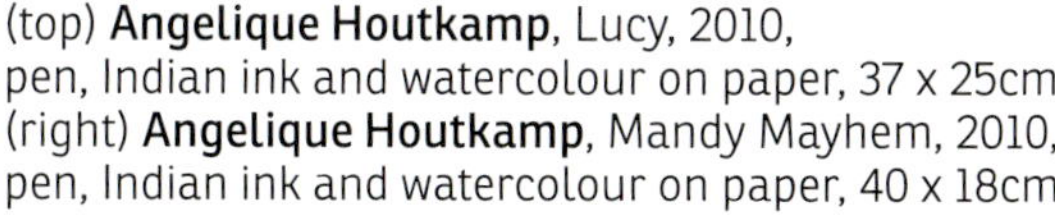

(top) **Angelique Houtkamp**, Lucy, 2010,
pen, Indian ink and watercolour on paper, 37 x 25cm
(right) **Angelique Houtkamp**, Mandy Mayhem, 2010,
pen, Indian ink and watercolour on paper, 40 x 18cm

(opposite) **Angelique Houtkamp**, Harper, 2010,
pen, Indian ink and watercolour on paper, 40 x 27cm

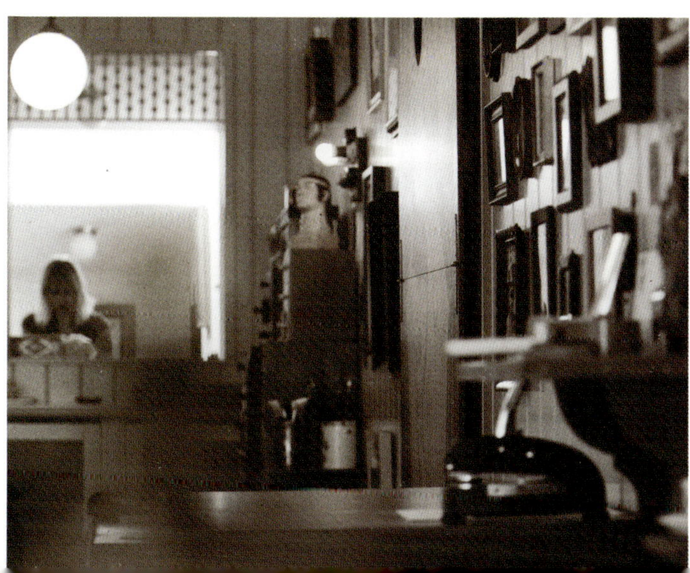

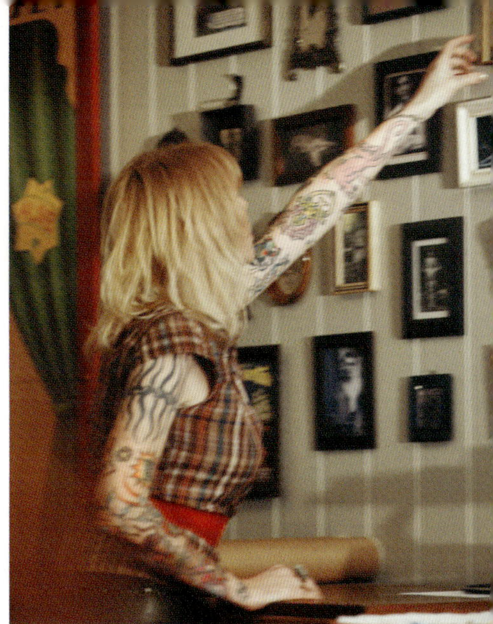

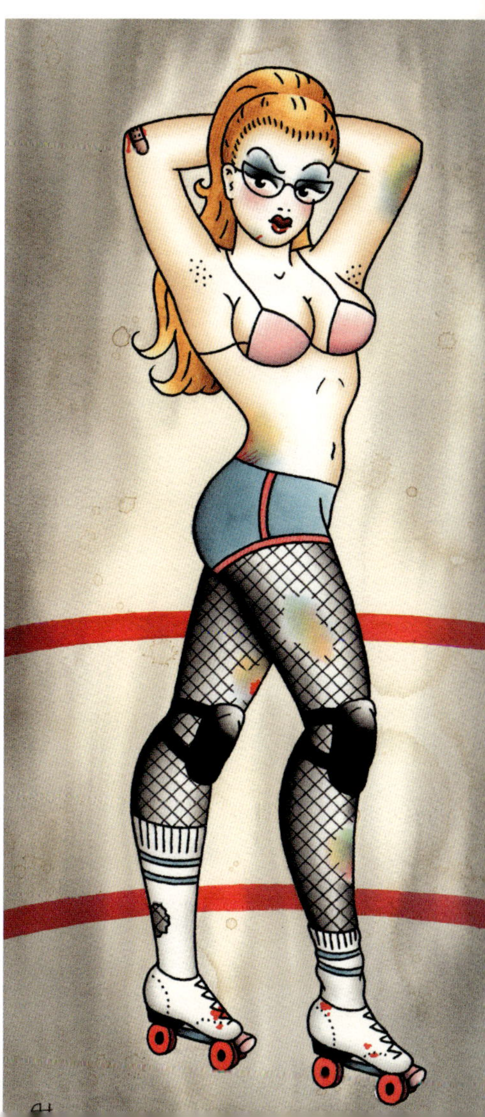

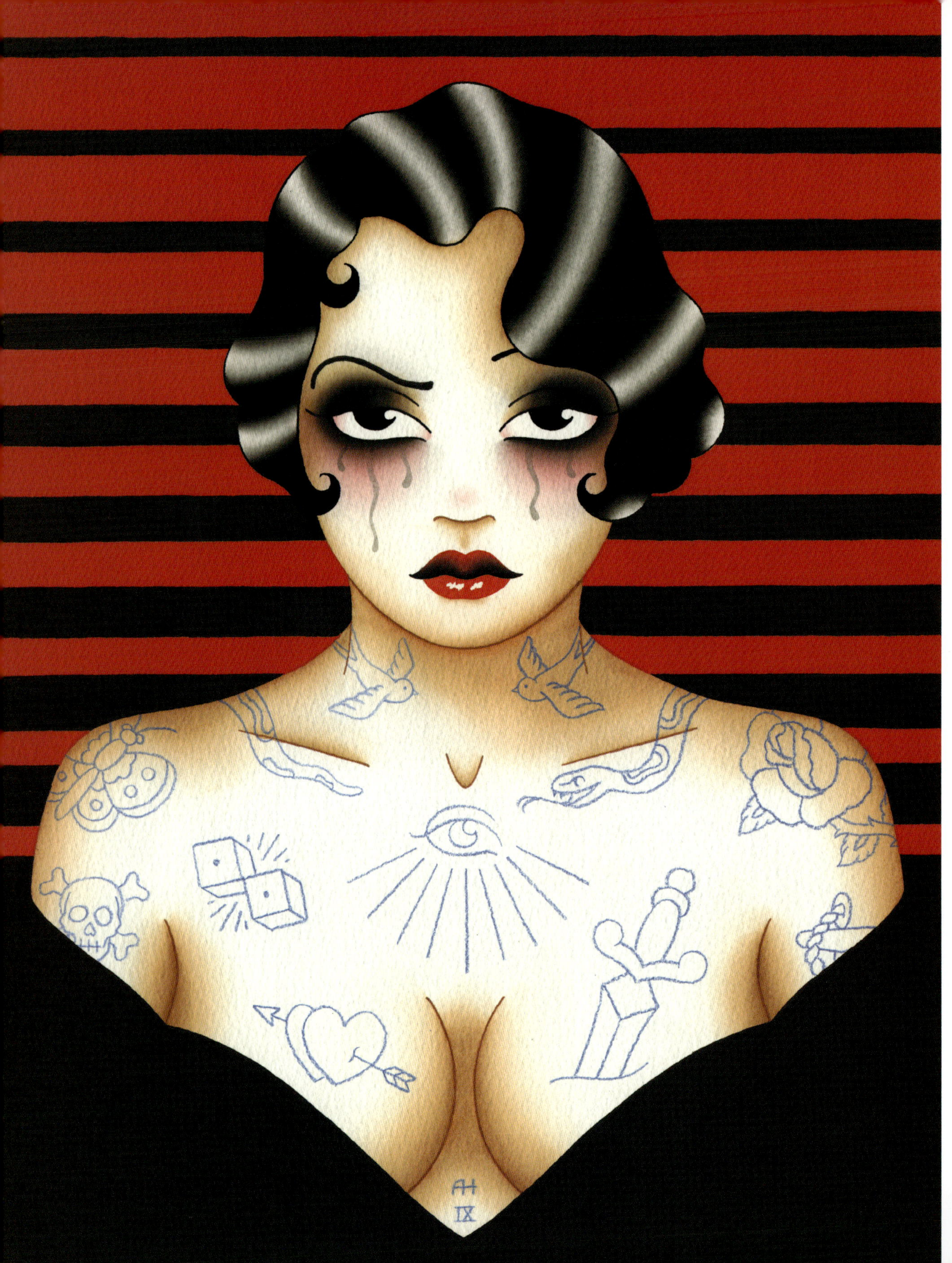

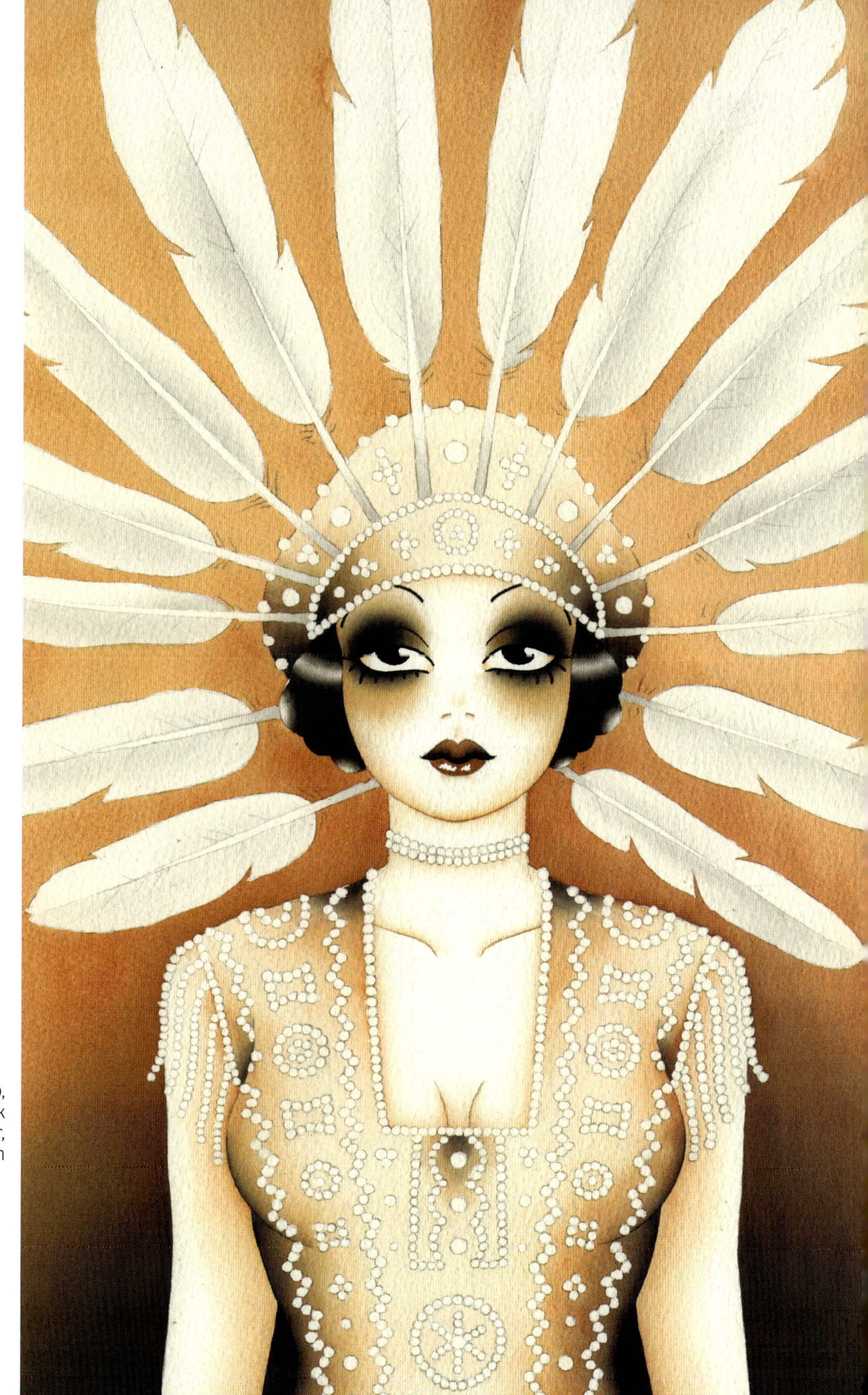

Angelique Houtkamp, Koko, 2010, pen, Indian ink and watercolour on paper, 40 x 24cm

(opposite)
Angelique Houtkamp, Frankie, 2010, ink and acrylic on watercolour paper, 38 x 29cm

CHRISTOPHER CONN ASKEW

Born – 1970
Hometown – Hollywood, California
Study / Apprenticeship – apprentice tattooist with Henry Goldfield.
No formal art schooling.
Lives and Works – San Francisco, California
Years as a tattooist – 16 years
Favourite medium – exclusively on paper

Christopher Conn Askew is one of the more mysterious figures to come out of the shadows of tattooing. Having turned his back on his professional life as a tattooist, Askew has chosen a solitary life as a painter and illustrator making works of intense dreamlike wonder and darkness.

Without any formal art school training, he drew obsessively from an early age, encouraged by his bohemian parents. "It was my first drug."

Askew has melded an incredibly original aesthetic that feels authentically old. His work is imbued with an authority of the ages and of an imagined history. He translates his deep knowledge of a variety of cultural, symbolic and narrative sources, including European folklore, Soviet propaganda art, Japanese watercolours, Victorian decoration, art deco design as well as tattoo symbolism, and makes it his own.

His compositions often include graphic motifs, borders and inexplicable icons loosely referencing the language of graphic design with a veiled symbolism. In this way the works take on a mysterious sense of importance and reference a place and past we cannot quite pin down.

This overt use of symbolism is at once something that has evolved out of his tattoo past, and from an innate or primal urge.

"My years in the skin trade have definitely left a big mark on my symbology, though the symbols I use are not always intended to indicate their currently perceived meaning. Any meaning behind them is based primarily on my own interpretation and feeling. For instance, I use a lot of crosses, but I am no Christian. Crosses can mean many things to me: death, a crossroads, the Western tradition, war, suffering, but mainly I have just been attracted to them for primal reasons I don't even understand myself. Many of the symbols I use have vague or multiple meanings..."

Askew turned from skin to paper, rendering his seemingly bejewelled pieces in a rich mix of water-colour, ink, graphite, gouache, gold leaf, and occasionally nail polish.

"What I enjoy most about working on paper is everything that separates it from skin: it has an even consistency, it's flat, and it doesn't move or talk. I am gradually trying to unlearn a lot of the habits I picked up while tattooing, to allow myself to take advantage of all the liberties that working on paper allows. I think that moving into new mediums as well, like printmaking, will help this process along."

Askew's departure from the world of tattoo was one based on feeling uncomfortable with the direction the industry was taking. But more so, an urge to retreat into his own self-determined world.

"I just wanted to be alone. I just can't deal with people on that intense and constant level anymore. Now I sit and work at home with my cats and have pretty minimal actual contact with others... This is what I'm comfortable with now."

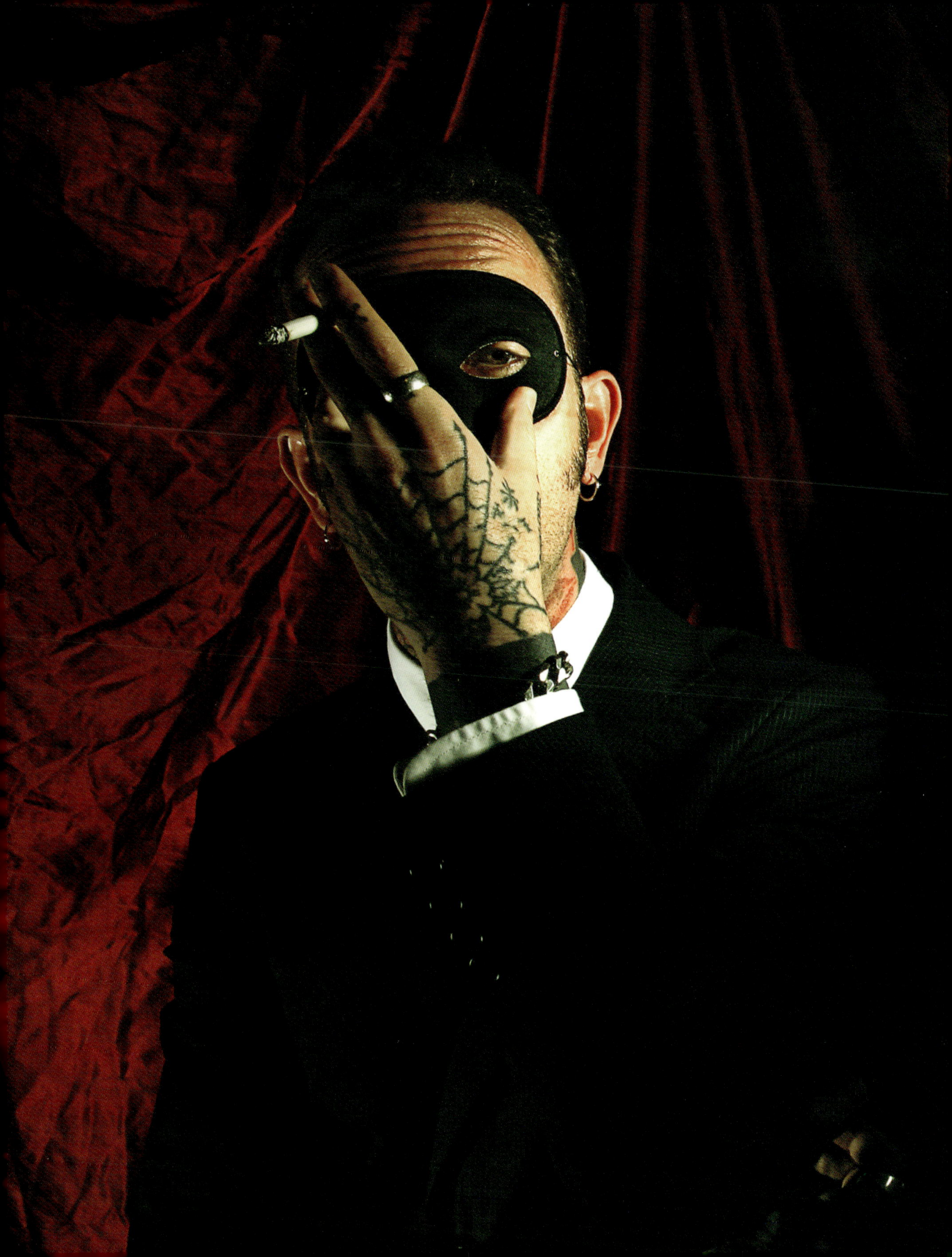

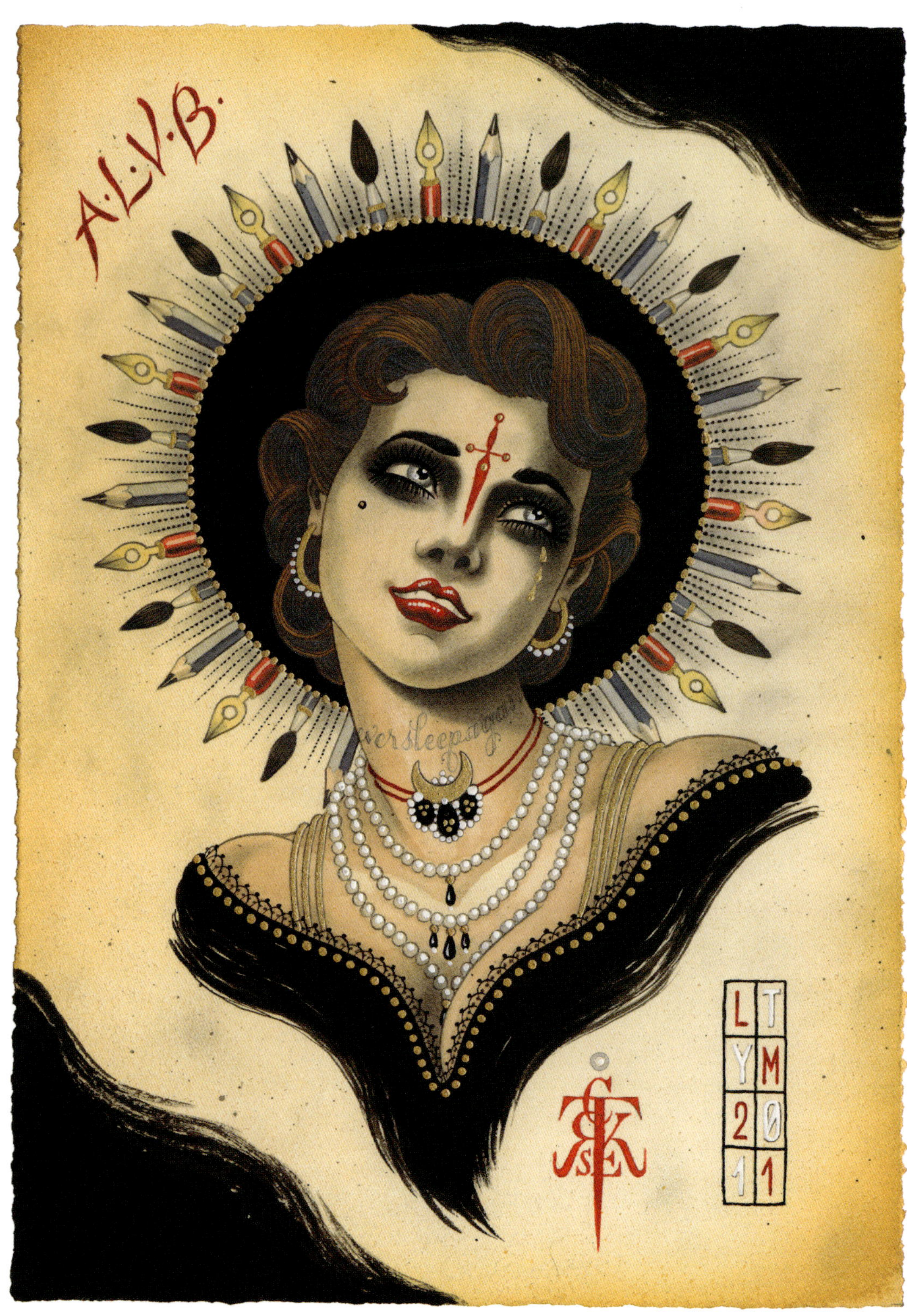

Christopher Conn Askew, A.L.V.B., 2011,
watercolour, ink, gouache, graphite, gold leaf, and nail polish on paper

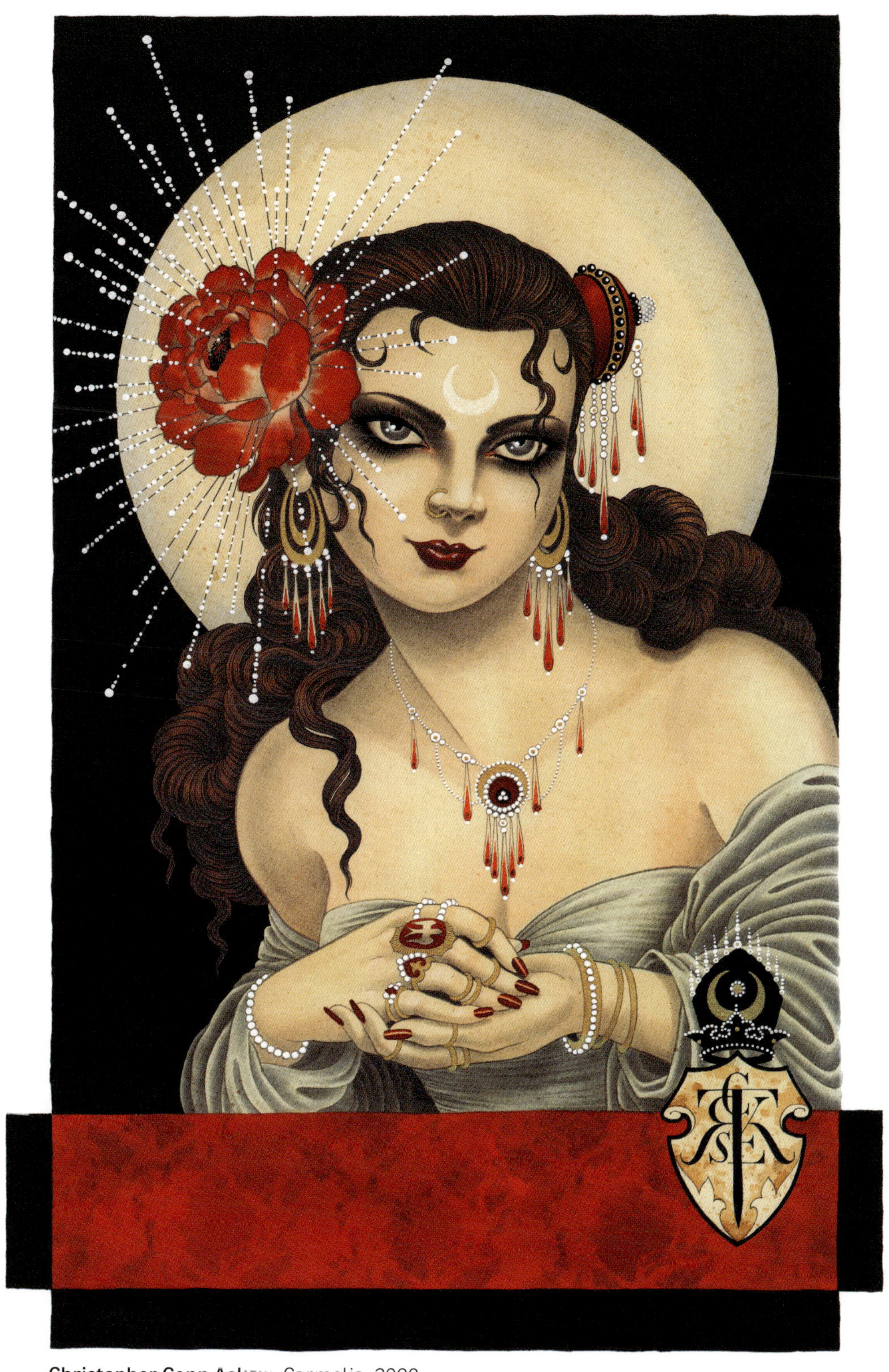

Christopher Conn Askew, Carmelia, 2009,
watercolour, ink, gouache, graphite, gold leaf, and nail polish on paper

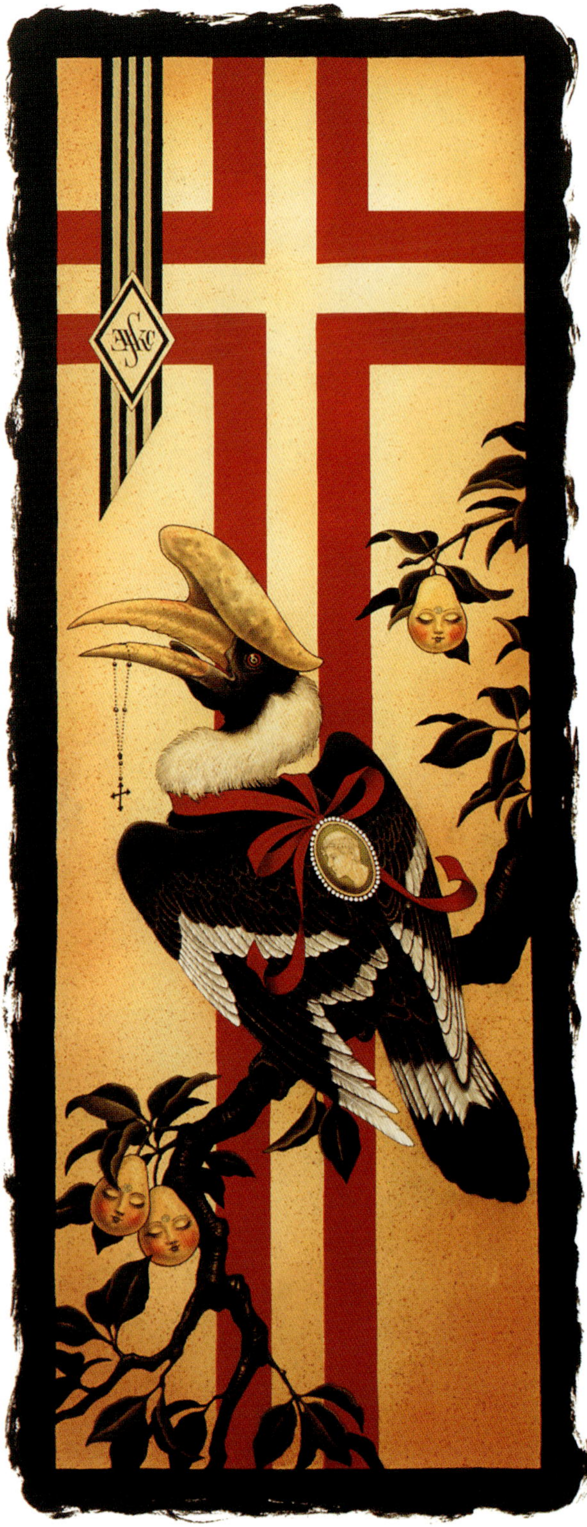

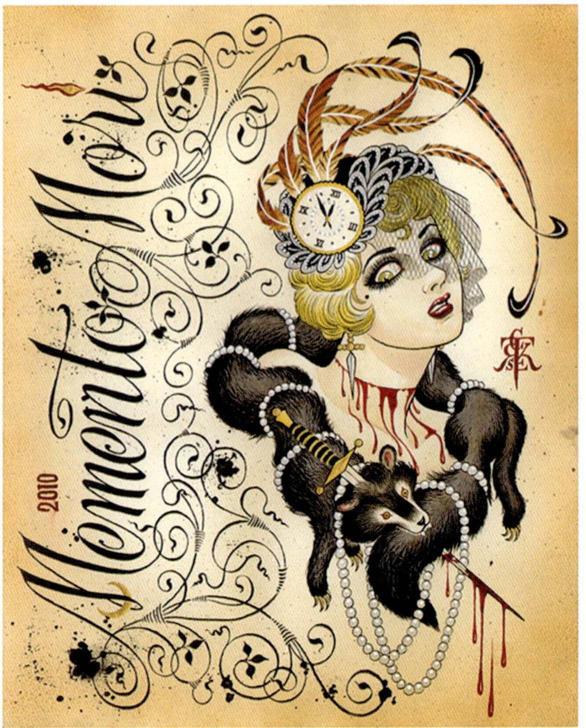
Memento Mori
2010

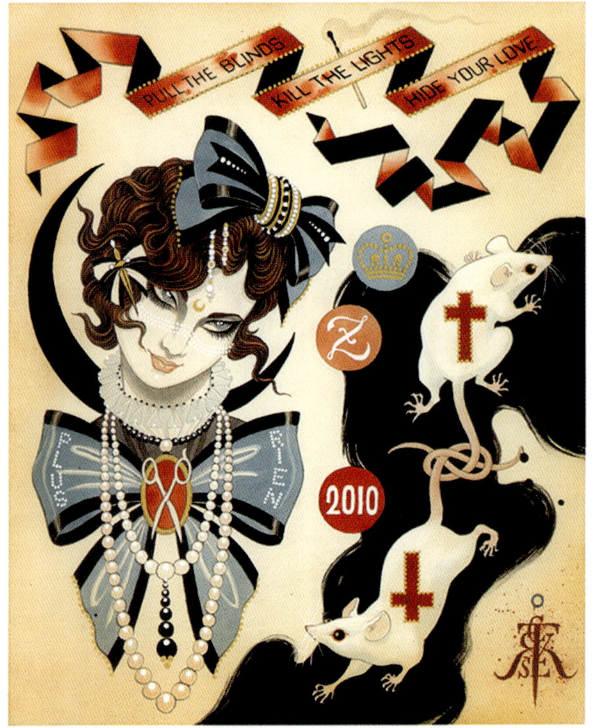
PULL THE BLINDS
KILL THE LIGHTS
HIDE YOUR LOVE
PLUS
RIEN
2010

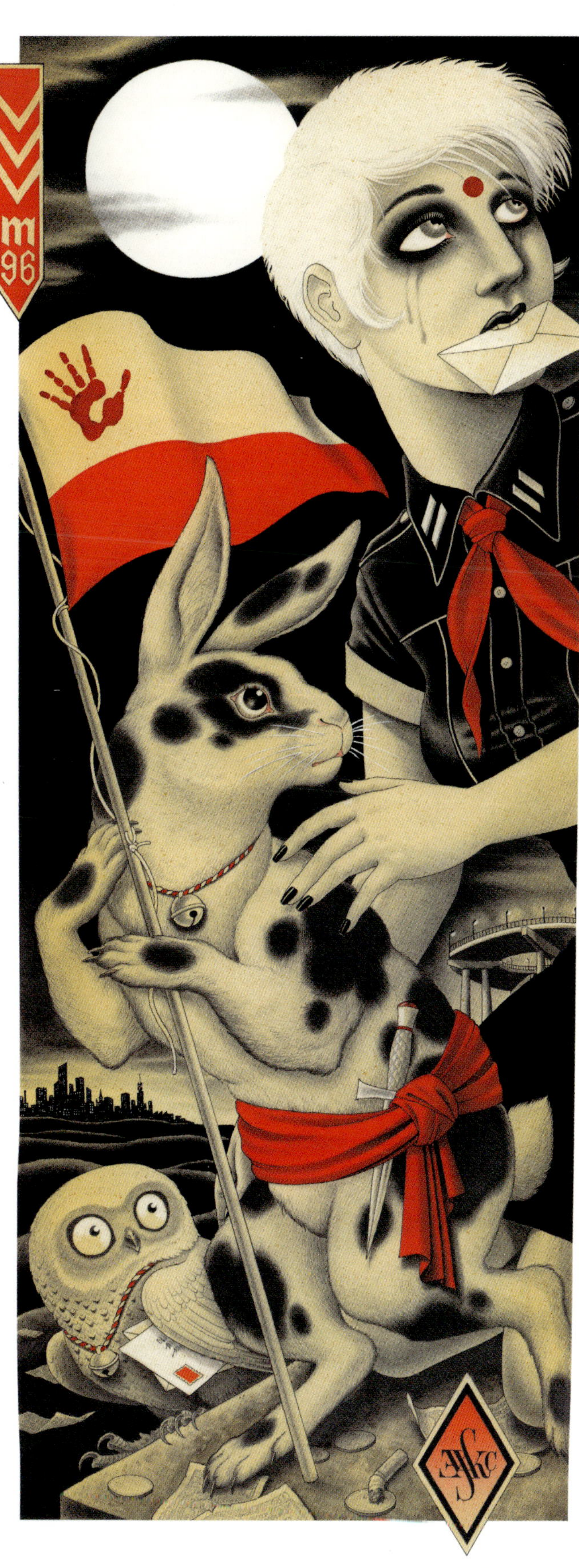

Christopher Conn Askew,
M96, 2006, watercolour, ink, gouache, graphite, gold leaf, and nail polish on paper

(opposite)
(clockwise from top right)

Christopher Conn Askew,
Memento Mori, 2010, watercolour, ink, gouache, graphite, gold leaf, and nail polish on paper

Christopher Conn Askew,
Pull The Blinds, 2010, watercolour, ink, gouache, graphite, gold leaf, and nail polish on paper

Christopher Conn Askew,
La Croix Rouge, 2006, watercolour, ink, gouache, graphite, gold leaf, and nail polish on paper

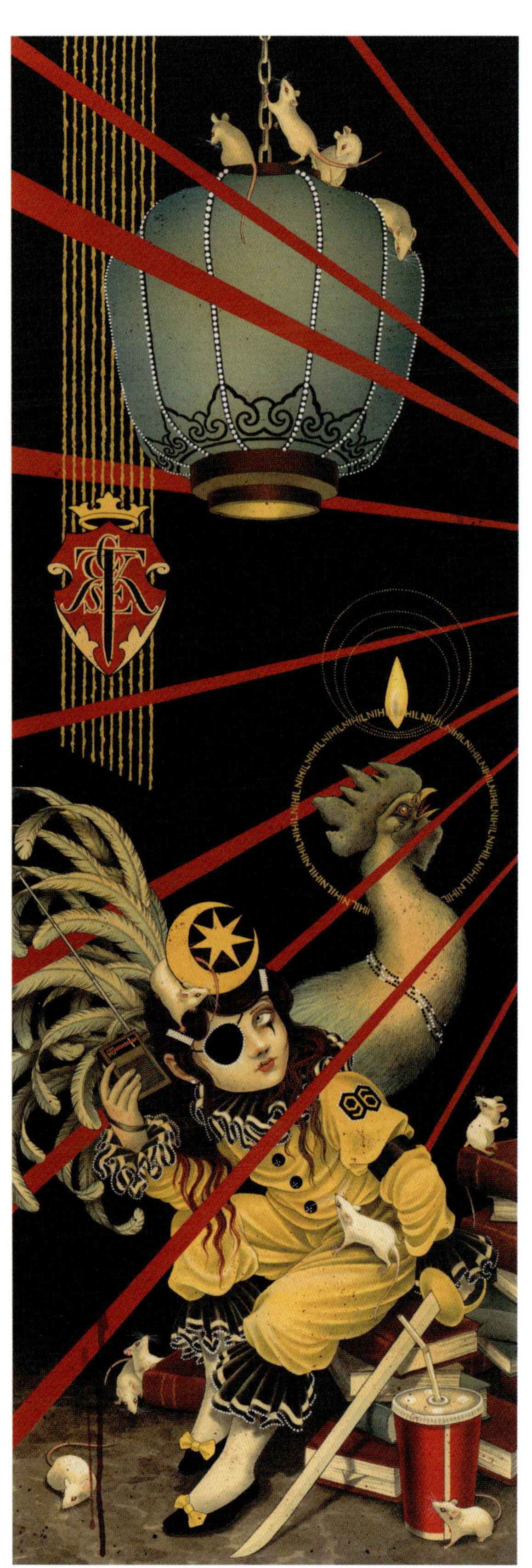

Christopher Conn Askew,
Annunciation, 2009,
watercolour, ink, gouache,
graphite, gold leaf,
and nail polish on paper

(opposite)
Christopher Conn Askew,
Maschere, 2010,
watercolour, ink, gouache,
graphite, gold leaf,
and nail polish on paper

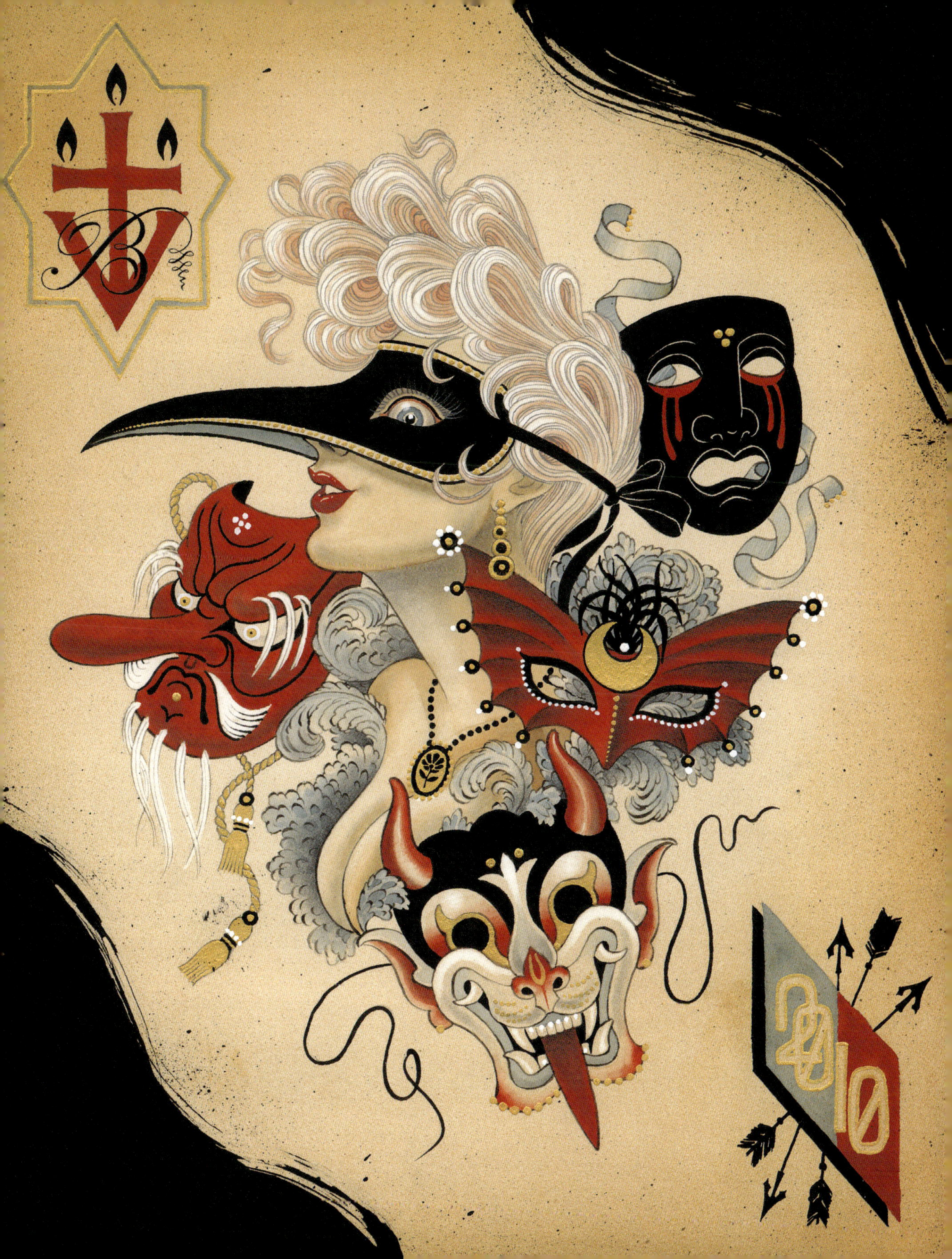
2010

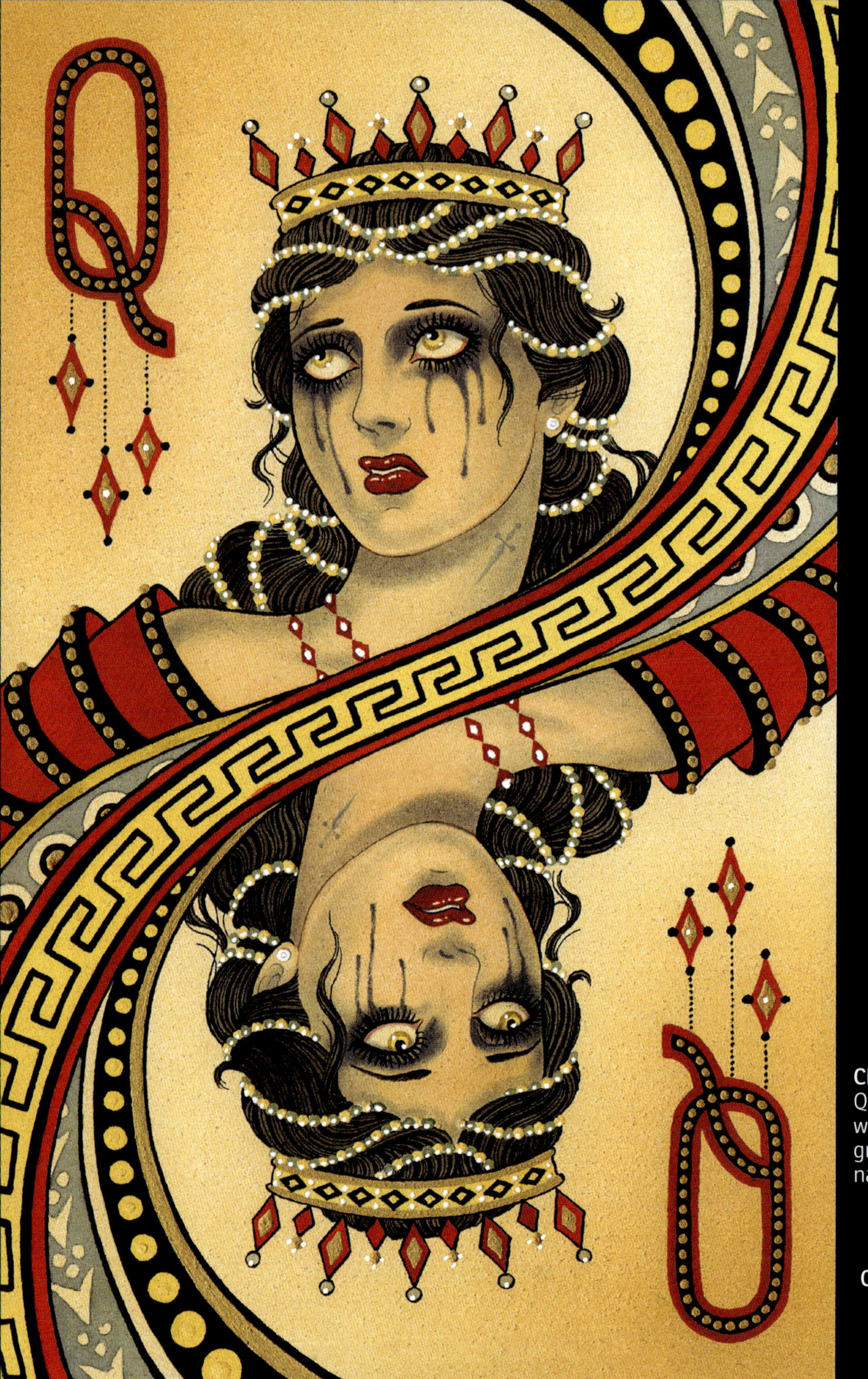

Christopher Conn Askew, Queen of Diamonds, 2011, watercolour, ink, gouache, graphite, gold leaf, and nail polish on paper

(opposite)
Christopher Conn Askew, Fox, 2009, watercolour, ink, gouache, graphite, gold leaf, and nail polish on paper

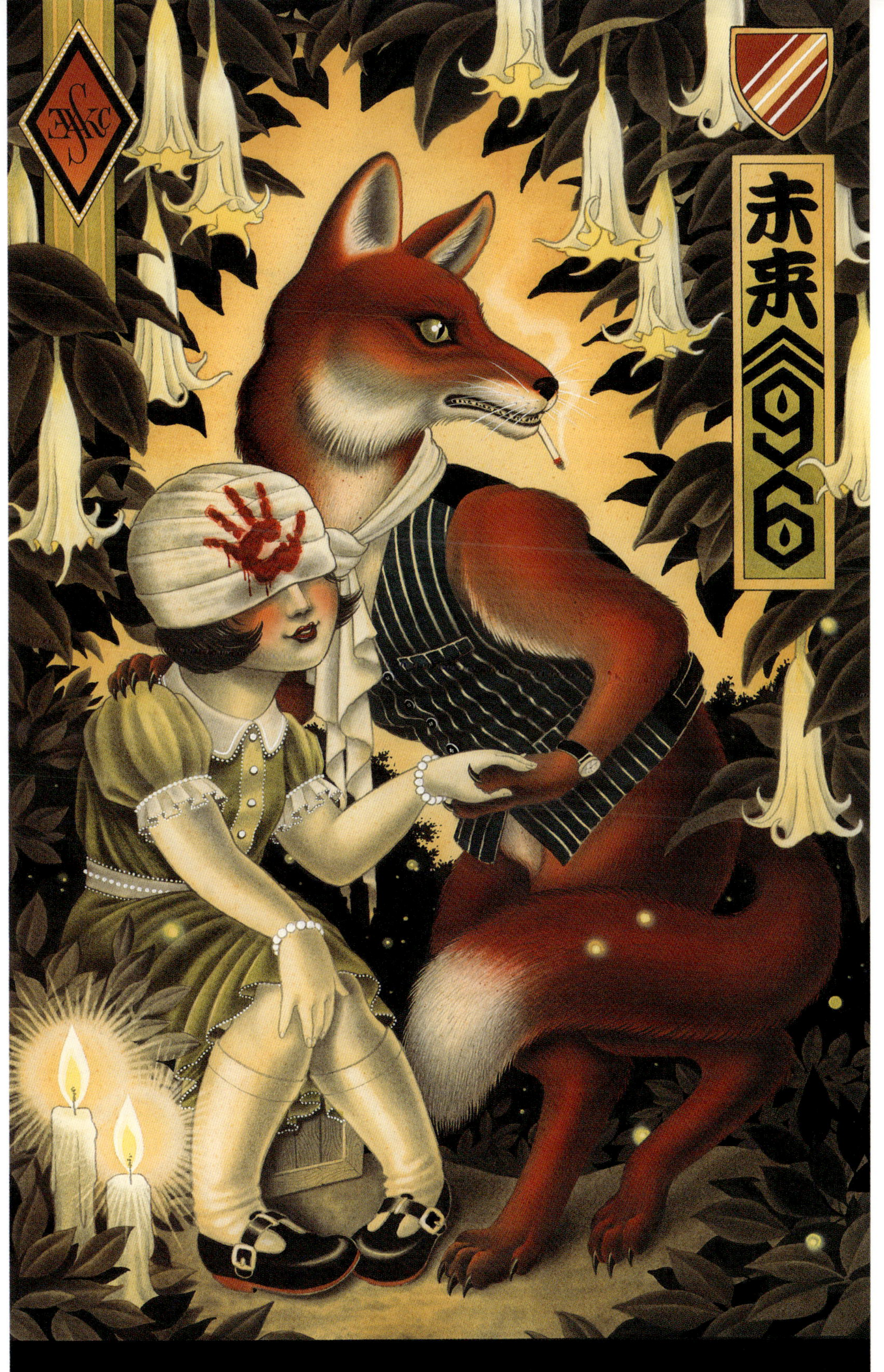

ET ENSUITE, LORSQUE LE SOIR AVANÇAIT...

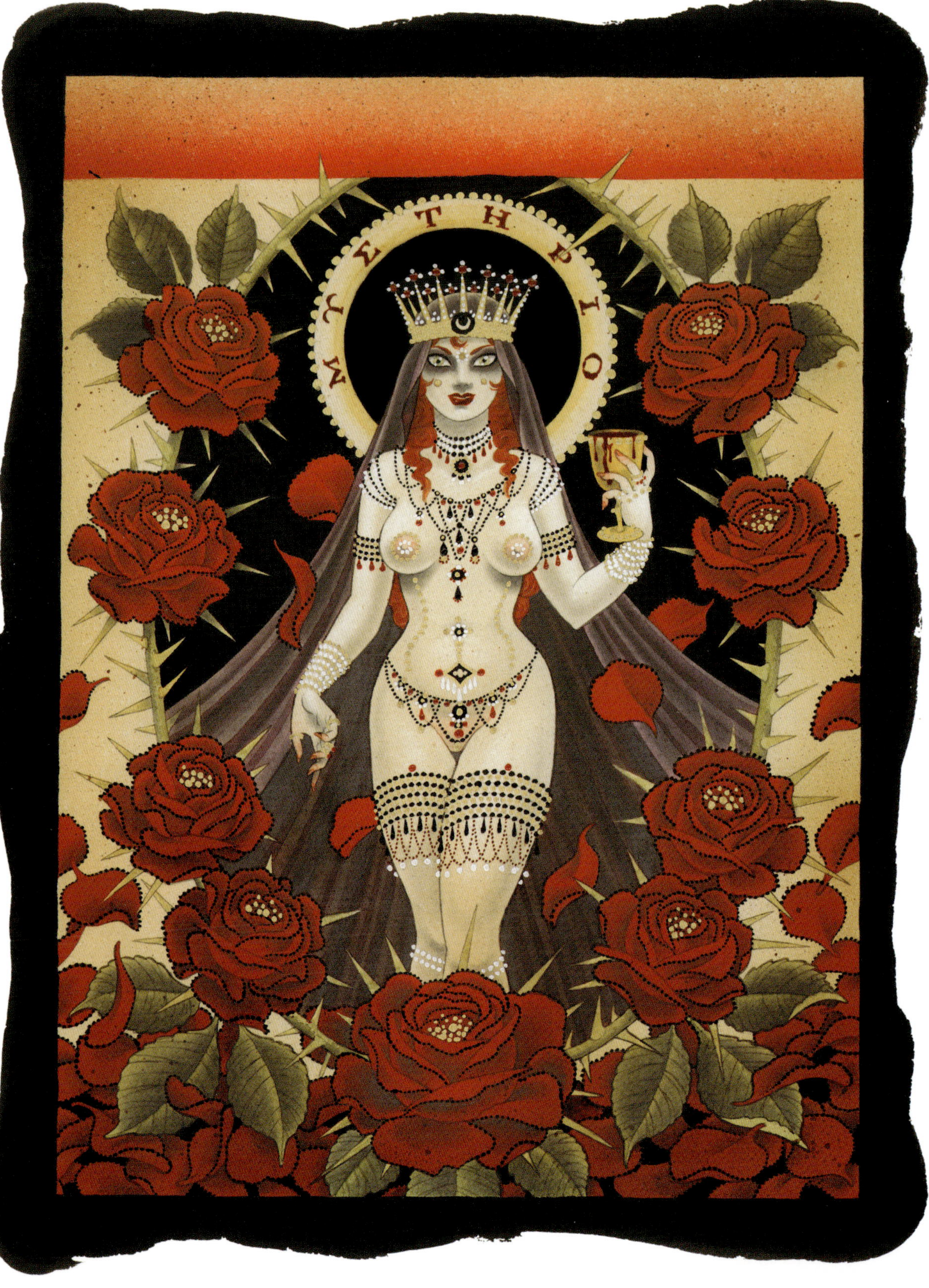
ΜΥΣΤΗΡΙΟ

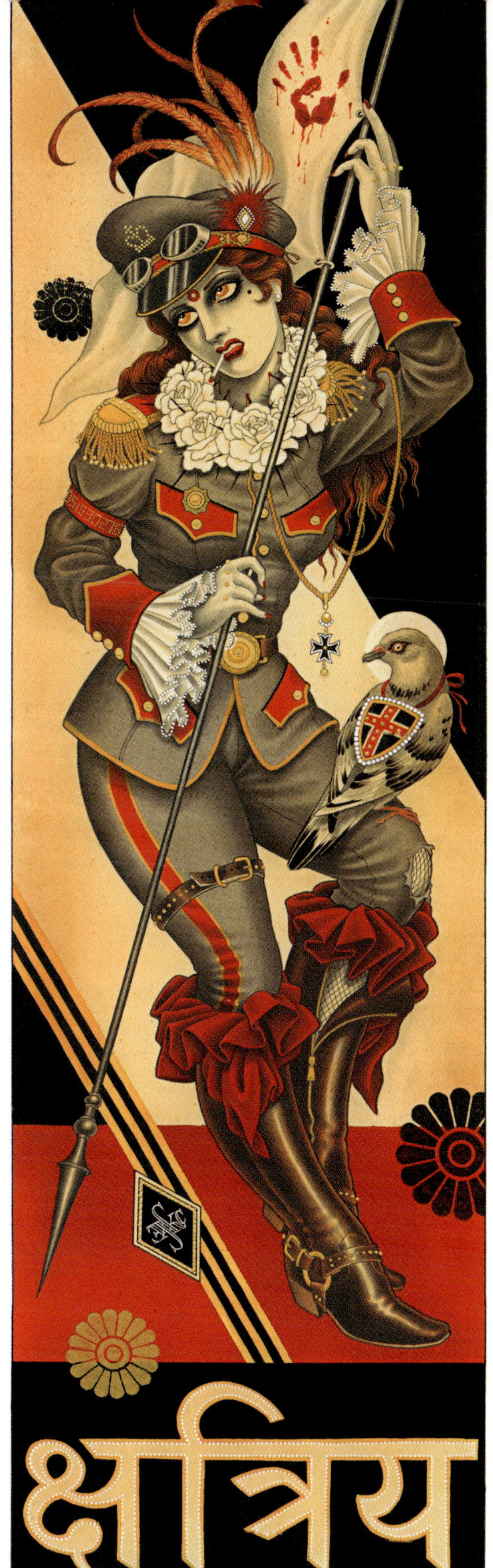

Christopher Conn Askew,
Kshatriya, 2009,
watercolour, ink, gouache,
graphite, gold leaf,
and nail polish on paper

(opposite)
Christopher Conn Askew,
Babalon, 2011,
watercolour, ink, gouache,
graphite, gold leaf,
and nail polish on paper

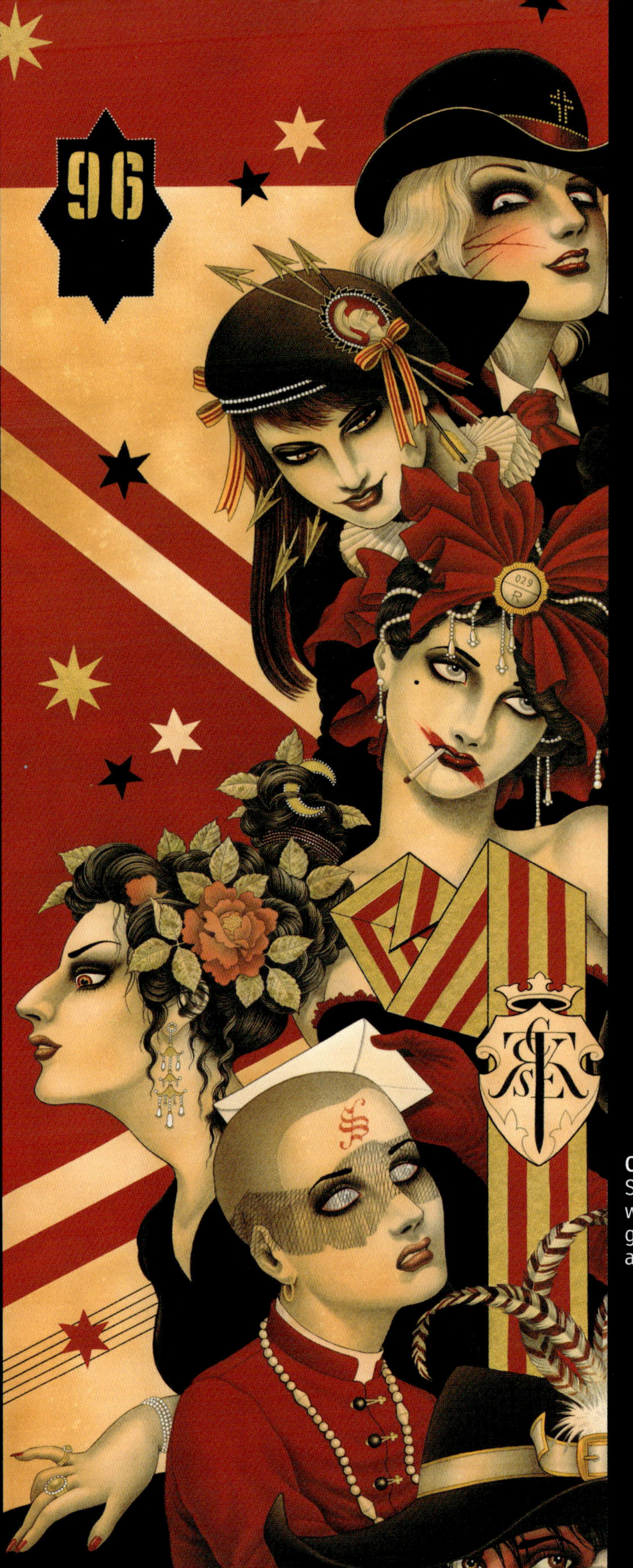

Christopher Conn Askew,
Six Girls, 2008,
watercolour, ink, gouache,
graphite, gold leaf,
and nail polish on paper

(opposite)
Christopher Conn Askew,
Eqvvs Novissimvs, 2010,
watercolour, ink, gouache,
graphite, gold leaf,
and nail polish on paper

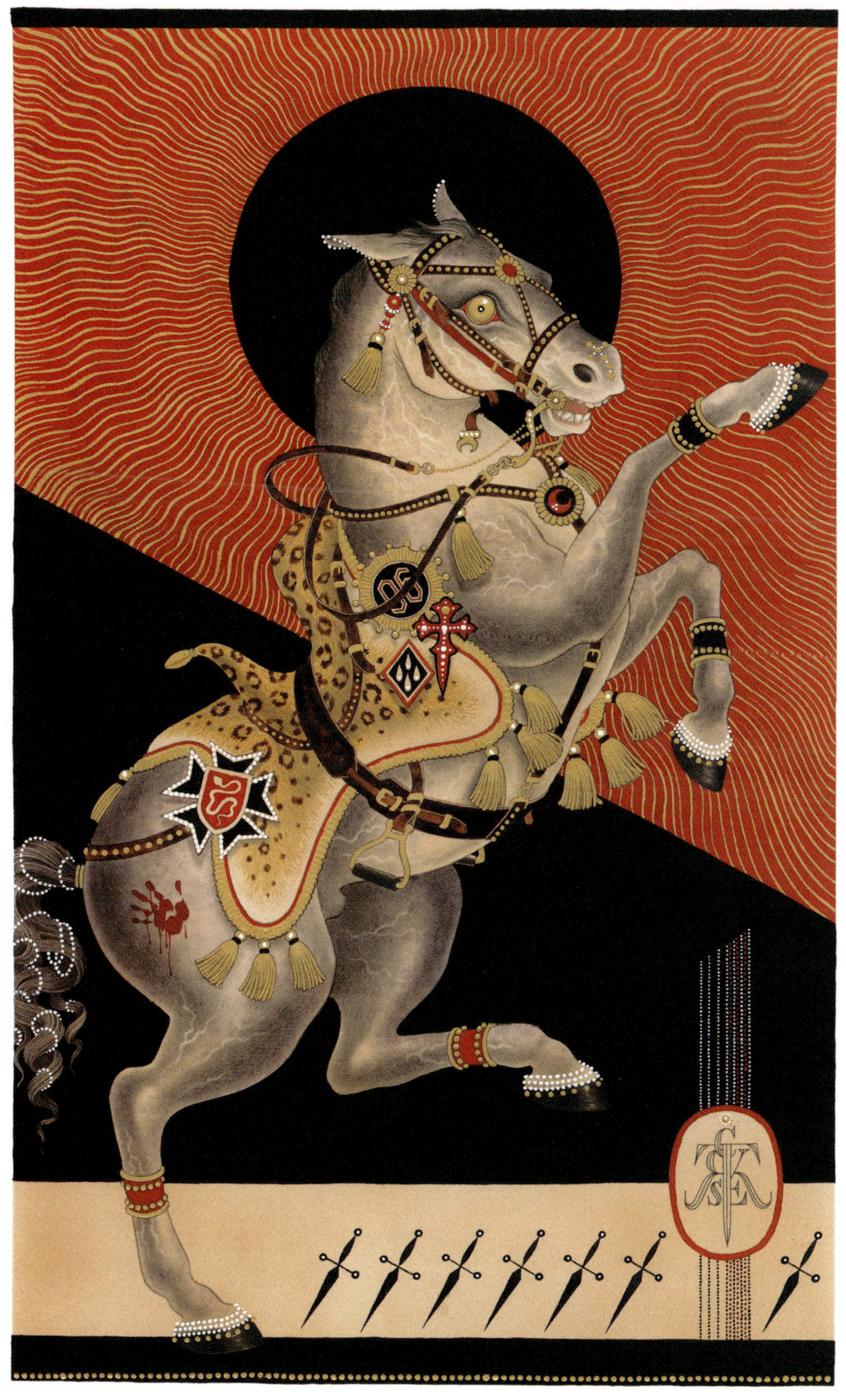

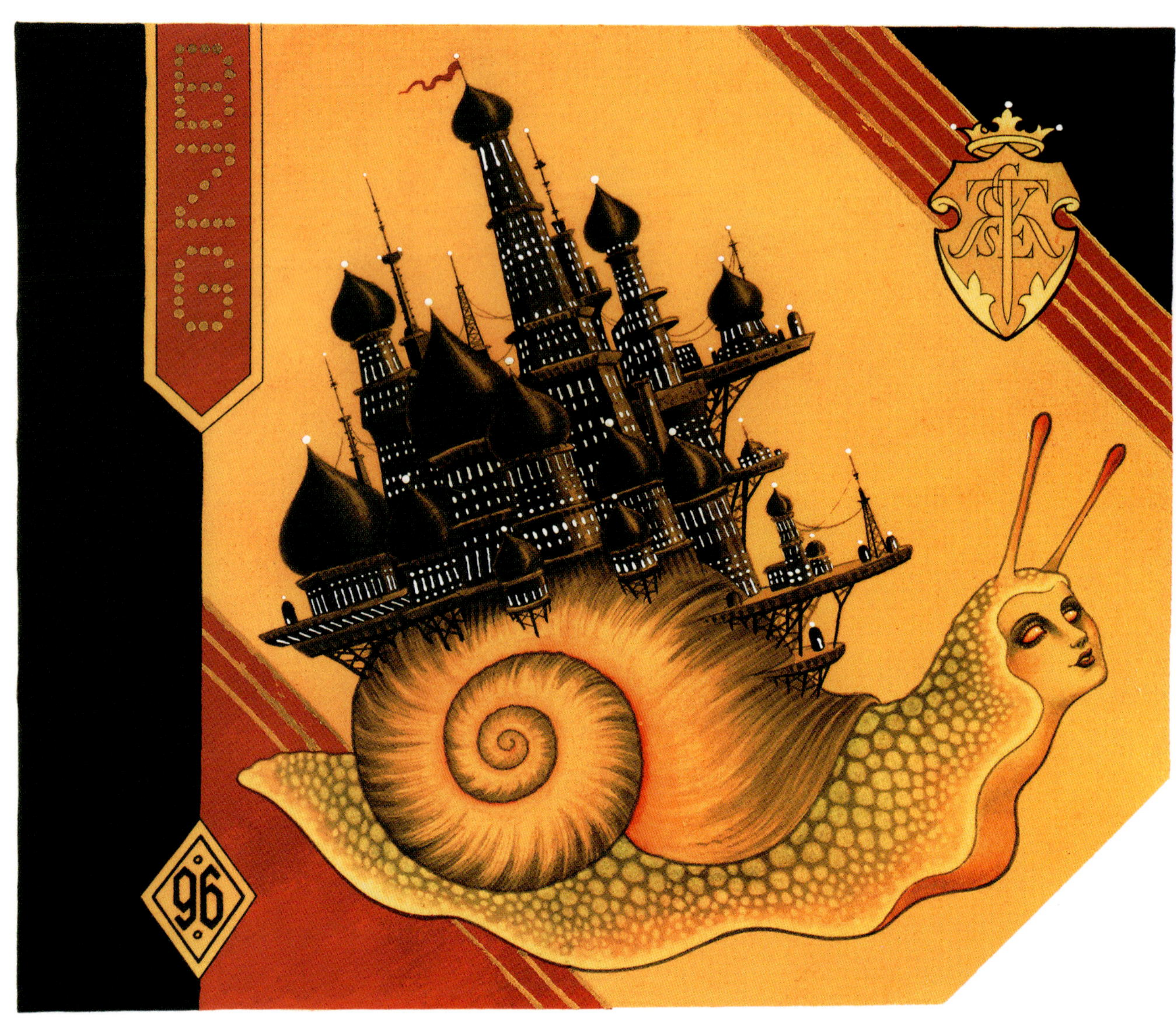

Christopher Conn Askew, B.Z.G., 2008, watercolour, ink, gouache, graphite, gold leaf, and nail polish on paper

(opposite) **Christopher Conn Askew**, Arcadia, 2010, watercolour, ink, gouache, graphite, gold leaf, and nail polish on paper

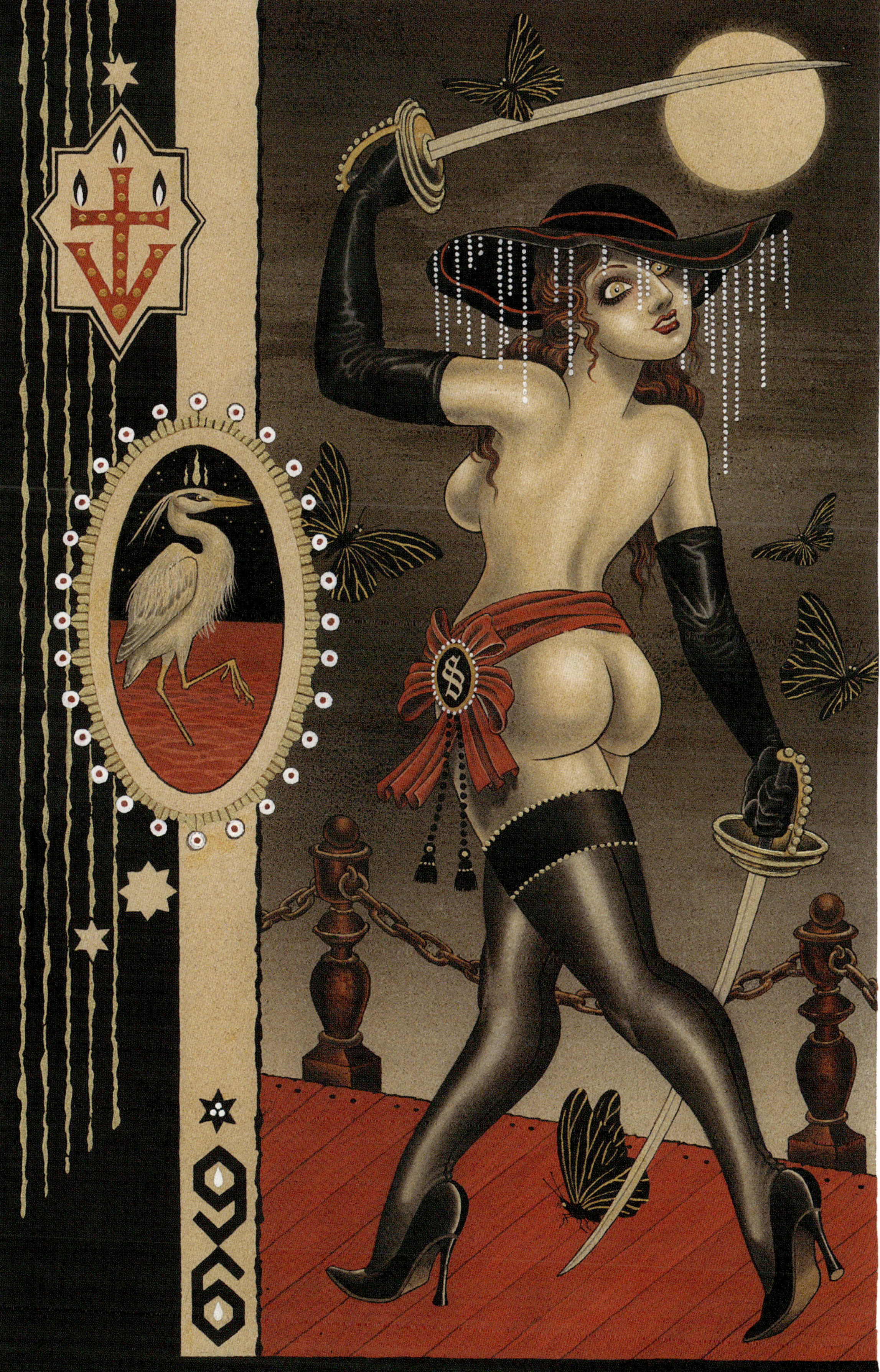

DR LAKRA

Born – 1972
Hometown – Mexico
Study / Apprenticeship – left school at 16, no apprenticeship
Years as a tattooist – since 1991
Favourite medium – ever changing

Of all the artists who have straddled the worlds of art and tattoo, the Mexican artist known as Dr Lakra has probably made the deepest inroads into the inner sanctums of white-cube galleries and museum-grade acceptability.

Born into a family of creatives, Lakra's father was a well known painter with whom he had an uneasy relationship. Rather than aspire to be a painter like his father, Lakra's compulsion to draw was fuelled by a love for cartoons and comic books like *MAD Magazine*.

Not surprisingly he's someone who is not only hard to pin down, but also feels himself somewhat at odds.

"I am sort of from everywhere... I'm not completely in the world of tattooing, but neither am I an illustrator. I'm everywhere and nowhere at the same time."[1]

Jerónimo López Ramírez adopted the moniker Dr Lakra doing rough tattoos out of a vintage doctor's bag in the early 1990s. "Lacra" appropriately translates to mean "scar" but also resonates another meaning – juvenile delinquent or lowlife.

"In Mexico no one was doing tattoos. No tattoo shops existed. Only punks and strange guys had tattoos. It wasn't a trend like it was now. It was more radical."[2]

One of Lakra's most significant early connections was meeting Ed Hardy at a tattoo convention around 1993. Hardy went on to invite Lakra to exhibit, traded him art for tattoo machines and on Hardy's recommendation saw him feature in the very first issue of *Juxtapoz* magazine.

Dr Lakra's works span a whole spectrum of different kinds of drawing. But he is best known for re-working and modifying found ephemera. He draws over vintage magazine images, mid-century pin-up girls, found photographs and old illustrations. Lakra virtually tattoos people from the past, obsessively covering unlikely beauty queens and the like with tattoo imagery and symbols. Often this new skin is crude, sexualised, wonderfully grotesque and down-right funny. Beautifully incongruous.

Lakra's technique and basis for drawing is closely connected with the way tattooists operate.

"A few years ago someone asked me how I had learned to draw. I remember I did tracings, I copied drawings on Albanene paper from the magazines I liked and then went over them with a pencil. When the tracing was finished I coloured them, which is basically what you do in tattooing. You put down a stencil, you make a line, and then you go over it. So I feel that yes, what I do has a lot of craft to it."[3]

It is drawing but also the brotherhood and bonds between people that is meaningful for Lakra as a tattooist.

"It's because of the social aspect of tattooing, of relating to someone else. It's not to create something graphic, or strange, or intentional, but rather a question of getting together with friends and creating ties"[4]

1 "Dr Lakra" by Amelia Hinojosa (ed) and Damian Ortega (ed), RM Verlag, Barcelona, 2010, p.34. **2** "Dr Lakra" by Caleb Neelon in Juxtapoz #115, August 2010, p.51. **3** Hinojosa, op. cit. **4** ibid.

Artwork photography by Estudio Michel Zabé, and Estudio Michel Zabé / Omar Luis Olguin. All artwork courtesy of the artist and kurimanzutto, Mexico City.

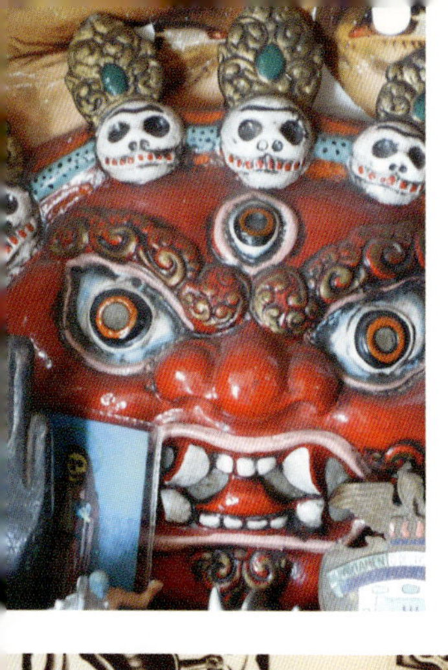

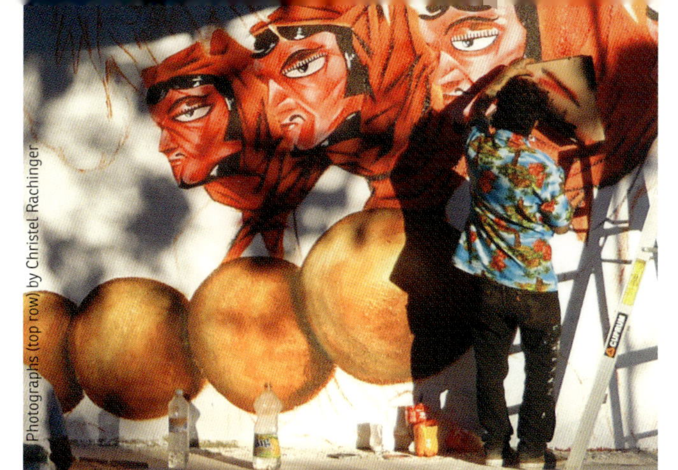

Photographs (top row) by Christel Rachinger

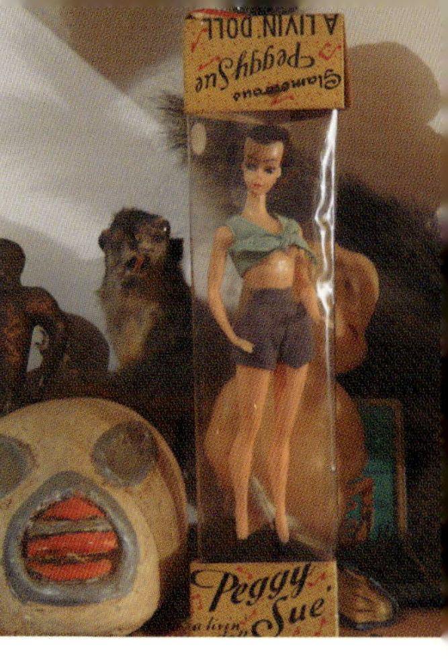

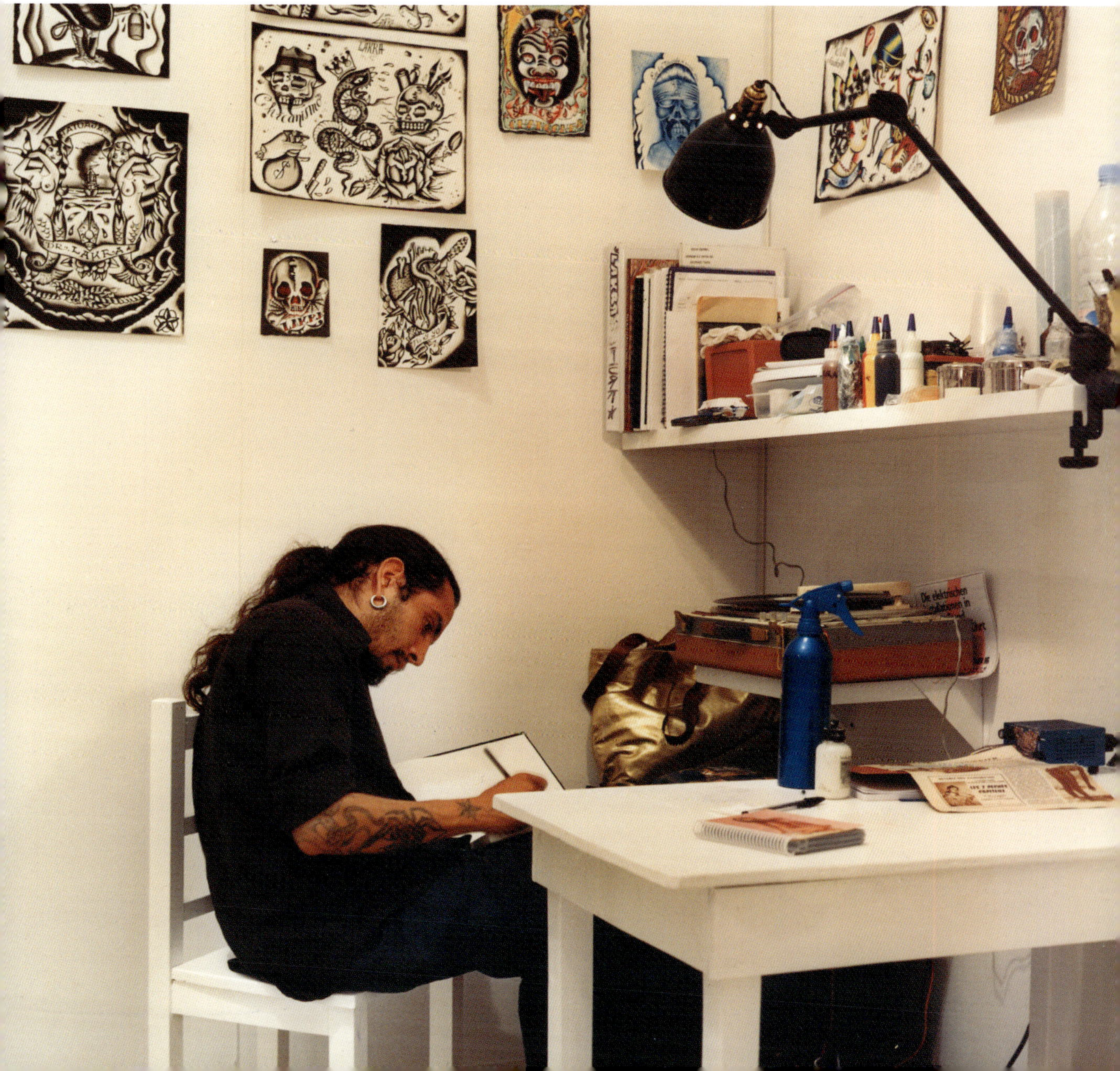

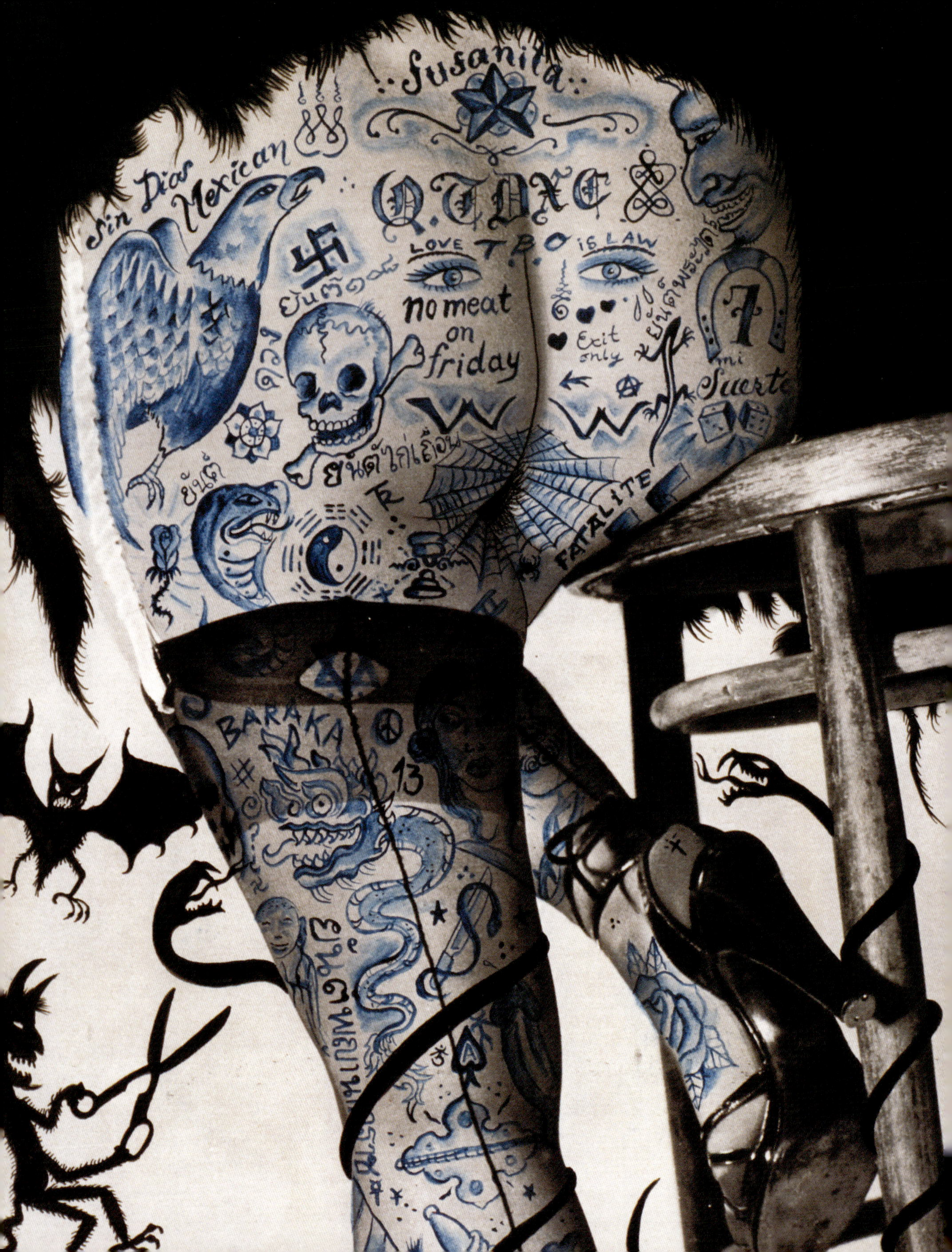
Susanita
Sin Dios
Mexican
LOVE
T.B.O
IS LAW
no meat on friday
Exit only
7
mi Suerte
FATALITE
BARAKA
13

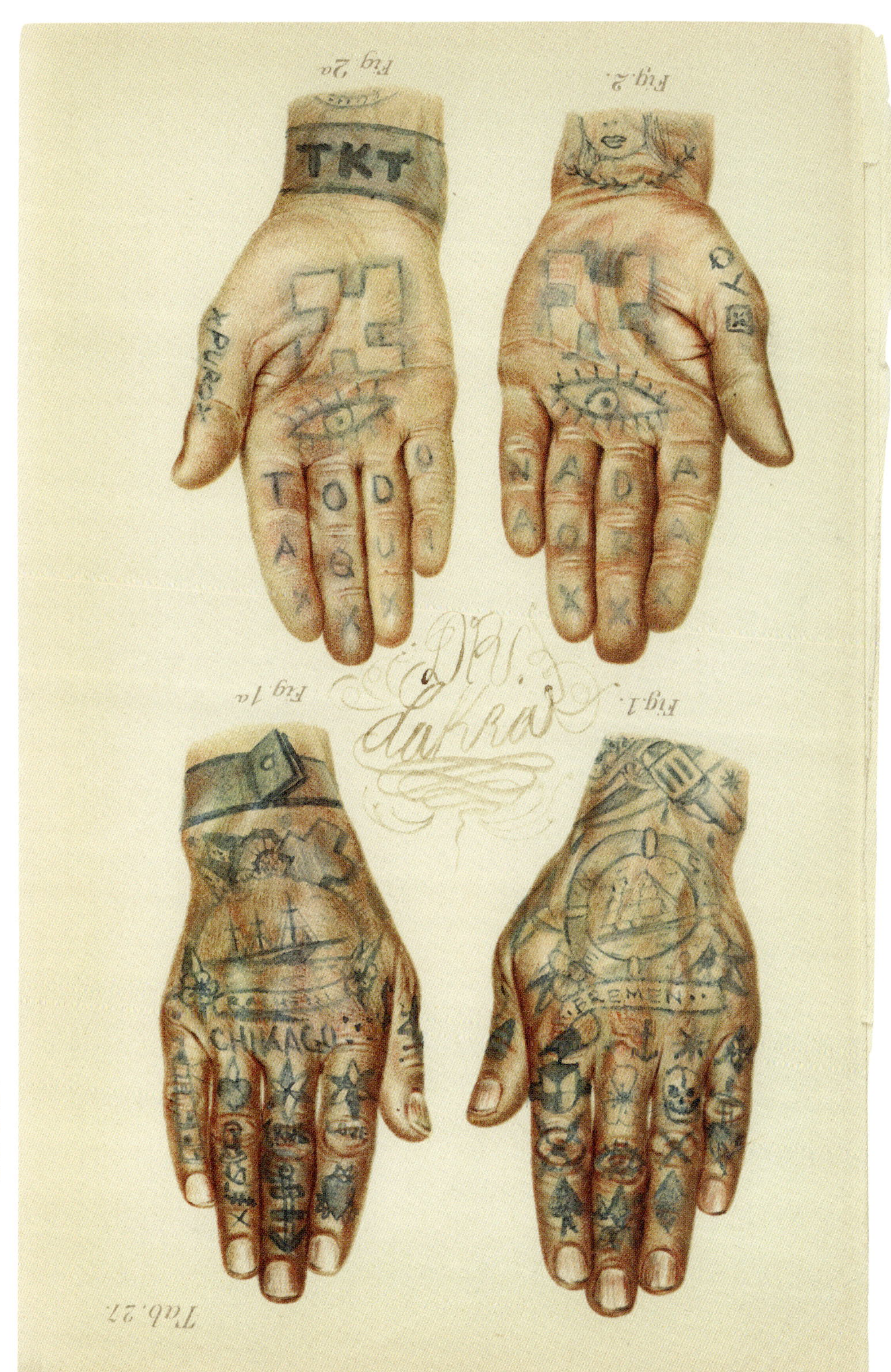

Dr Lakra,
Sin título / Untitled (Tab. 27), 2009, ink on vintage lithography, 18 x 11cm

(opposite)
Dr Lakra,
Sin título / Untitled (Nalgas), 2003, ink on antique magazine 23.5 x 31cm

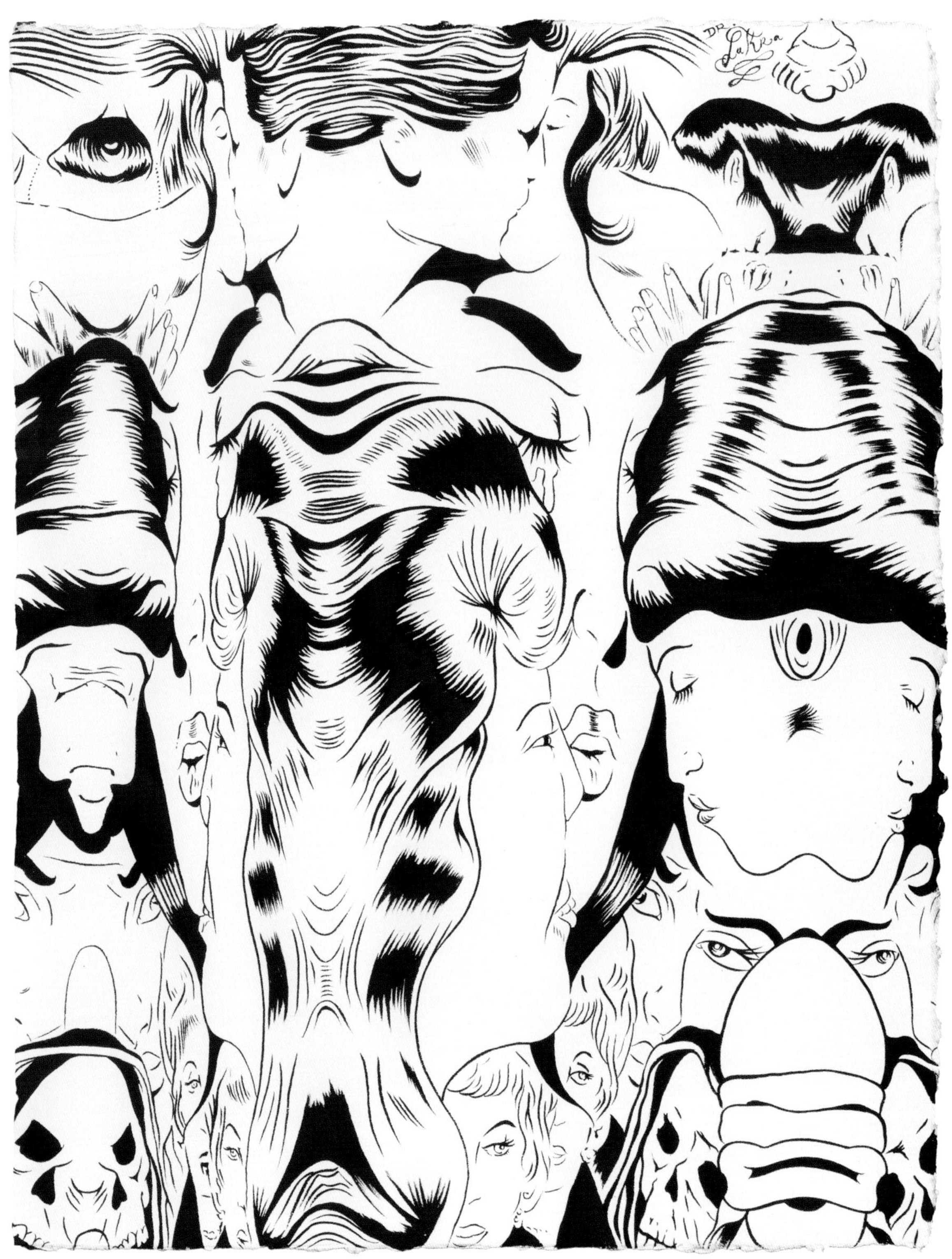

Dr Lakra, Sin título/Untitled (Espejo en blanco y negro), 2009, ink on cotton paper, 76.5 x 56cm

(opposite) **Dr Lakra**, Sin título/Untitled (Estrella blanca), 2005, ink on poster, 48 x 34cm

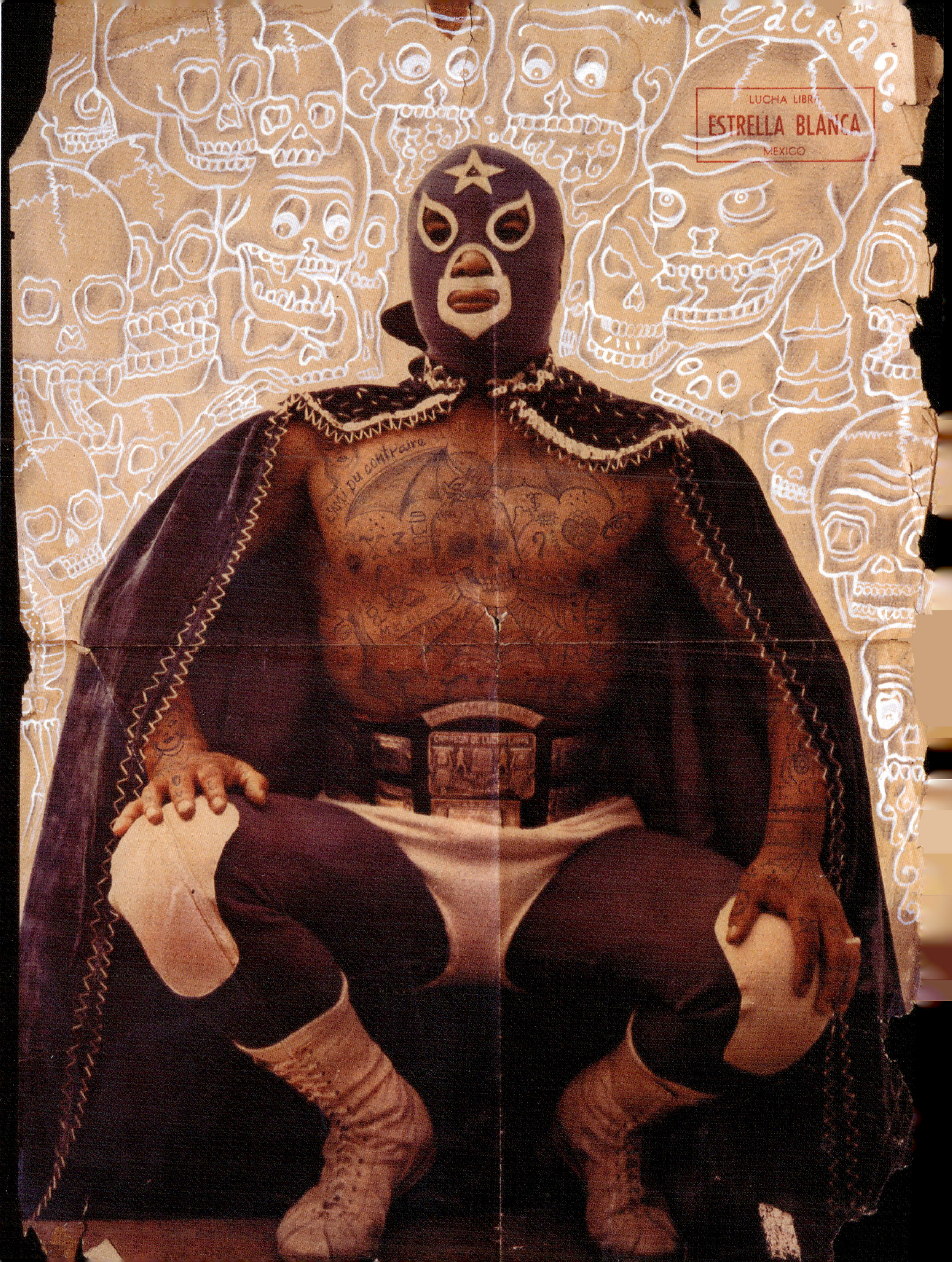
LUCHA LIBRE
ESTRELLA BLANCA
MEXICO

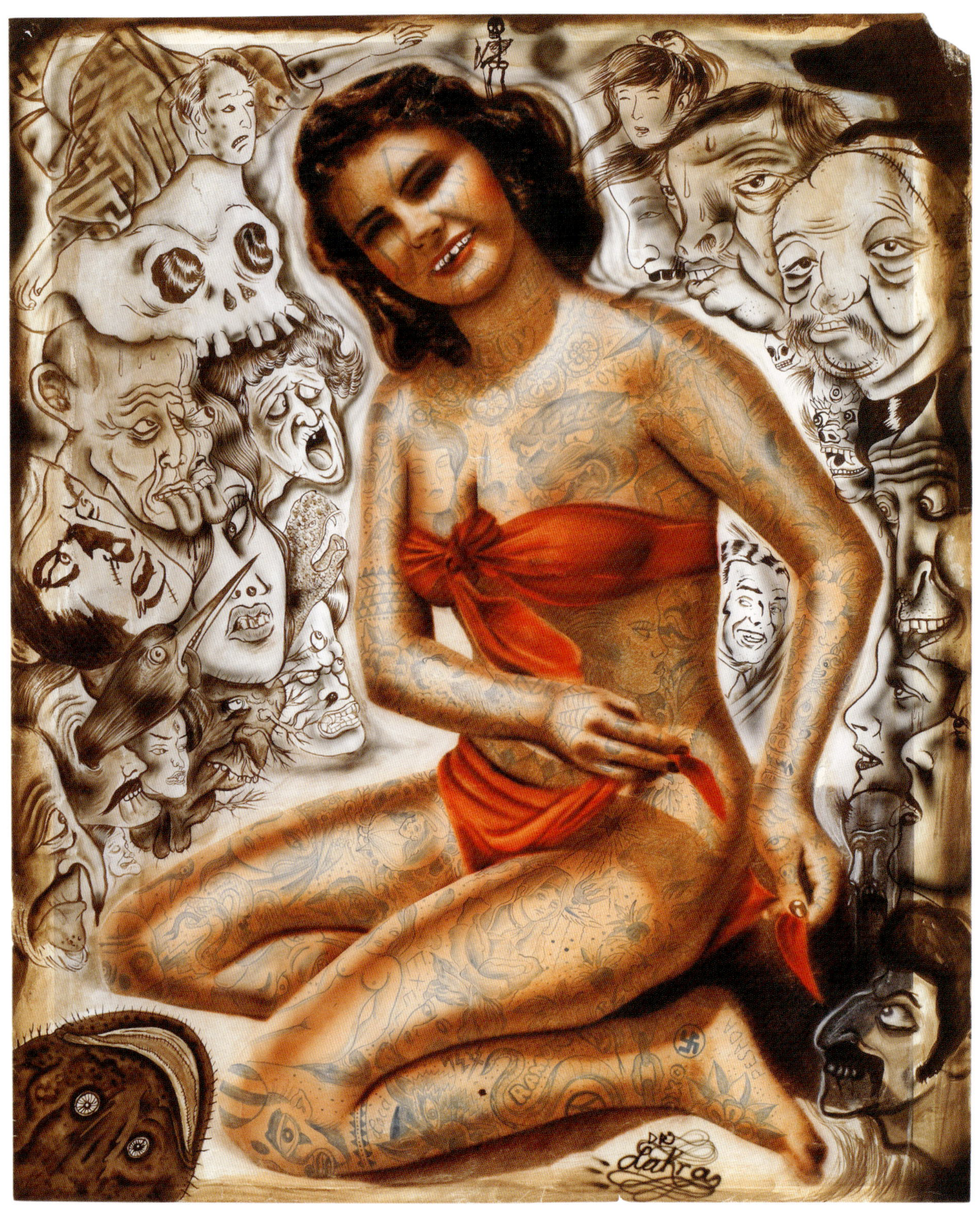

Dr Lakra, Sin título / Untitled (Mujer en bikini con dibujo), 2009, ink on digital print on paper, 139.5 x 101.6cm

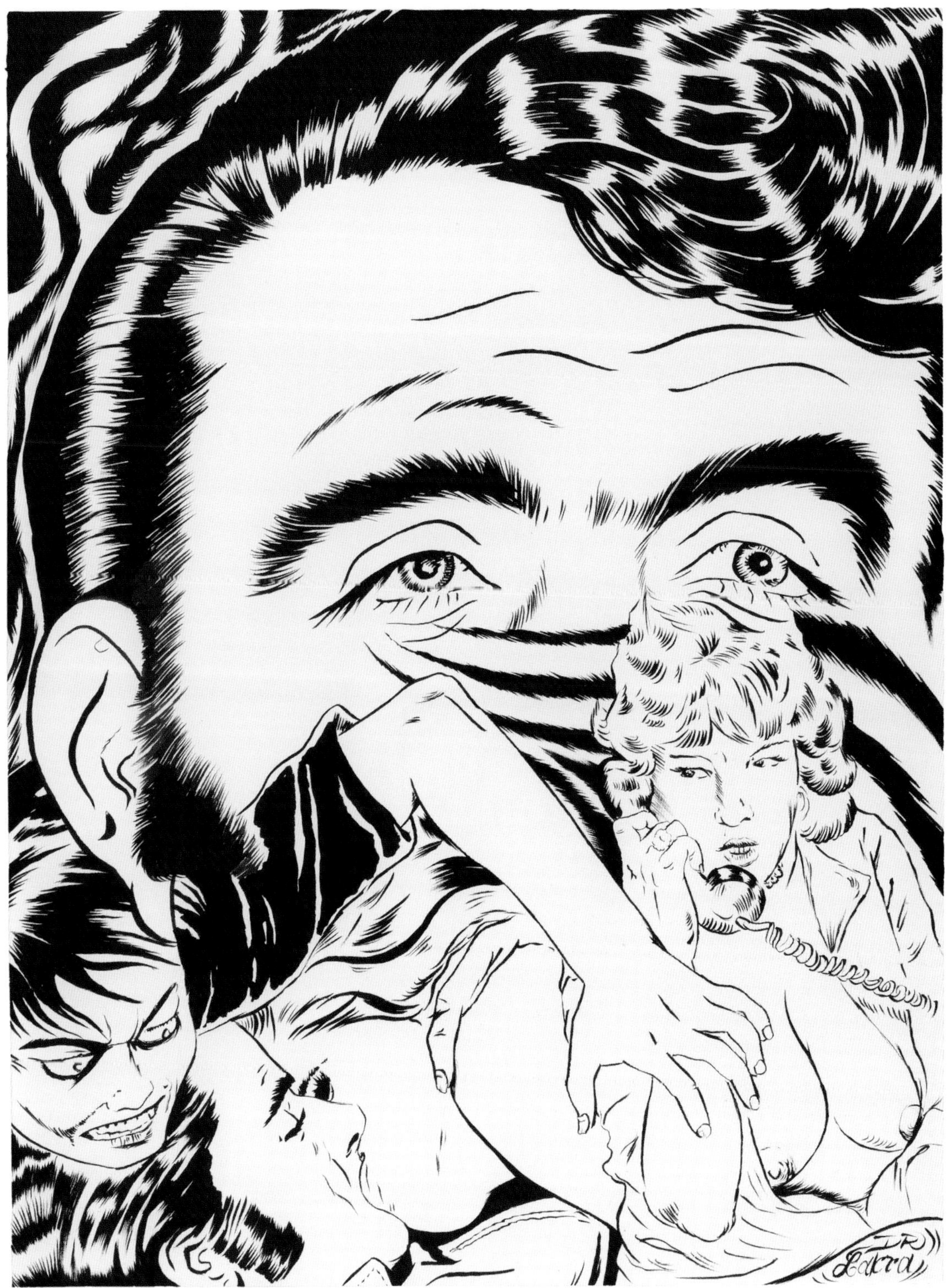

Dr Lakra, Sin título/Untitled (Blanco y negro V), 2009, ink on cotton paper, 76 x 55.5cm

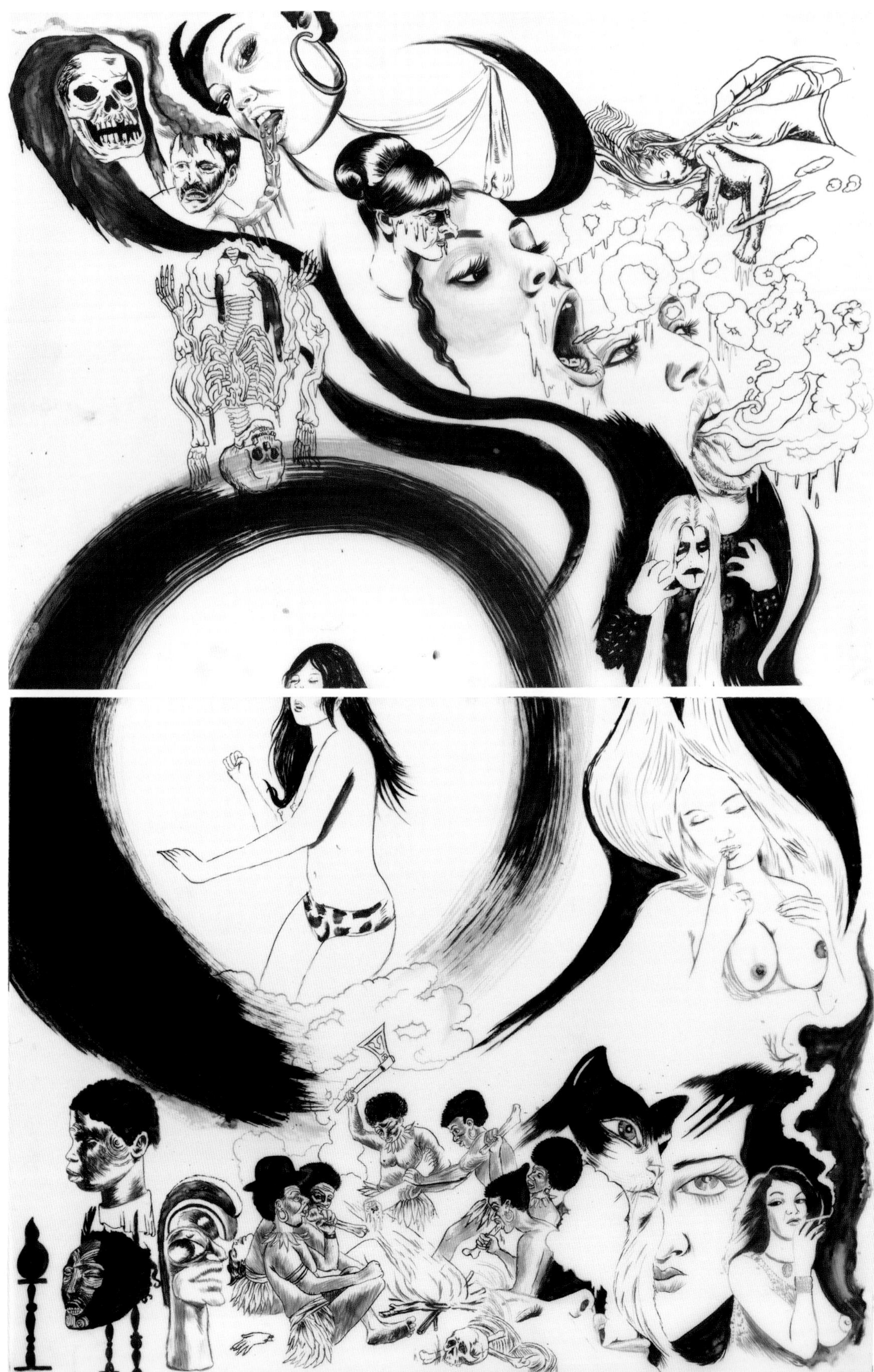

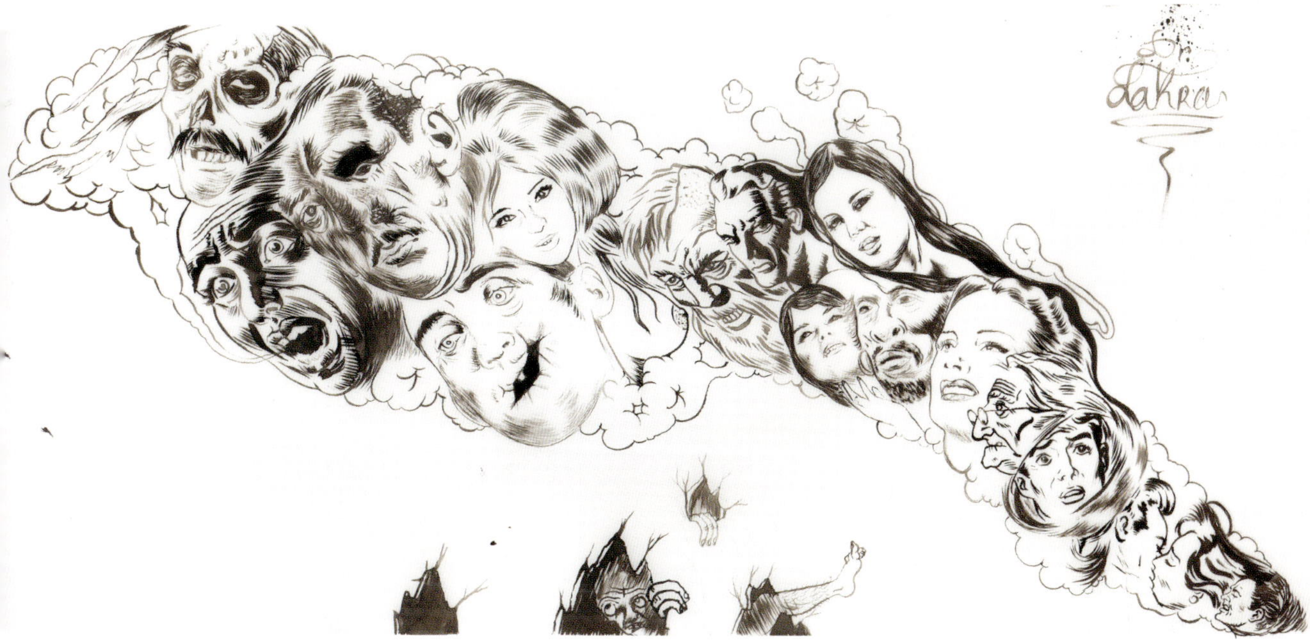

top) **Dr Lakra**, Sin título / Untitled (Boceto 33), 2009, ink on tracing paper, 23.4 x 47.5cm
bottom) **Dr Lakra**, Sin título / Untitled (mural), 2010, ink and paint, both sides of wall, each 396.2 x 1493.5cm,
nstallation view at ICA / Boston, photograph: John Kennard

opposite) **Dr Lakra**, Sin título / Untitled (Boceto 77), 2010, ink on tracing paper, 48 x 61cm / 48.5 x 61cm

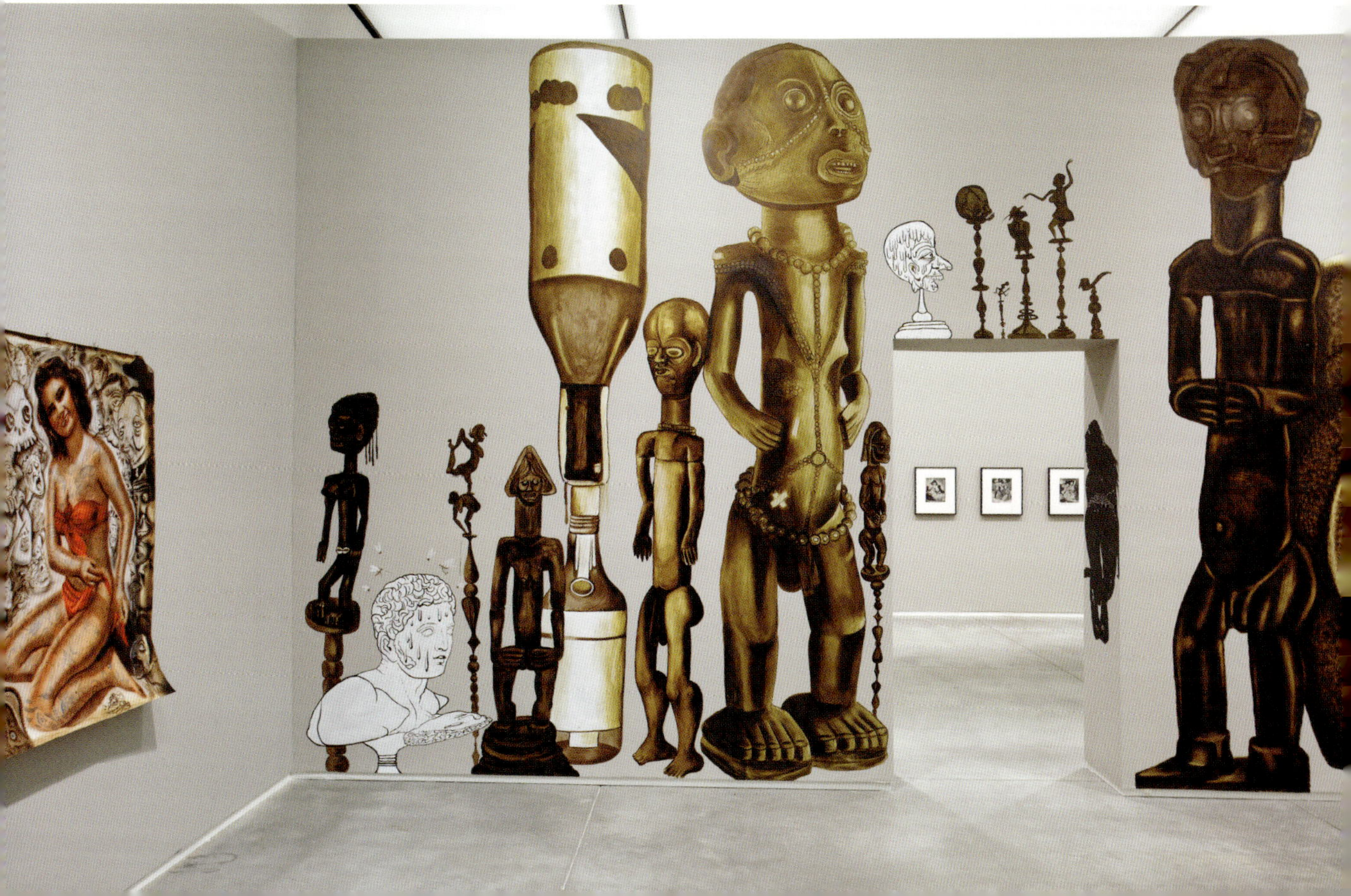

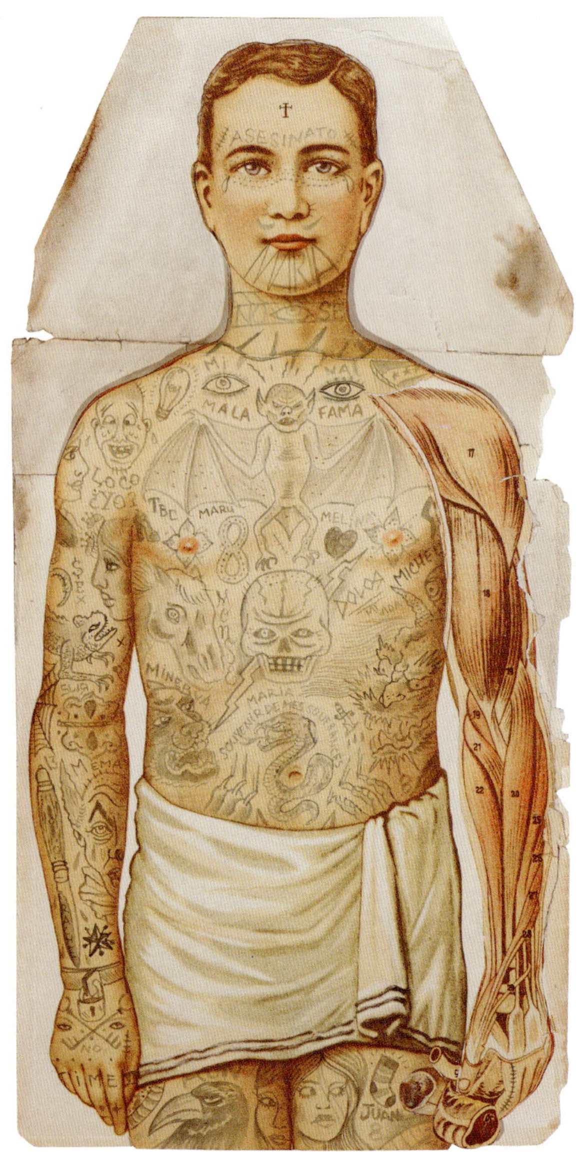

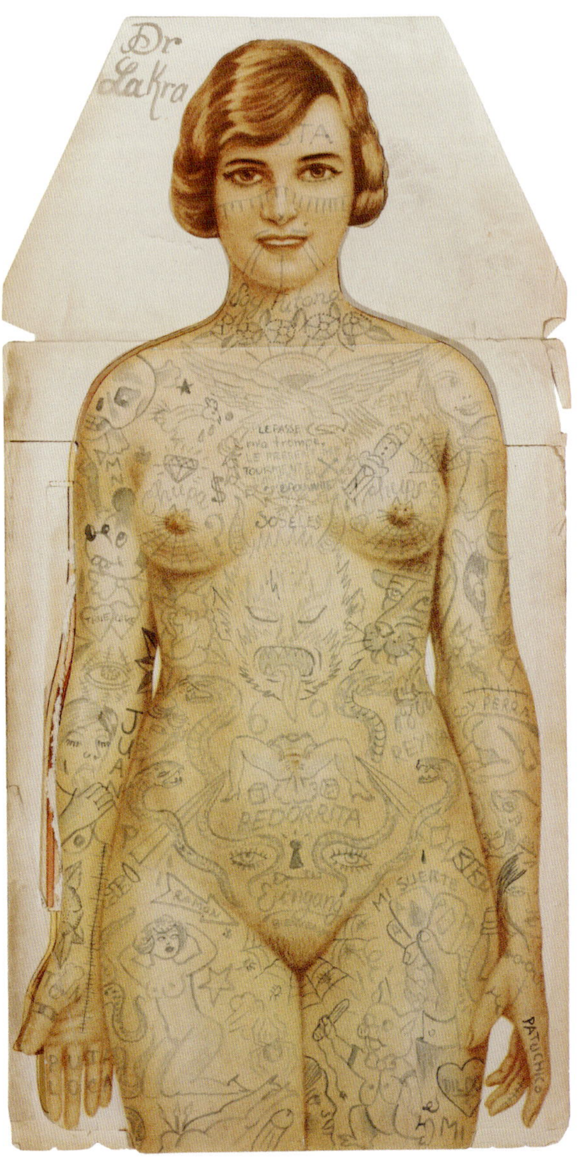

Dr Lakra, Sin título / Untitled (Anatomía Él y Ella), 2009, ink on lithography 30.3 x 15cm / 30.4 x 15cm,

(opposite)
Dr Lakra, Sin título / Untitled (Toñito), 2010, ink on vintage lithograph, 36 x 29.5cm

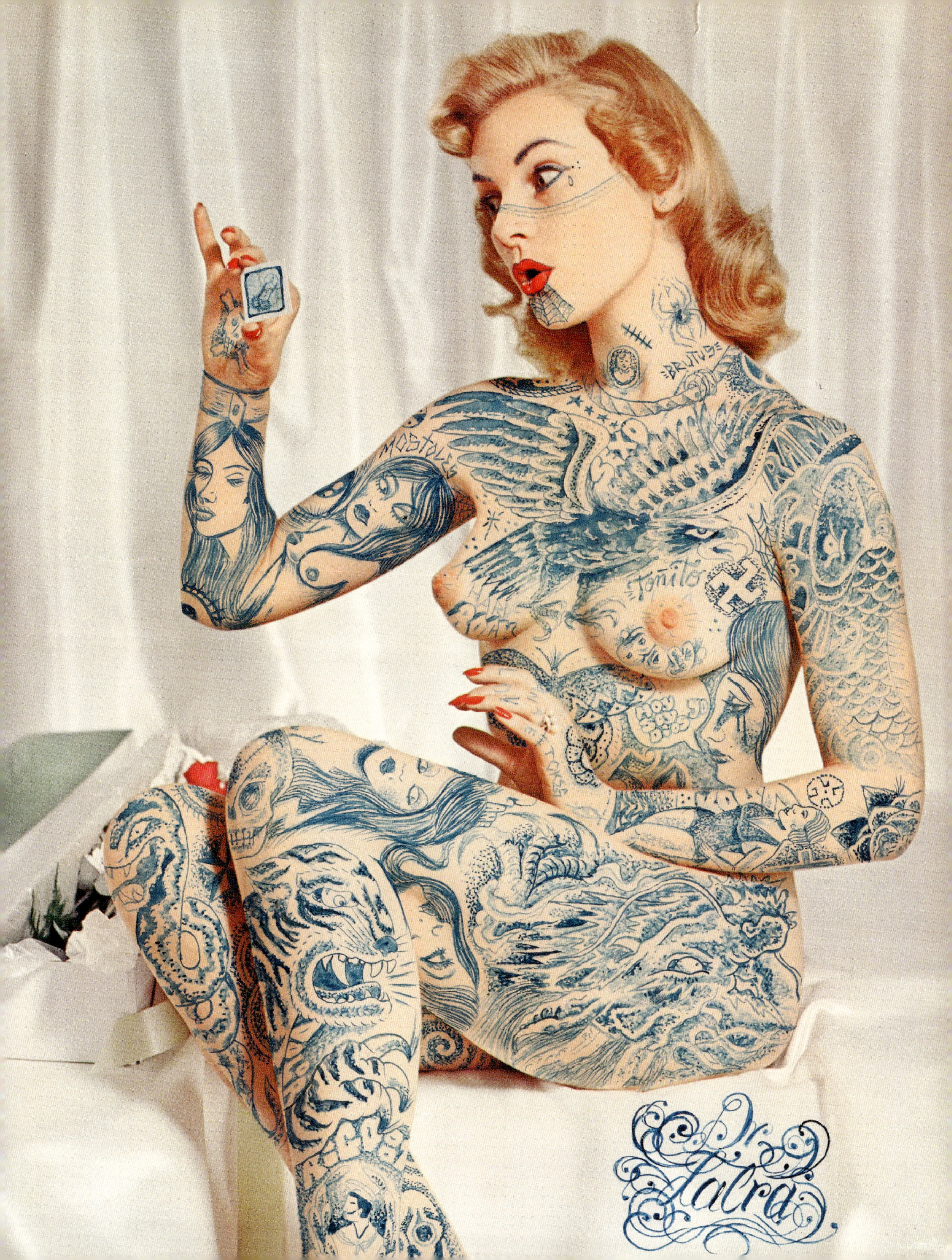
Dr. Lakra

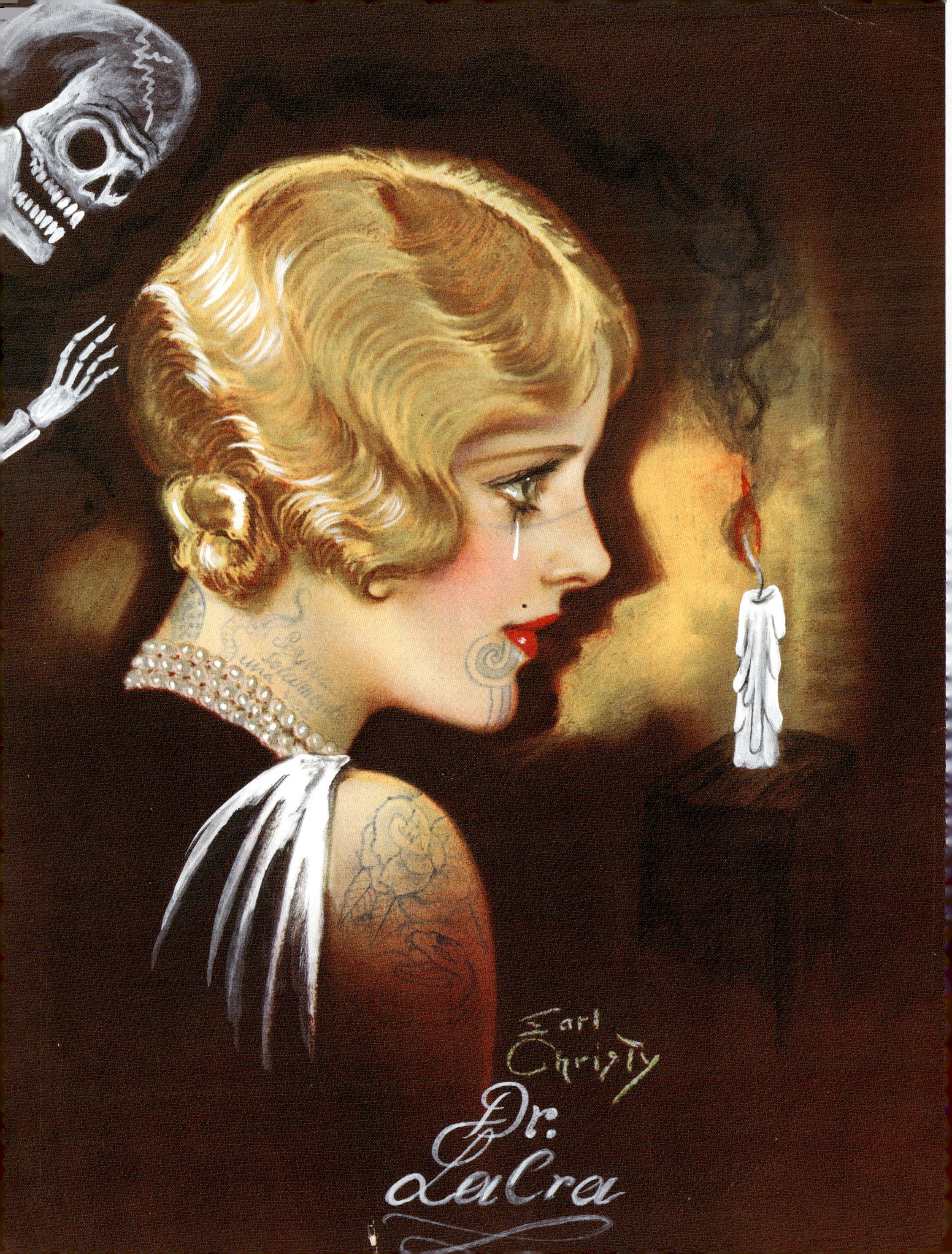
Earl Christy
Dr. Lakra

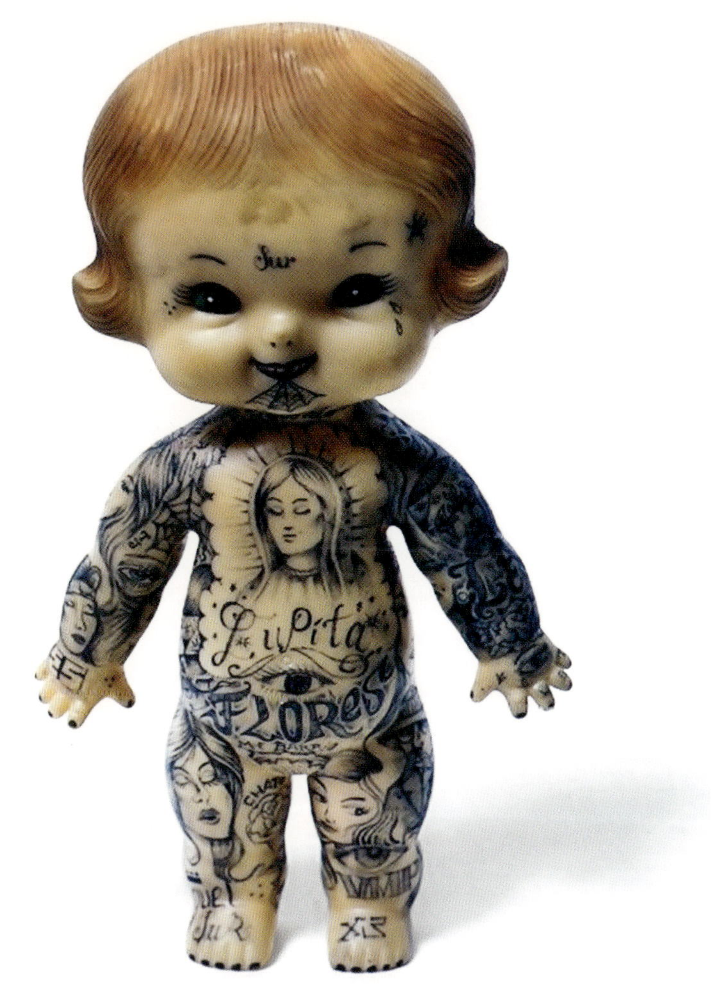

Dr Lakra, Sin título / Untitled (Cupido Lupita), 2006, tattooed plastic doll, 32 x 19 x 7.5cm

(opposite)
Dr Lakra, Sin título / Untitled (Vela), 2010, ink on vintage magazine page, 30.2 x 22.7cm

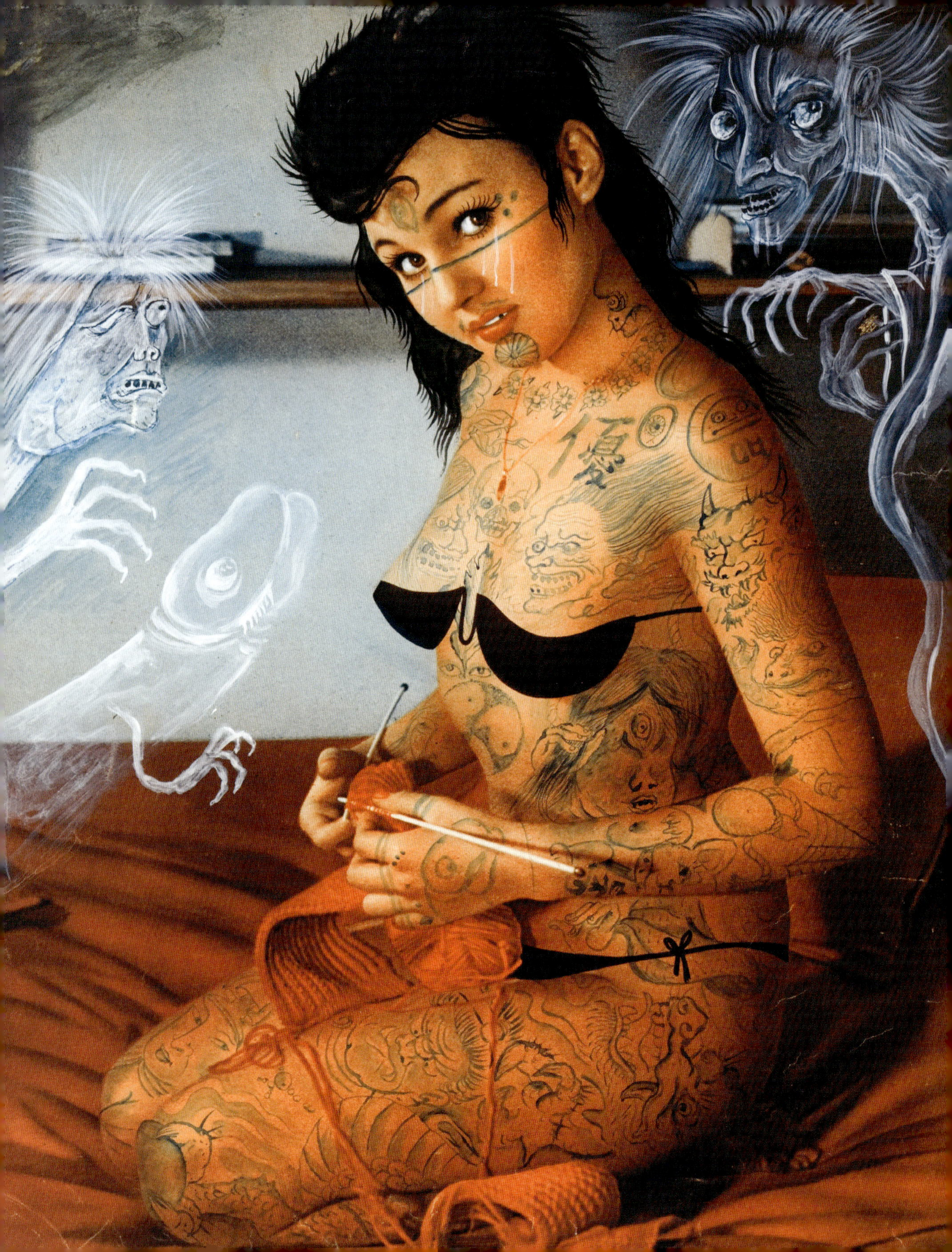

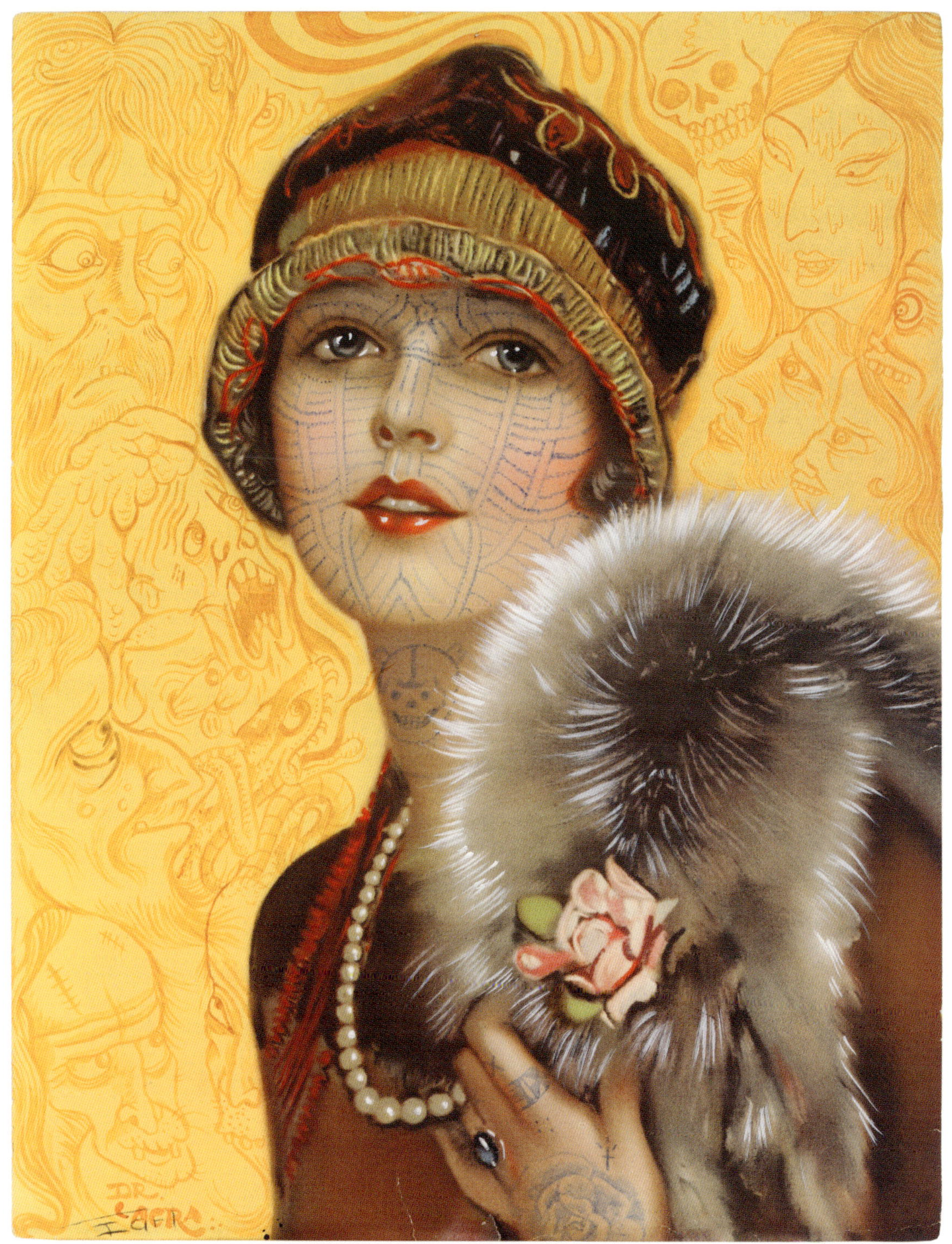

Dr Lakra, Sin título / Untitled (Zorro), 2010, ink on vintage lithograph, 30.2 x 22.9cm

(opposite) **Dr Lakra**, Sin título / Untitled (Joven tejiendo y espectros), 2007, ink and acrylic paint on page of vintage magazine, 31 x 24cm

MIKE GIANT

Born – 1971
Hometown – Brockport, New York
Study / Apprenticeship – University of New Mexico 1989 - 1993, Architecture major
Lives and Works – San Francisco, California
Years as a tattooist – 12 years
Favourite medium – Sharpie permanent marker on paper

Michael Le Sage adopted the tag Giant in 1989 as a graffiti writer in New Mexico. As a towering and influential figure in underground pop culture, it's a name that rings true.

A self-confessed "grandpa hipster", Giant mixes his love for San Francisco, bike riding, tattoo culture and meditation with his background in skating, architecture, graffiti and an amazing work ethic. From graffiti to architecture to tattoo to illustration, one has a sense that this journey is a loop for Giant that is going to keep informing and feeding on itself.

Giant is known for his stark, powerful, simple black and white line work, executed with Sharpie markers. Being colour blind, for him, this was the natural way to work. But it also comes down to the strength of the image, which directly translates into the language of a good tattoo.

"I just like the black and white, I love how it reads from a distance. When you strip something down to it bare, simple essentials, there's so little room for error and I think that's when your craft can come through. I think that's something that universally impresses people, when you can kinda dumbfound them with your craft."[1]

And his particular brand of handmade craft is at the core of all of his creative endeavours – be it graffiti, illustration or tattoo work. "I'm really into craft. I think your skill with your medium is super important. I don't think your individual style can really shine until you've mastered your medium. I love to see artwork with a high degree of craft."

The necessity of speed and efficiency he learnt from graffiti has pervaded the way he works in general. He is infamous for his technique of ink straight to paper. No sketching.

"It's always better to nail your outline straight away so you can get the fuck on to the next spot. In that way, lining (graffiti) pieces can be a lot like lining with Sharpies, or even a tattoo machine. It requires a directness of concentration that can't be faked. Precise action."[2]

Giant gave up tattooing some years ago for a number of reasons; the physical toll on his own body, the demands of perfection and the overwhelming sense of pain.

"It's heavy I think, you're marking people, you're making them bleed and hurt and a lot of the time you're manifesting things that they feel so compelled in their heart to put into their skin and at the risk of all kinds of financial loss and pain and being judged by their family, all kinds of stupid shit. It's a lot different than just drawing on paper, that's for sure."[3]

Despite giving up professional tattooing, Giant maintains a strong link to tattoo culture through his palpable love for tattoo imagery and his sincere desire to perpetuate the symbolic power of tattoos in his artwork.

1 "Mike Giant: Black and White" by L. Ruano on Hypebeast, www.hypebeast.com, 15 June 2009. **2** "Mike Giant Interview" on Fecal Face, www.fecalface.com, 31 December 2008. **3** Ruano, op. cit.

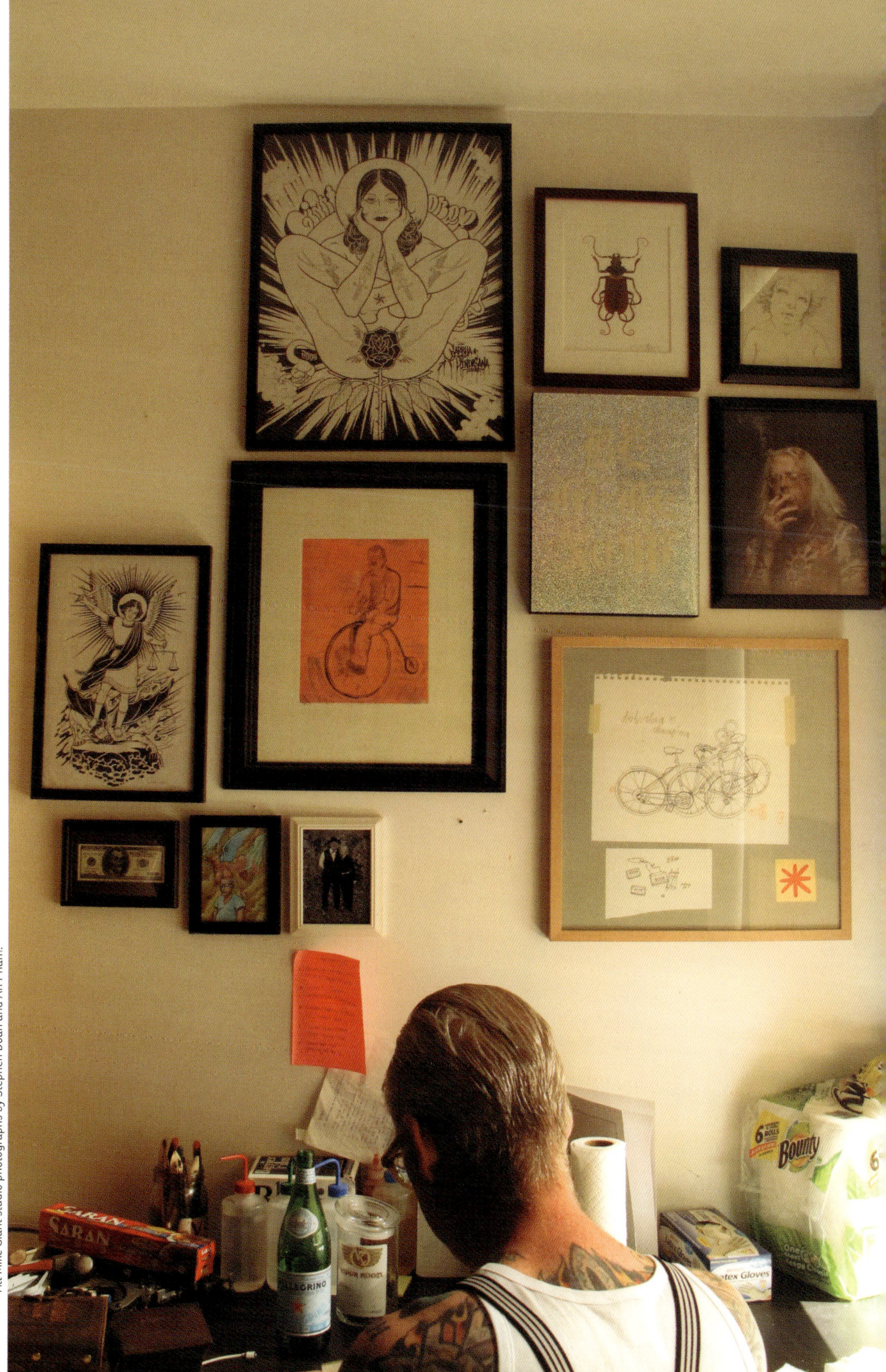

All Mike Giant studio photographs by Stephen Doan and An Pham.

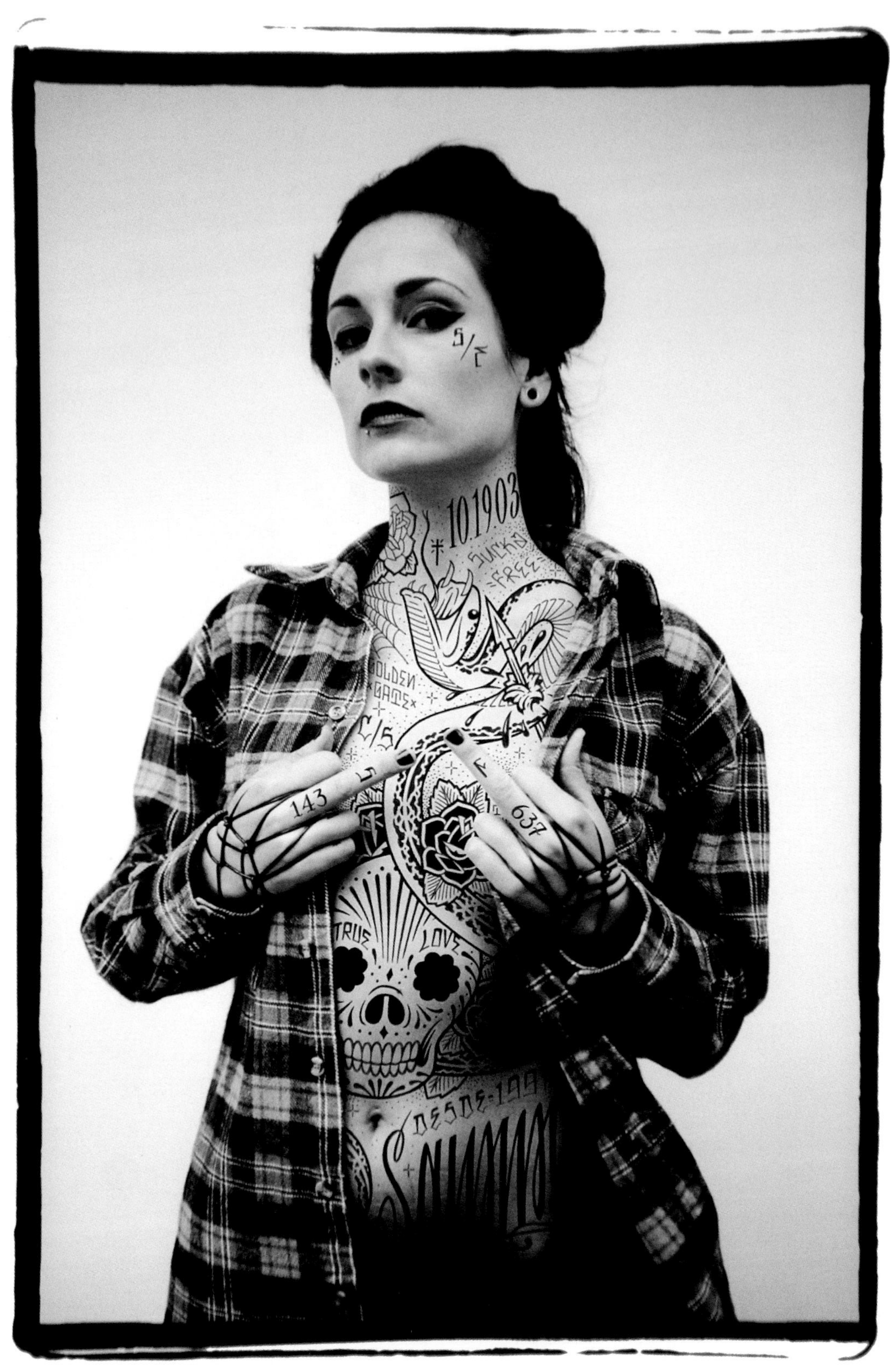

Mike Giant, Kristene, 2010, Sharpie on digital print, 61 x 45.5cm

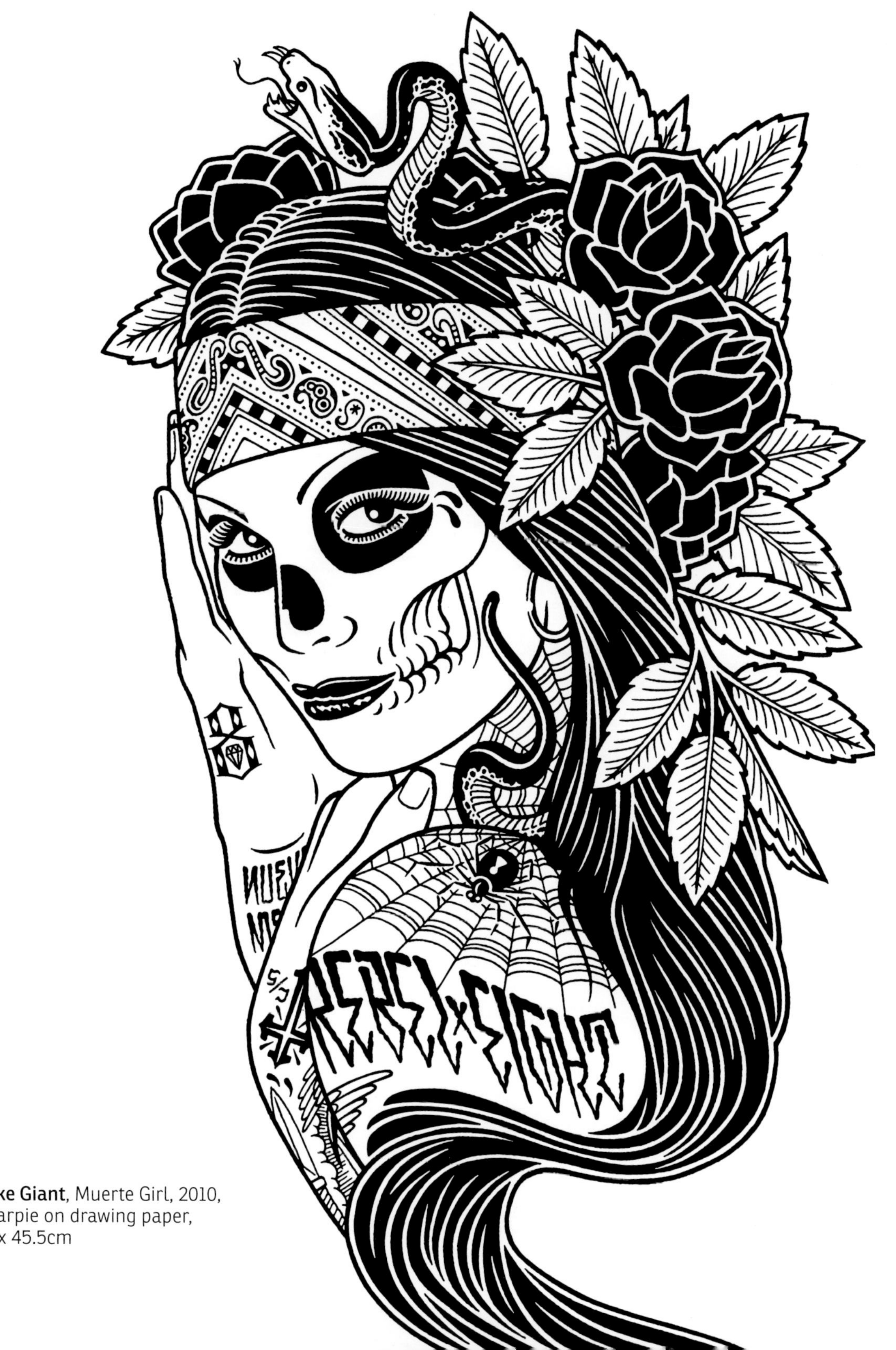

Mike Giant, Muerte Girl, 2010,
Sharpie on drawing paper,
61 x 45.5cm

Mike Giant, Skater Girl, 2010,
Sharpie on drawing paper,
61 x 45.5cm

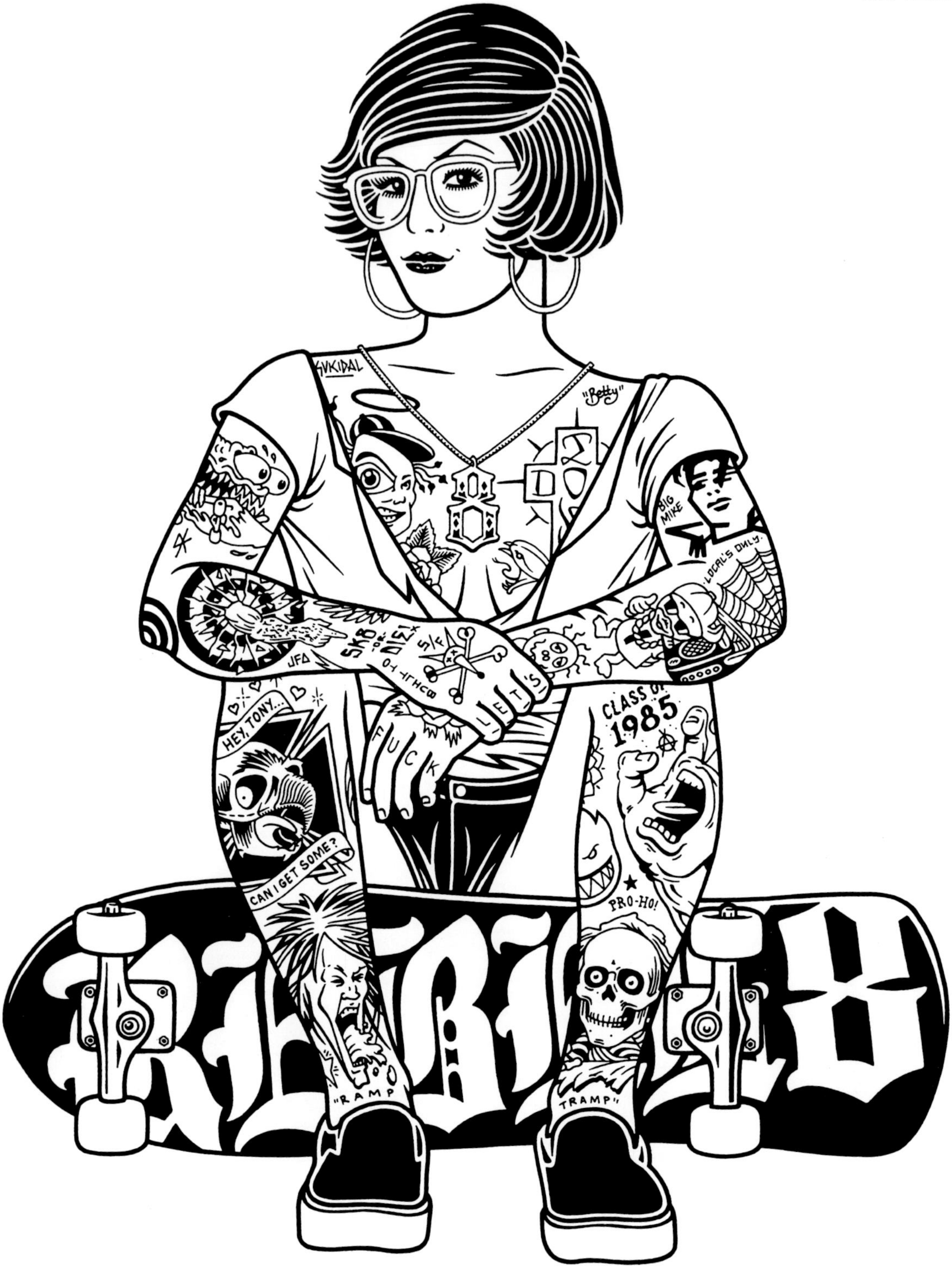

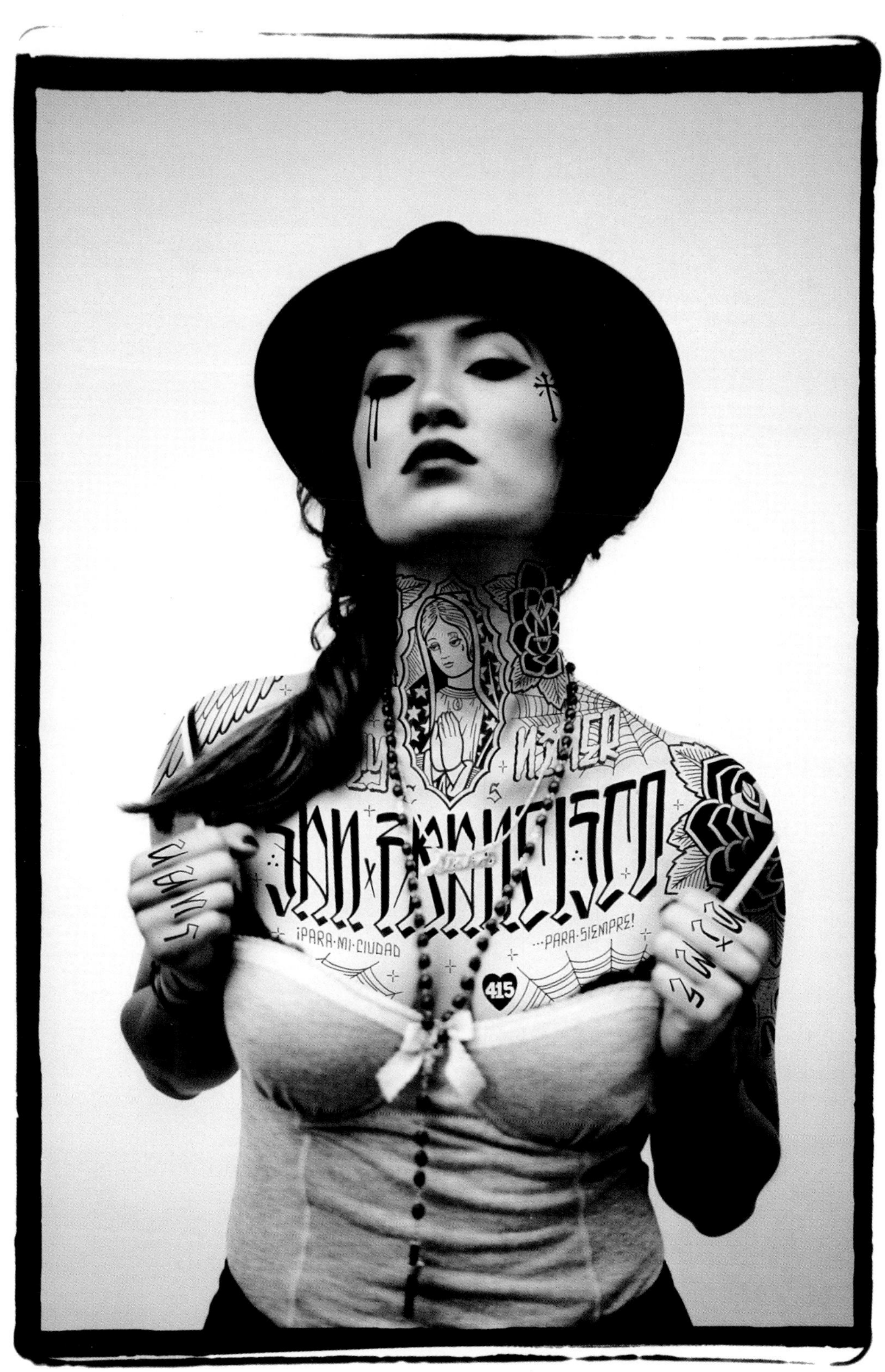

Mike Giant, Aisha, 2101, Sharpie on digital print, 61 x 45.5cm

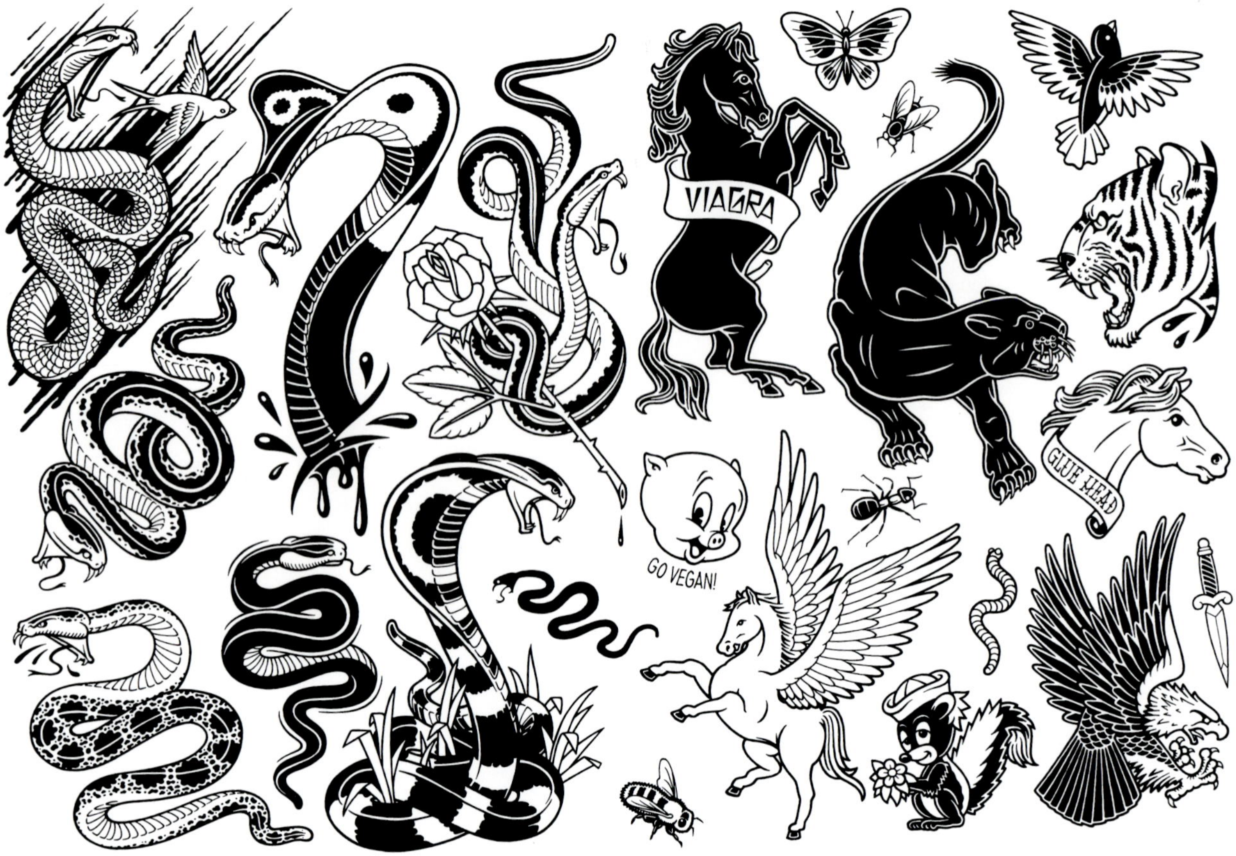

Mike Giant, Americana Flash Set #2 – Animals, 2010, Sharpie on drawing paper, 45.5 x 61cm

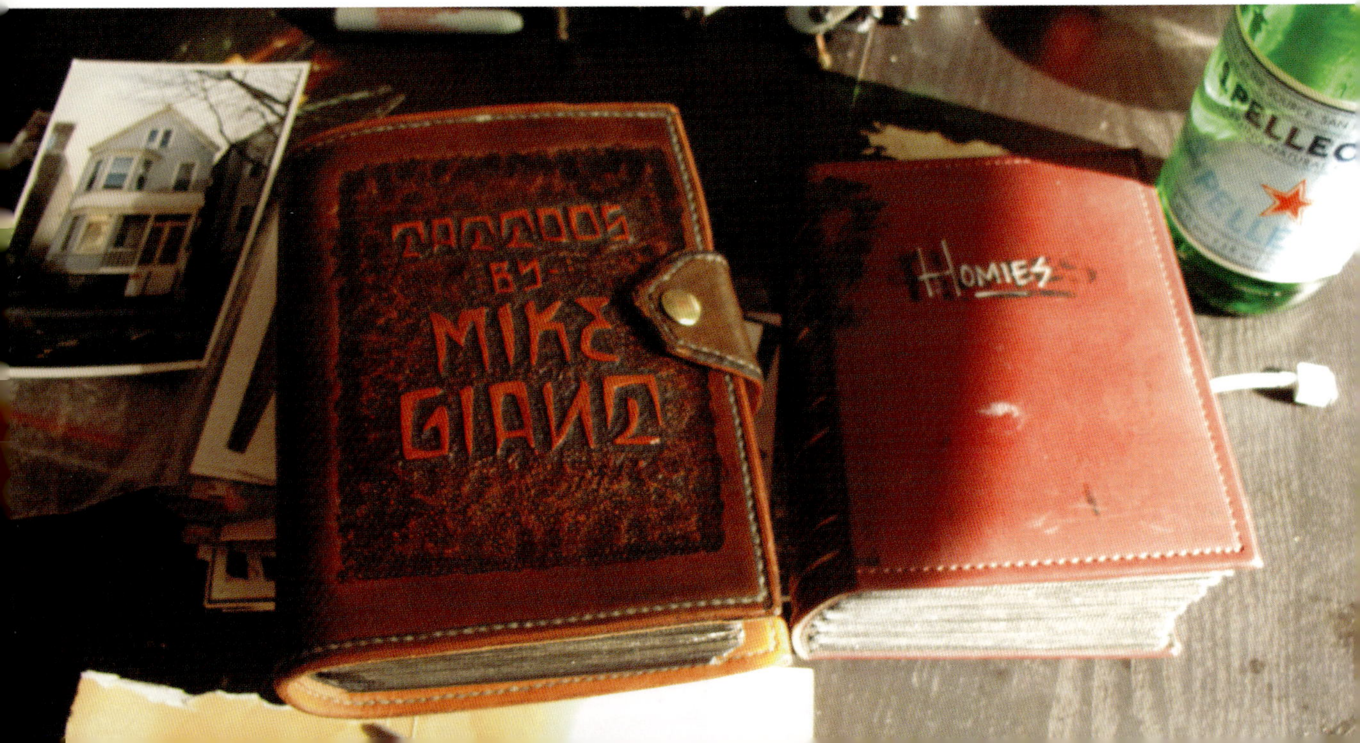

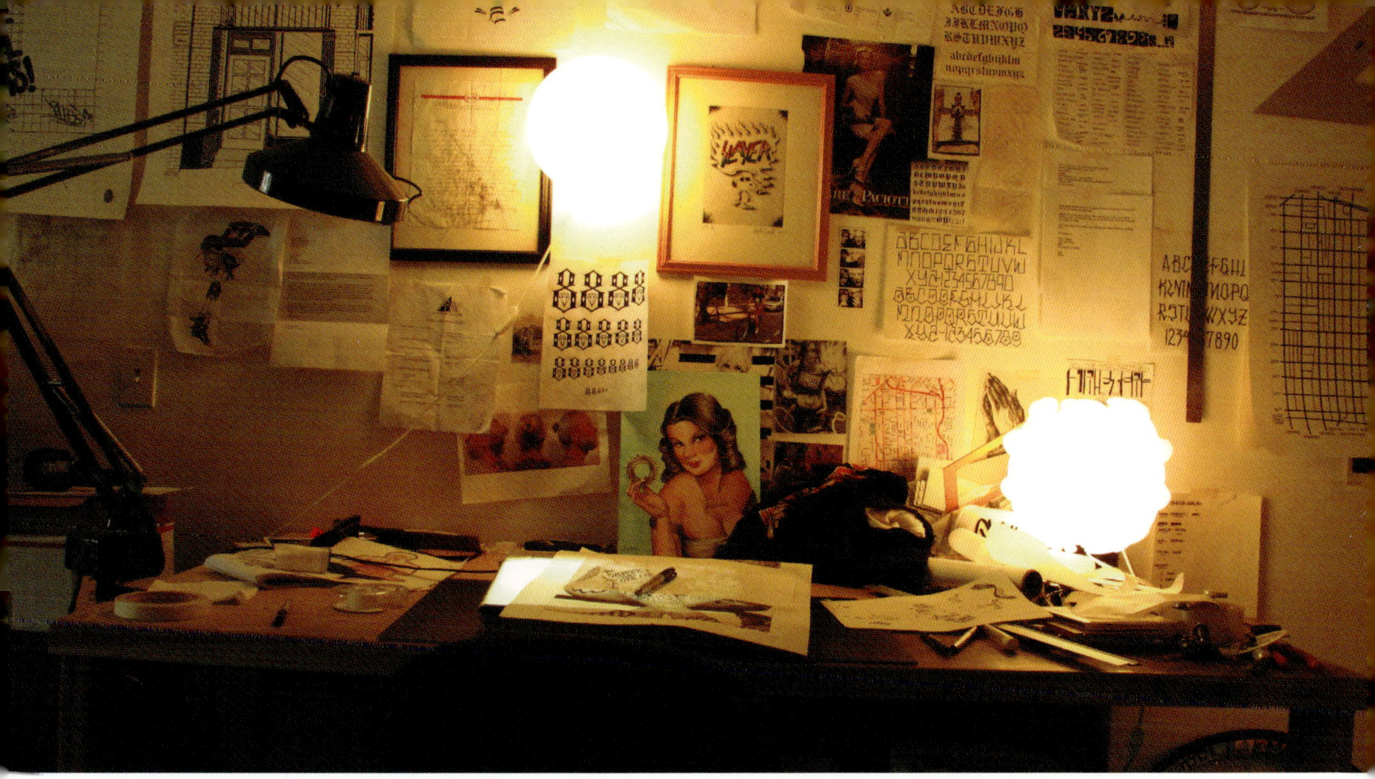

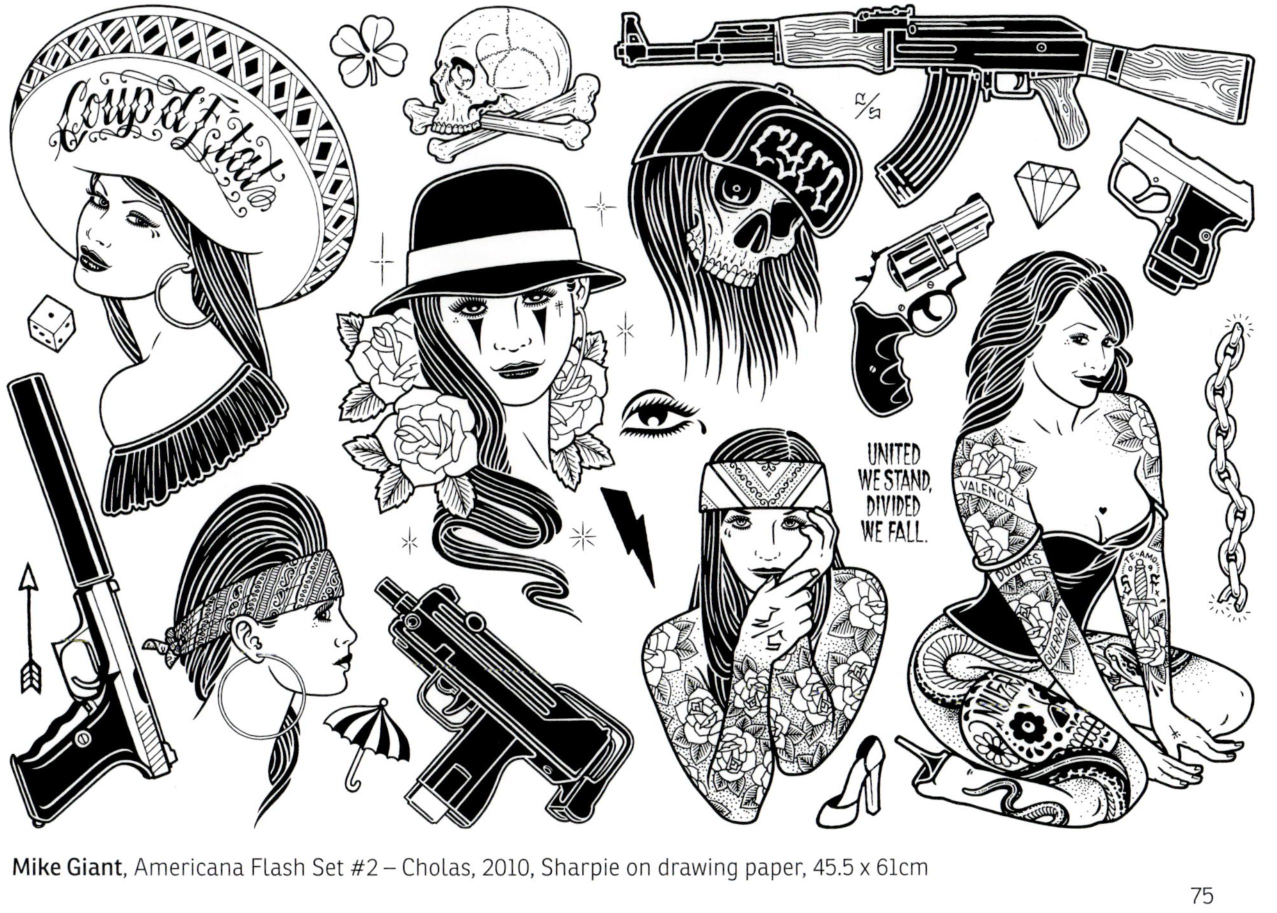

Mike Giant, Americana Flash Set #2 – Cholas, 2010, Sharpie on drawing paper, 45.5 x 61cm

Mike Giant, Hand of the Mysteries, 2008,
Sharpie on drawing paper,
61 x 45.5cm

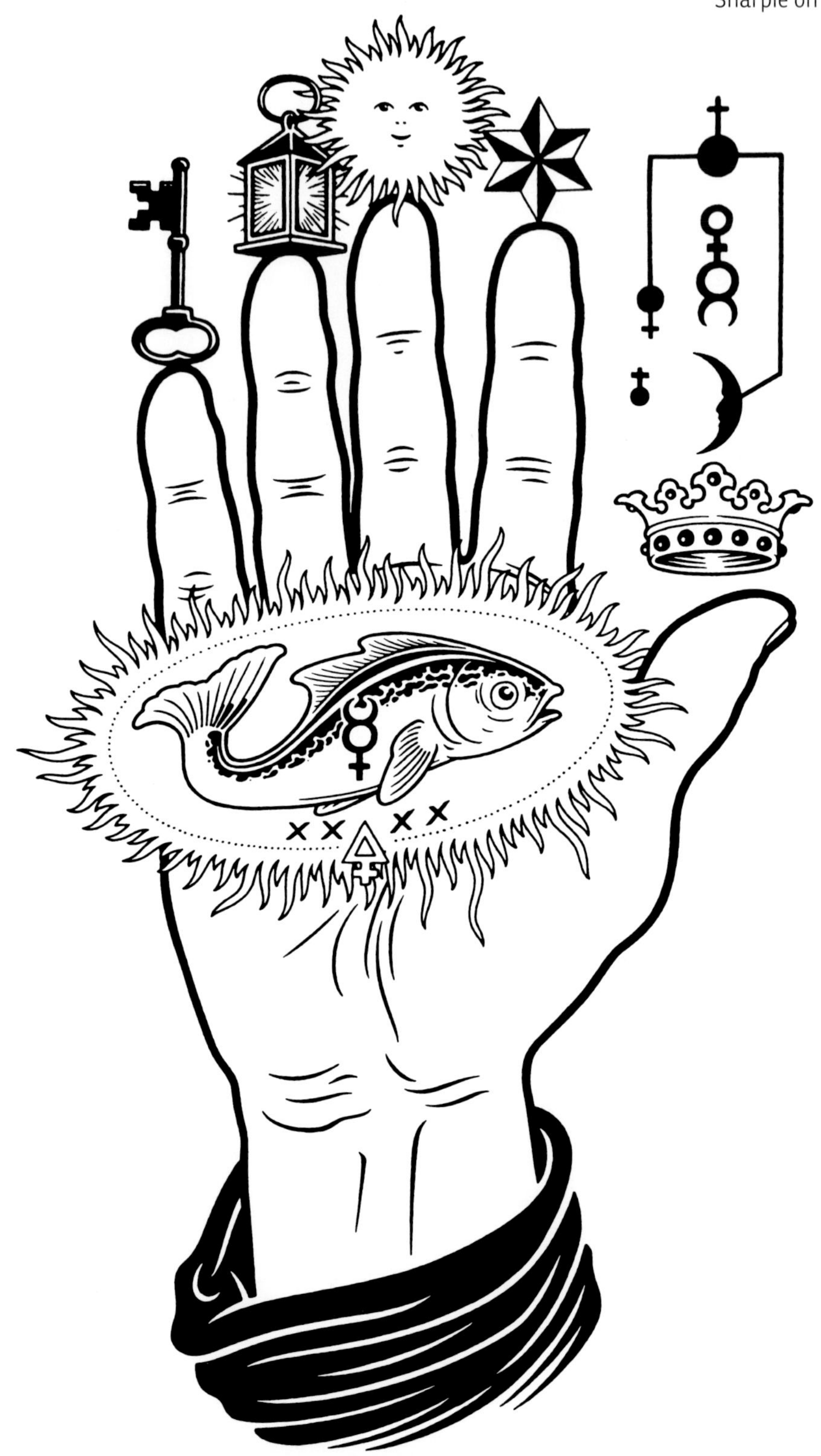

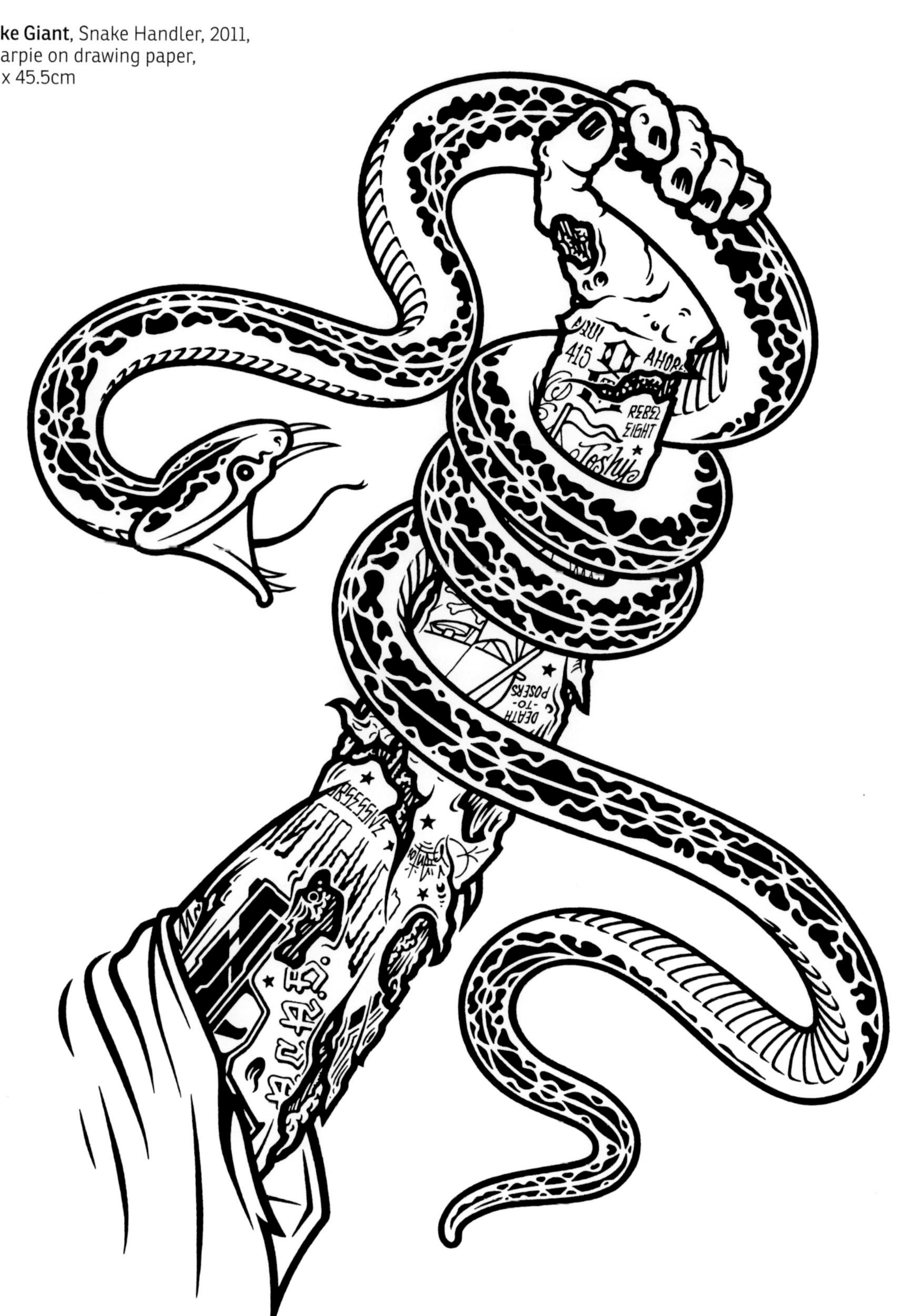

Mike Giant, Snake Handler, 2011,
Sharpie on drawing paper,
61 x 45.5cm

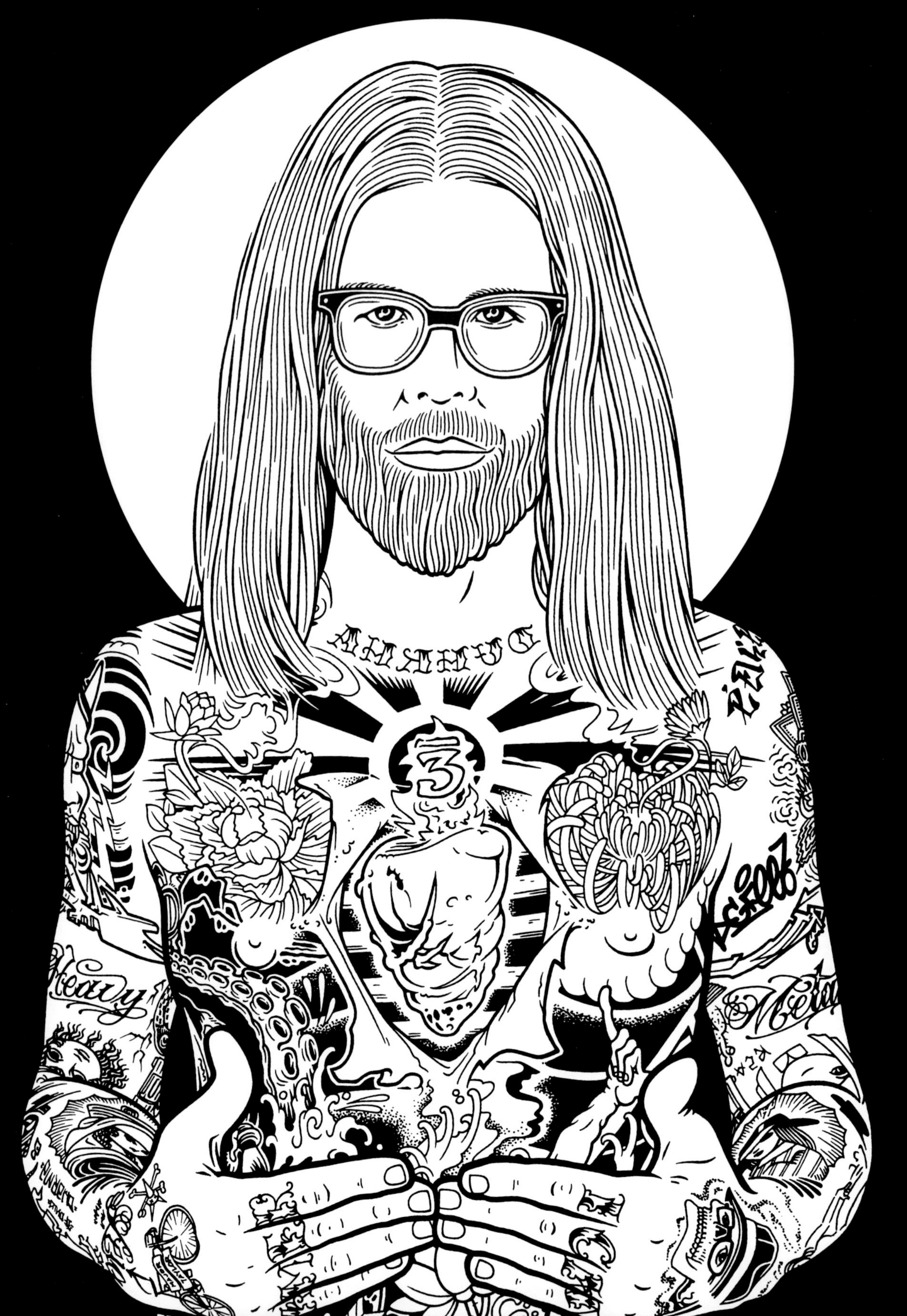
Heavy

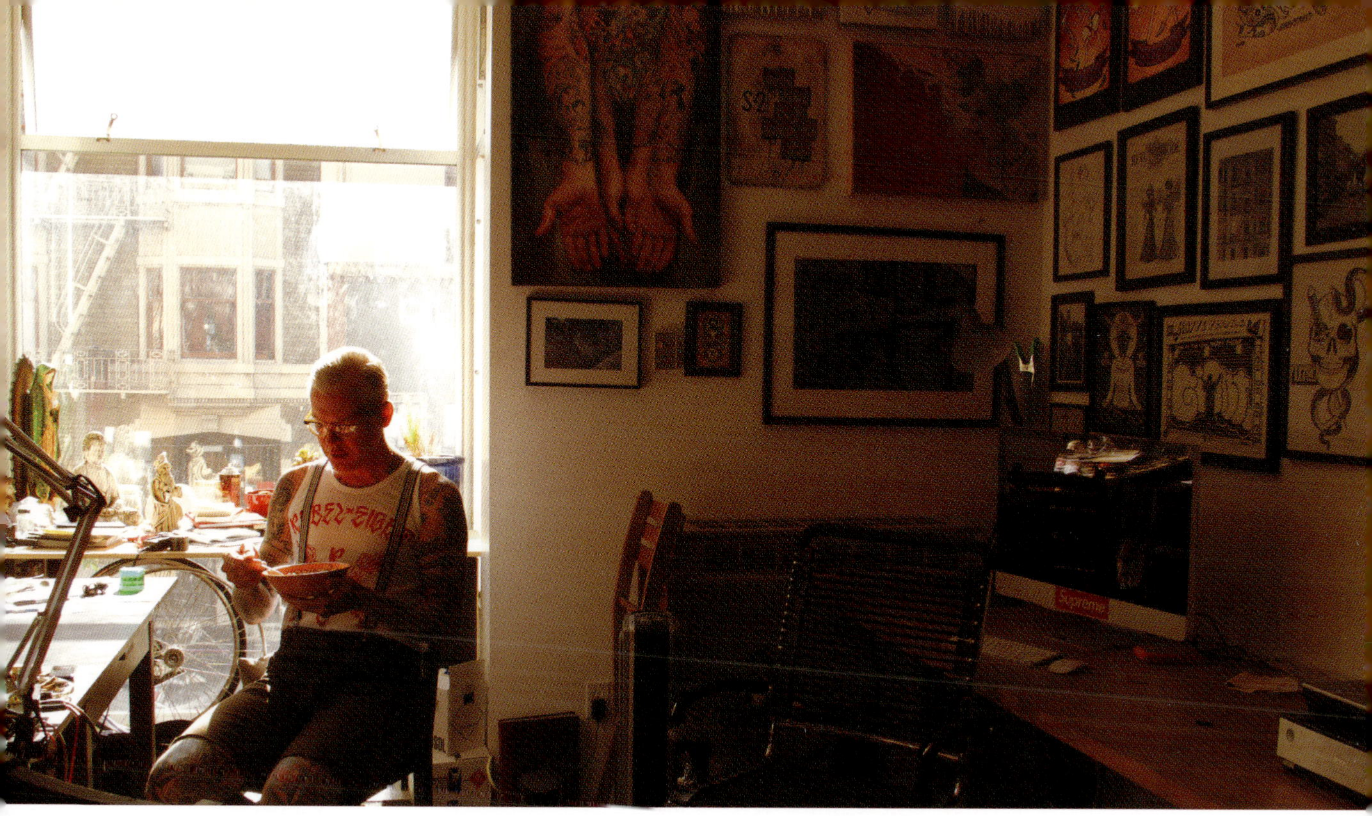

(opposite) **Mike Giant**, Self Portrait, 2011, Sharpie on drawing paper, 61 x 45.5cm

(overleaf left) **Mike Giant**, Home, 2008, Sharpie on drawing paper, 61 x 45.5cm
(overleaf right) **Mike Giant**, Graffiti Collage, 2011, Sharpie on drawing paper, 61 x 45.5cm

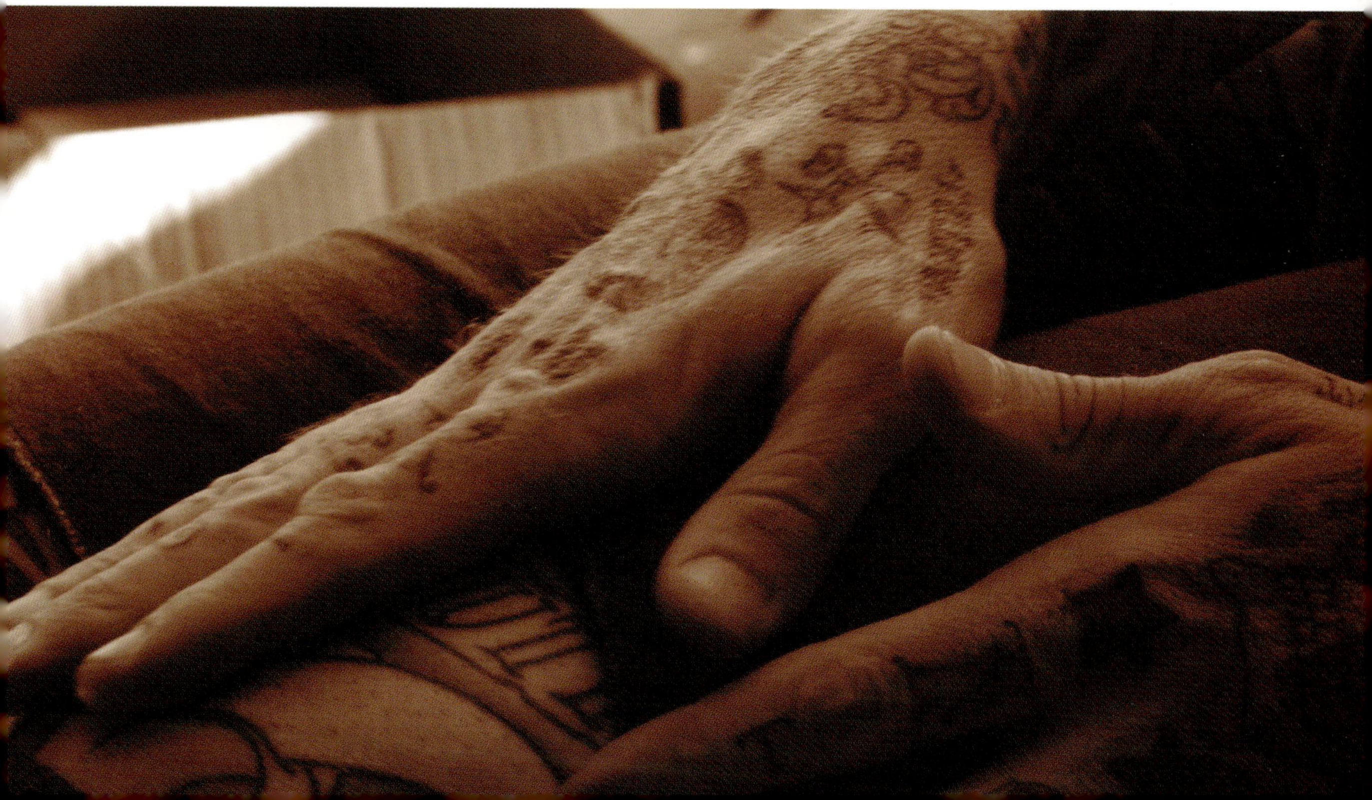

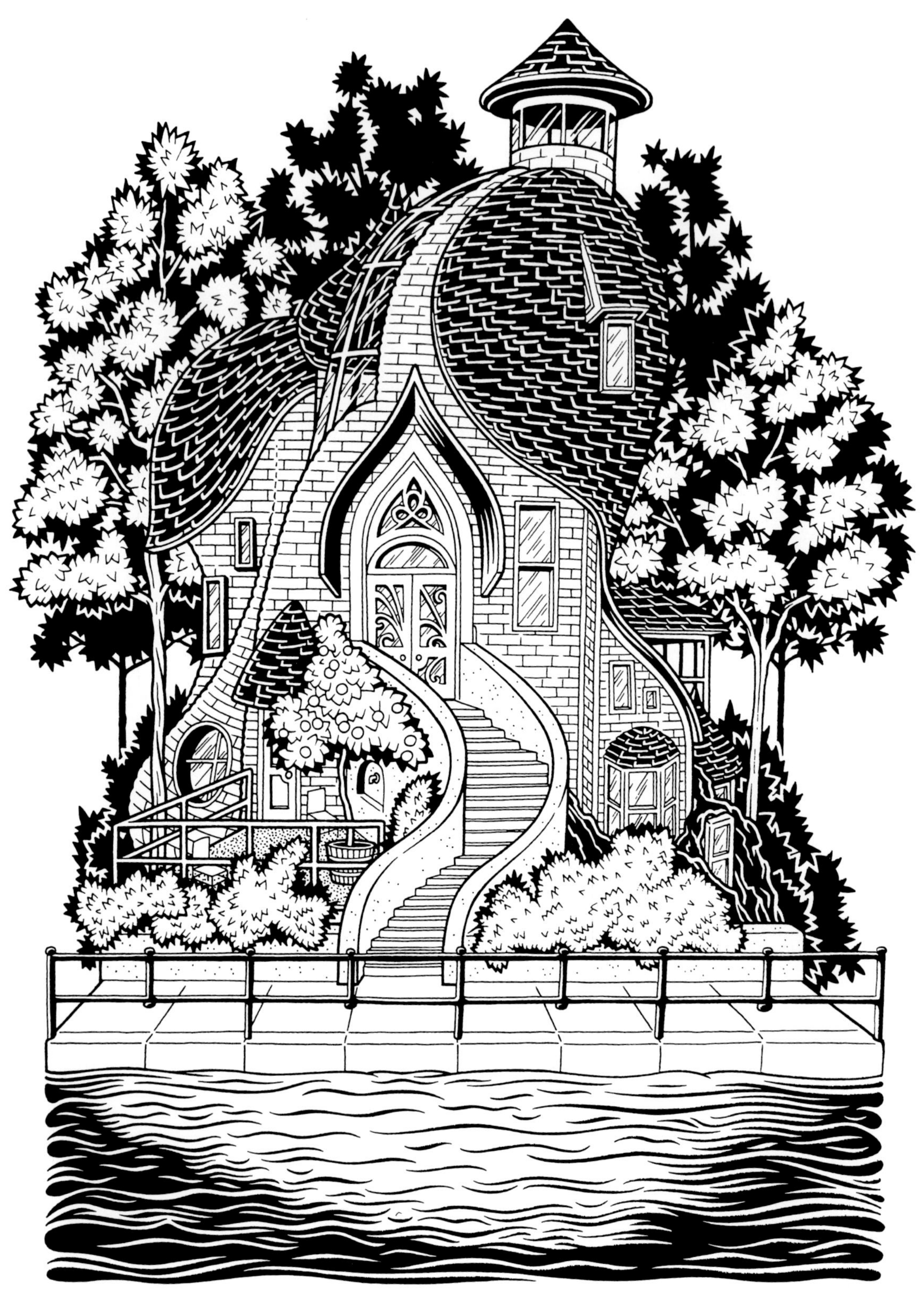

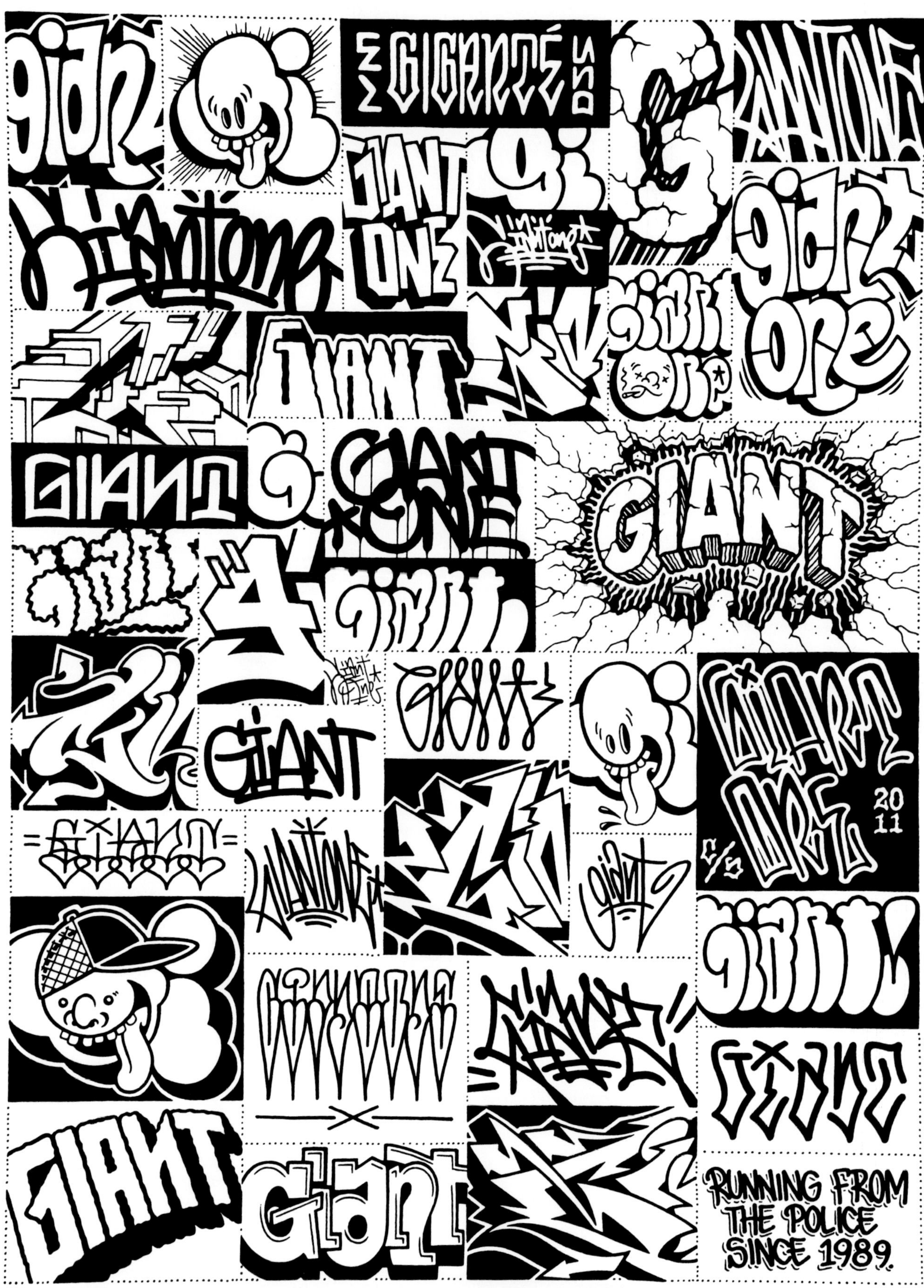
GIANT ONE
GIANT
GIANT
GIANT ONE
GIANT
GIANT
20
11
GIANT
RUNNING FROM
THE POLICE
SINCE 1989.

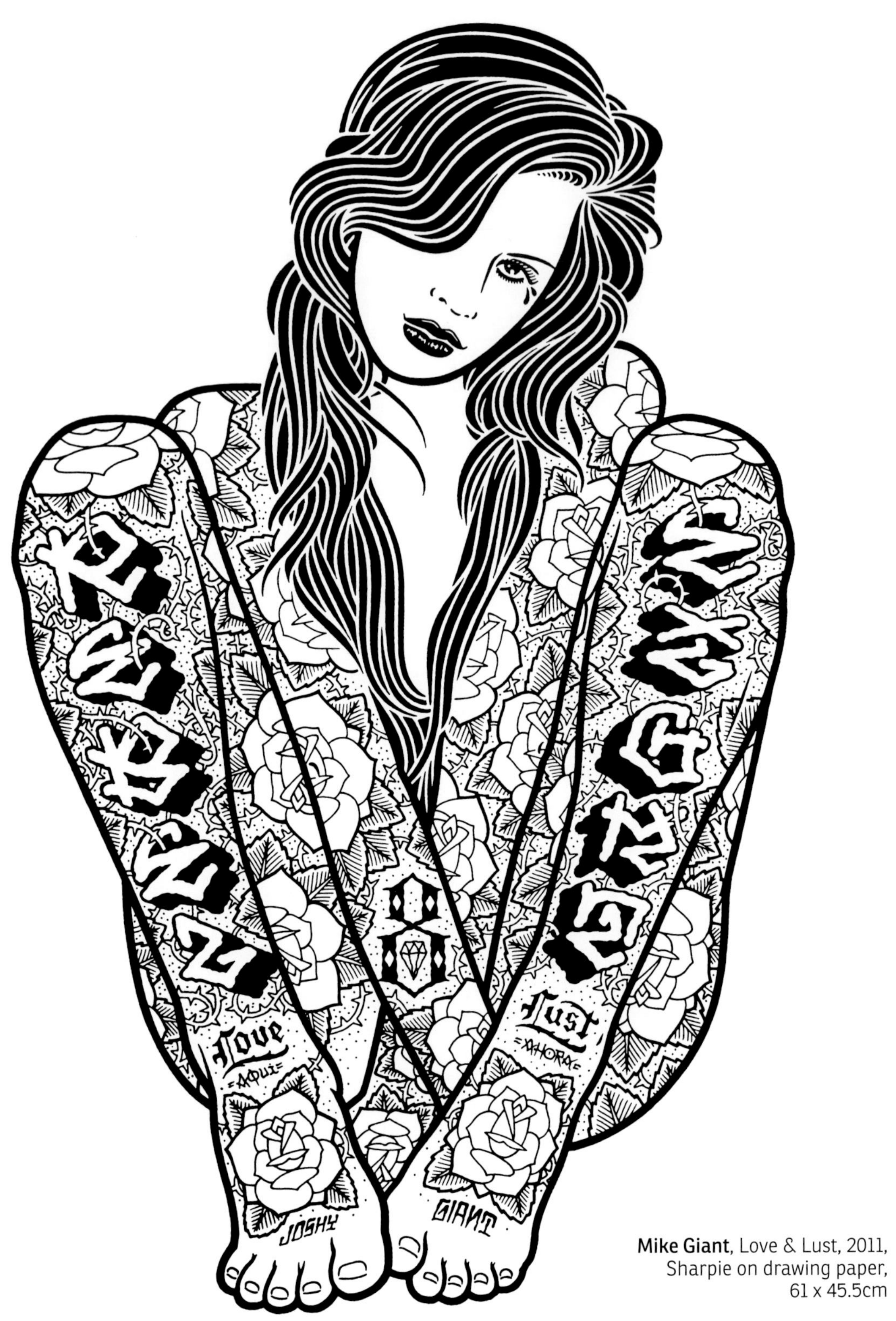

Mike Giant, Love & Lust, 2011,
Sharpie on drawing paper,
61 x 45.5cm

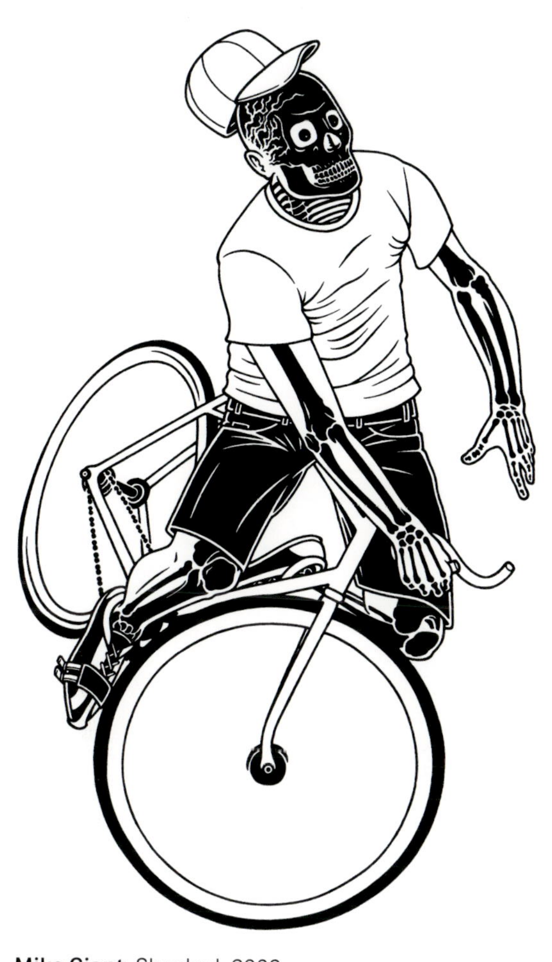

Mike Giant, Shocked, 2008,
Sharpie on drawing paper, 61 x 45.5cm

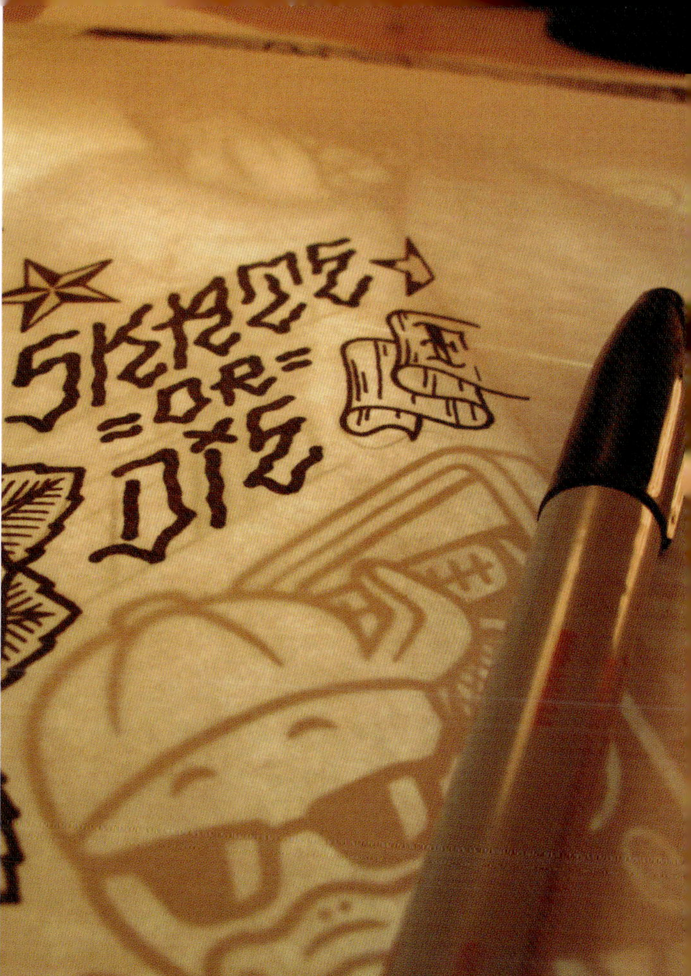

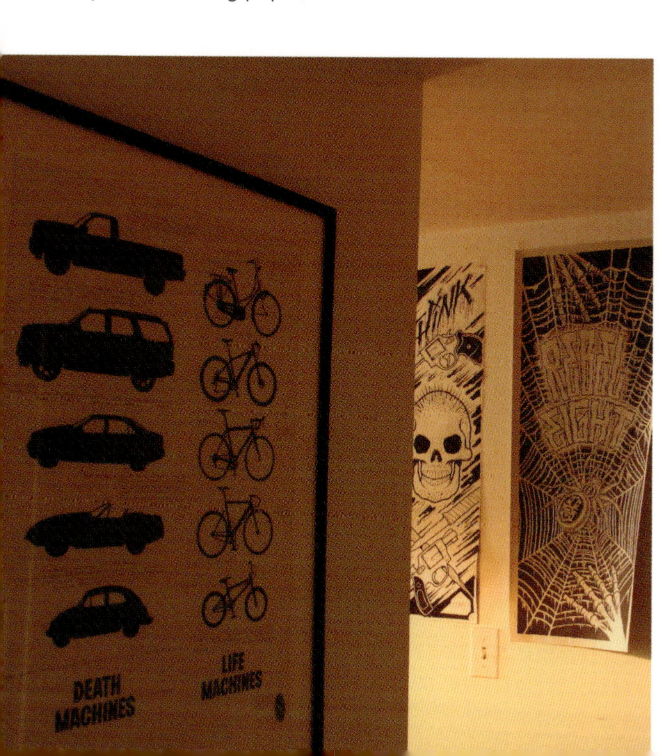

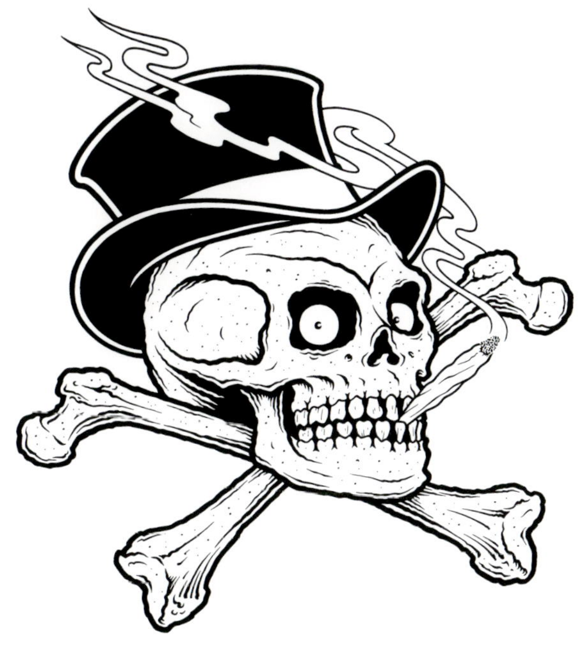

Mike Giant, Tokin' Skull, 2011,
Sharpie on drawing paper, 61 x 45.5cm

SCOTT CAMPBELL

Born – 1977
Hometown – New Orleans, LA
Study – self taught
Lives and Works – Brooklyn, New York
Years as a tattooist – 12+
Favourite medium – all of the above

Scott Campbell says, "I'm just the dirty kid who snuck in the back door."[1] This backdoor lead him to become the well respected tattoo-go-to for the likes of Marc Jacobs, Heath Ledger, Courtney Love and Nan Goldin.

To sum up the Scott Campbell story as a classic college-drop-out-to-celebrity narrative, while true, would gloss over his hard won place as a craftsman, thinker and confidant.

Campbell left the South with a desire to re-create his identity and rebel against his conservative Baptist parents. The beginning of this journey is marked by a small skull tattoo. "It was the most efficient way to irritate my father I could find."[2]

He spent the better half of his twenties travelling the world working in different studios, learning his trade on the move. In 2001 he settled in New York and went on to open Saved Tattoo – "the name refers to our being saved from 'real' jobs."[3]

For Campbell the craft of tattooing is a very human act that brings together a handmade experience with a emotional connection. "Still, because of that folk art aspect, because of the purely analogue nature of it, it remains special. It can never be mass produced. Every experience is one-on-one, for each individual."[4]

It is this ability to bring tight execution and good craft together with heartfelt and sincere ideas that Campbell translates from tattooing into his fine art.

Drawing on the history, iconography and language of tattoos in his mixed media gallery work, he then re-writes it with humour, irony and big questions about value, permanence and death. With a direct line to the US Mint, Campbell is best known for his laser-cut stacked sheets of dollar bills into which he irreverently carves imagery and text otherwise reserved for flash. Not to be pinned down, he also plays with neon lights, ostrich eggs, as well as beautifully rendered watercolours and etching plates engraved with a tattoo gun.

The common idea that tattoos are "forever" and are about "permanence" is something that the artist questions. He talks a lot about the way that tattoos are relatively ephemeral. People walk away, they die, skin gets burnt and scarred. As such he's less precious about the concrete ownership of all the things he makes. "The magic is in the idea and the execution. What hangs on the wall is just an artefact of an action."[5]

And, while he values being able to create works which are "a bit more archival than somebody's arm,"[6] he is just as comfortable to see an intricate tattoo walk away from him forever, as he is to burn down a sold-out show.

"It's important not to be controlled by the objects I make, to not hesitate to burn it all down and start over at the slightest hint of insincerity, in order to keep things evolving."[7]

1 "Drawn to a Larger Scale" by Alex Williams in The New York Times, April 14, 2010. **2** "Icons: Scott Campbell" by Suzanne Weinstock in Inked Magazine, 2011. **3** "The Tattoo and the Word" by Victoria Cambun (text), Matthew Evans and Pierre Alexandre de Looz (interview) in 032c, issue 21, Summer 2011, p.54. **4** ibid. p.55. **5** ibid. **6** Weinstock, op. cit. **7** Cambun, op. cit.

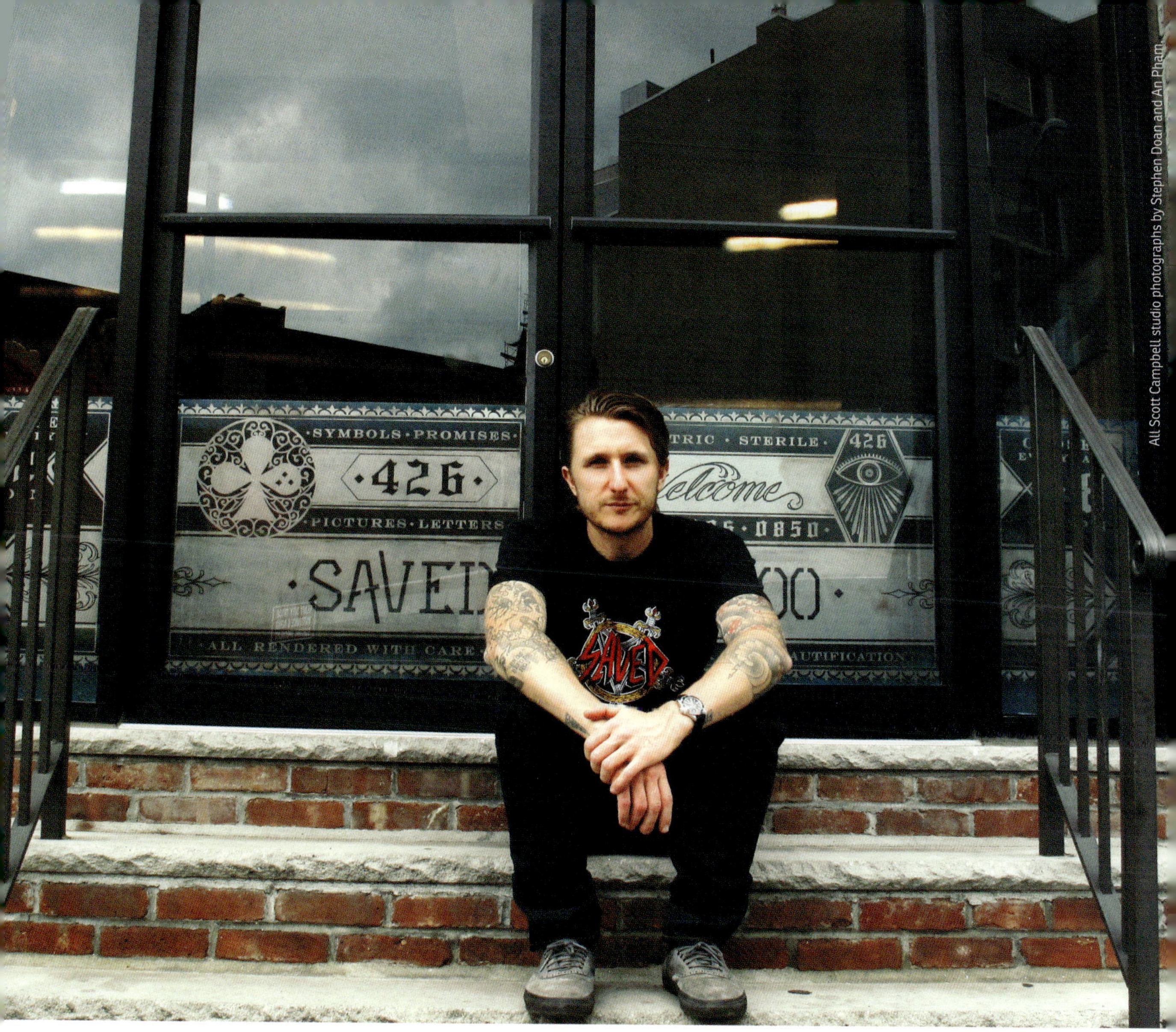

All Scott Campbell studio photographs by Stephen Doan and An Pham.

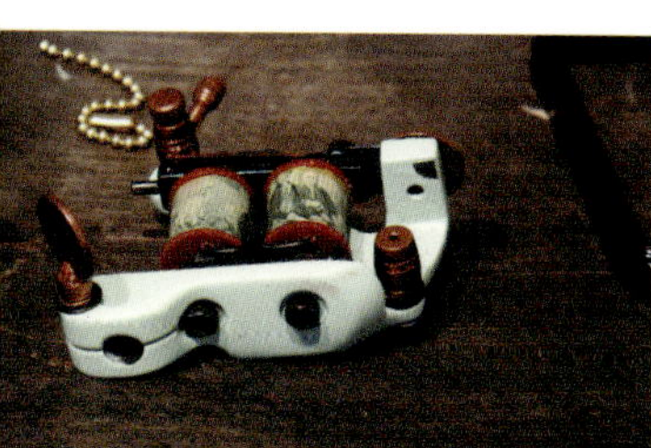

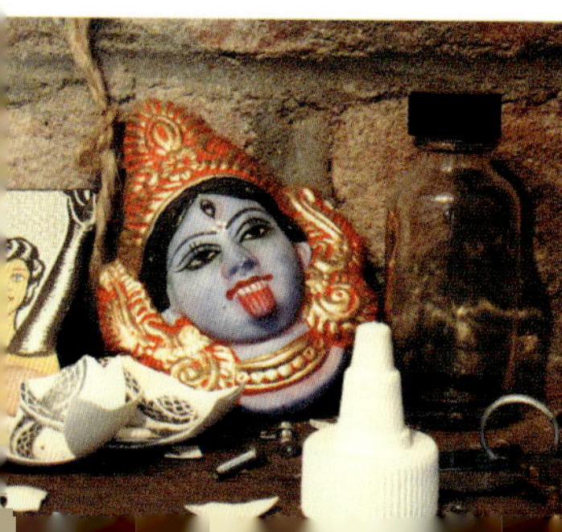

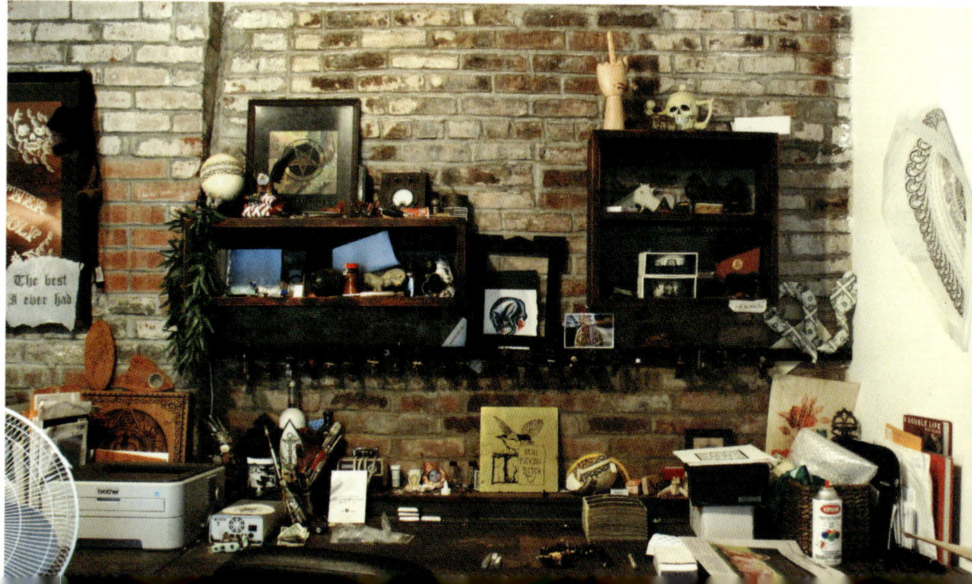

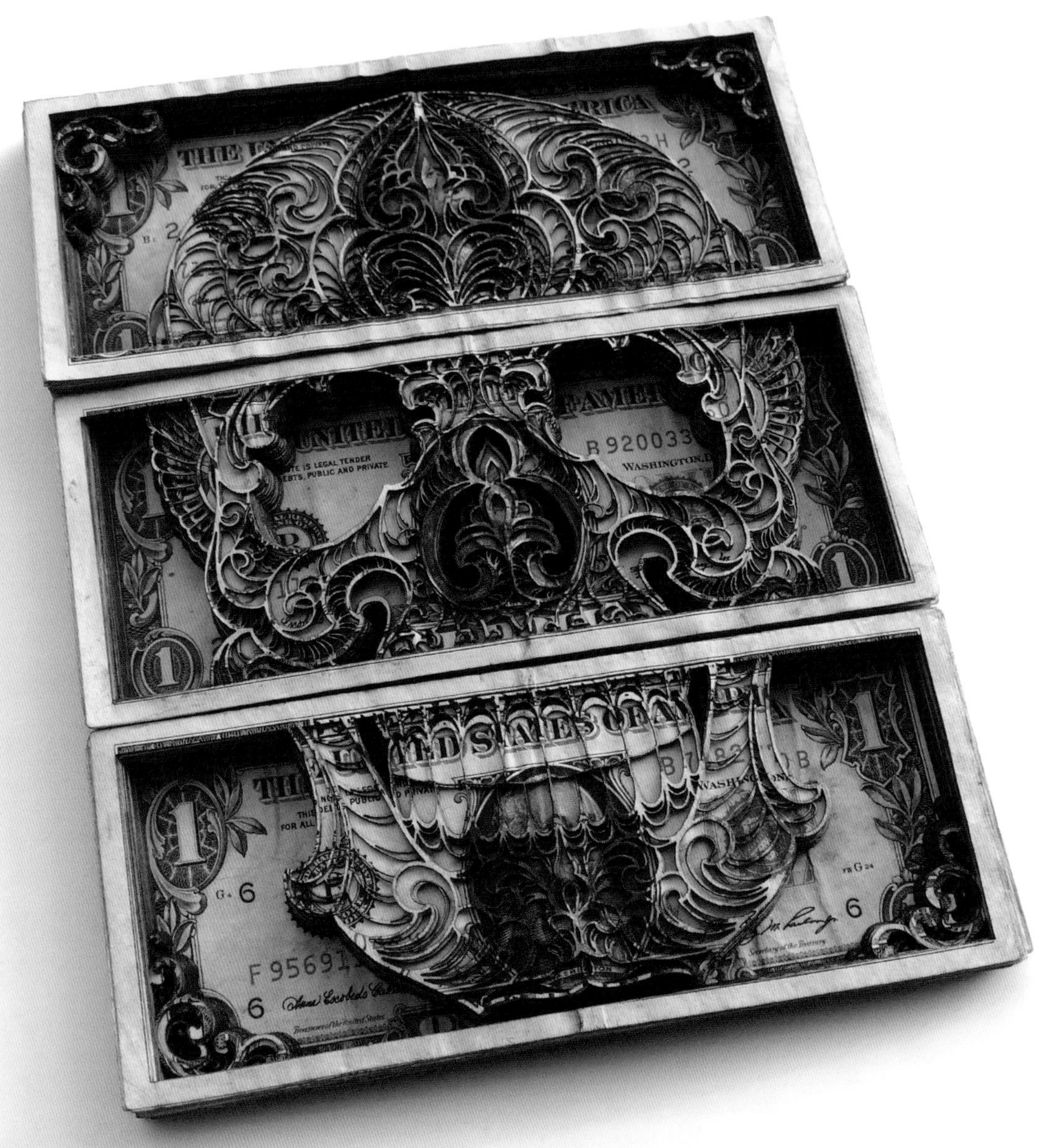
THE
AMERICA
B 920033
WASHINGTON, D
TE IS LEGAL TENDER
EBTS, PUBLIC AND PRIVATE
WASHINGTON
F 95691
Secretary of the Treasury

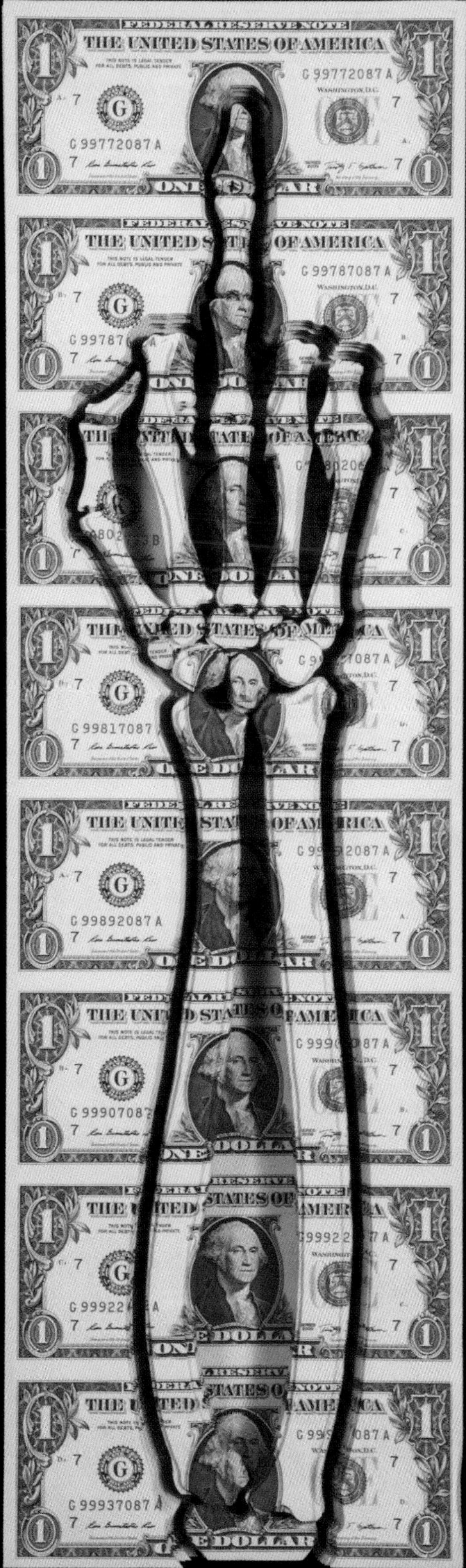

Scott Campbell,
Good Morning, 2011,
cut uncut US
currency sheets,
53.3 x 15.2cm

(opposite)
Scott Campbell,
Day of the Dead, 2009,
US cut dollar bills,
22.8 x 15.2 x 5cm

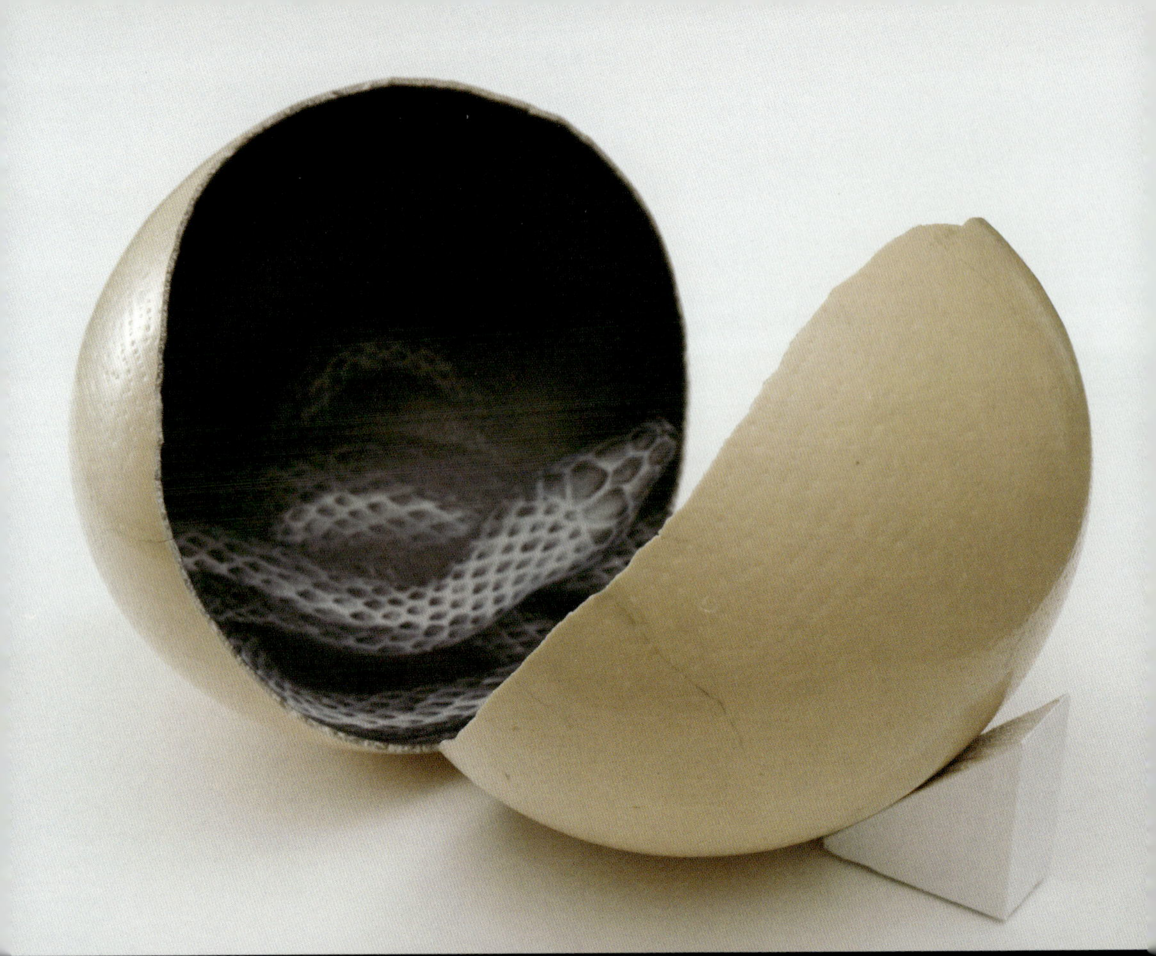

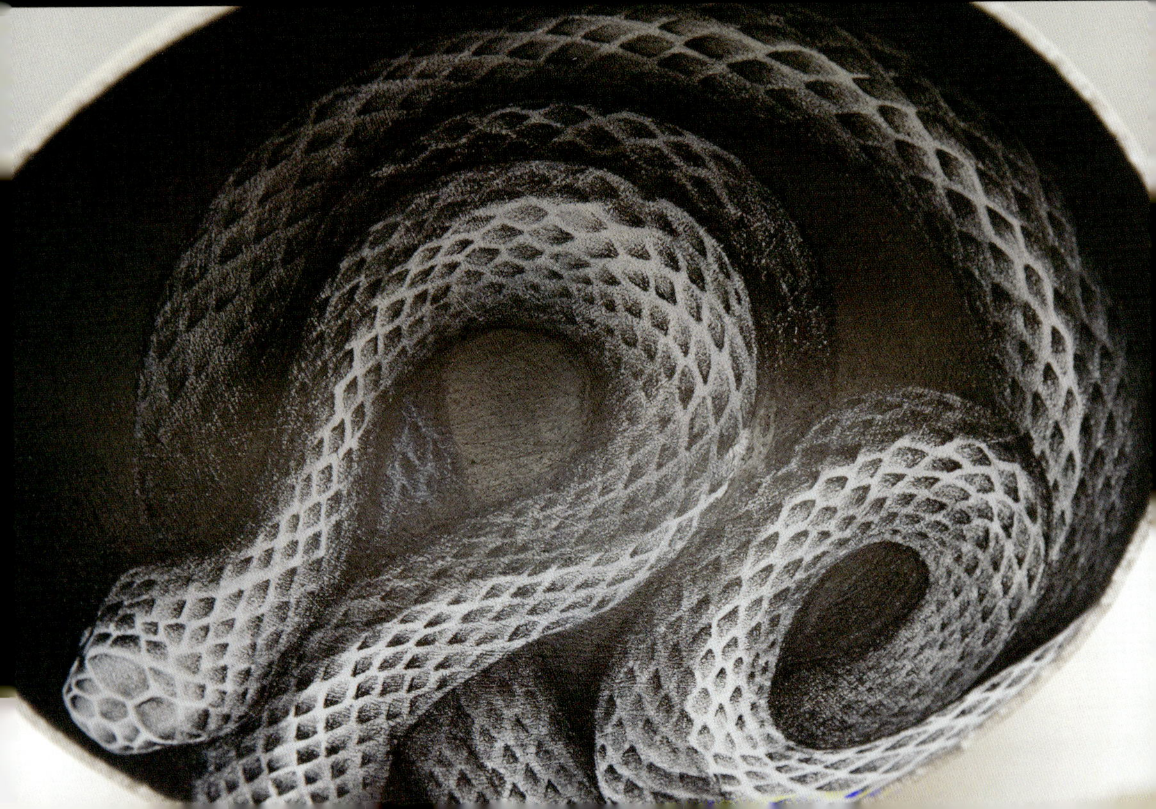

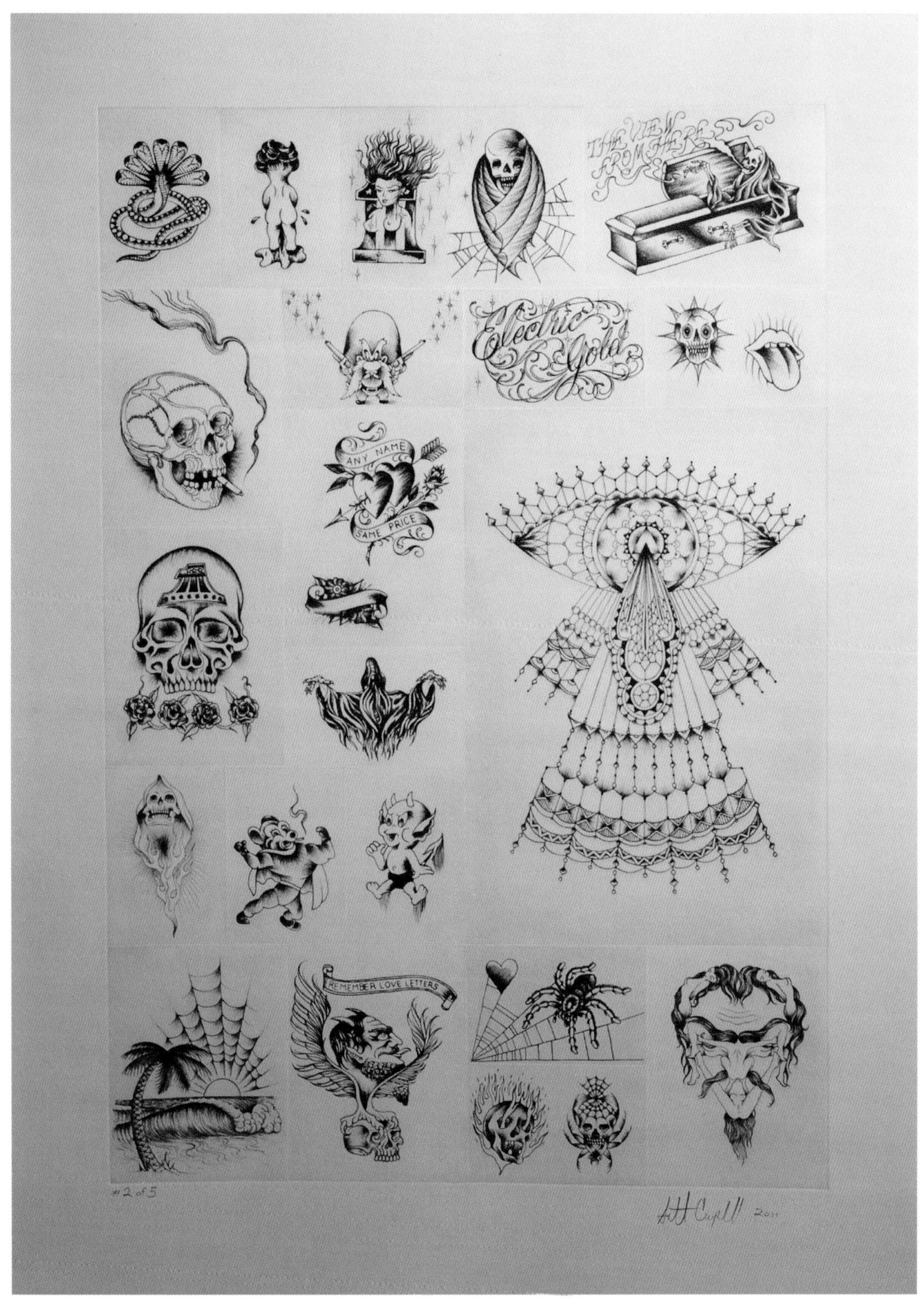

Scott Campbell, When Walking Through Hell, Keep Walking, 2011, intaglio print, 111.7 x 76.2cm

(opposite) **Scott Campbell**, Untitled, 2011, graphite on ostrich egg, variable size

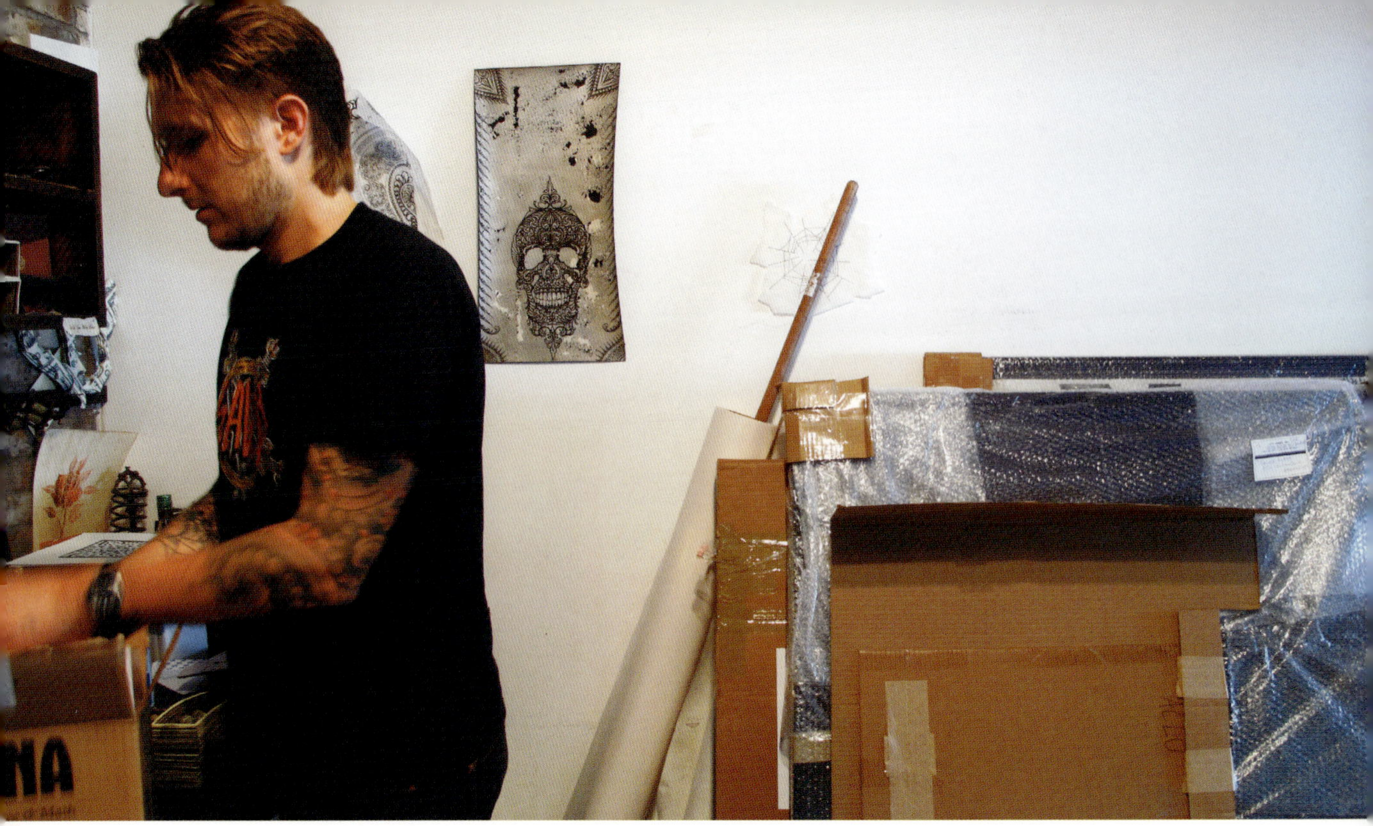

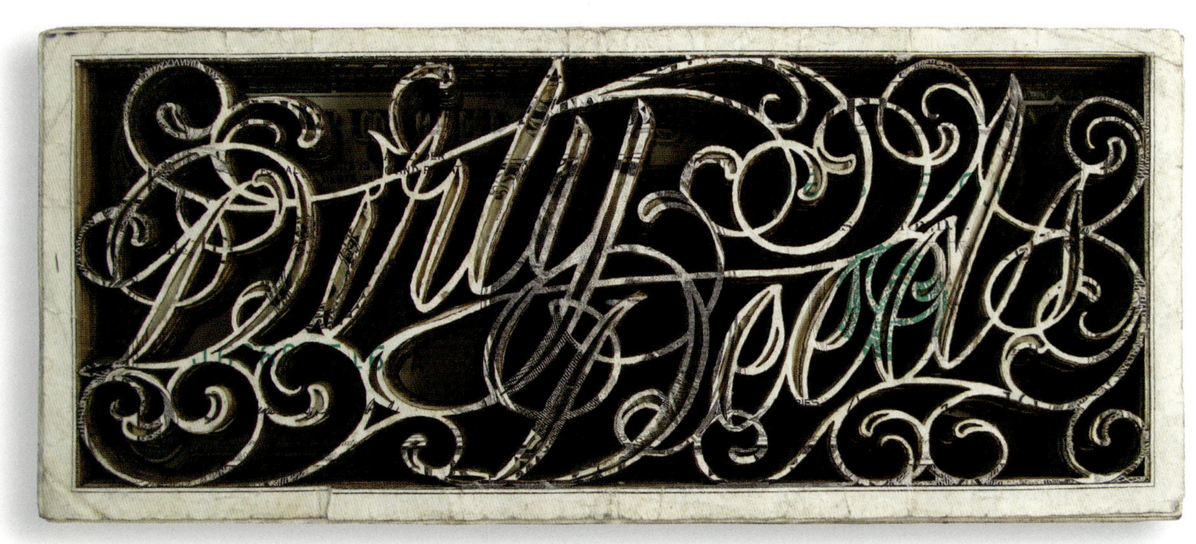

Scott Campbell, Dirty Deeds, 2009, US cut dollar bills, 7.6 x 15.2 x 5cm

(opposite) **Scott Campbell**, Prison Machine 1, 2009, ink on paper, 152.4 x 101.6cm

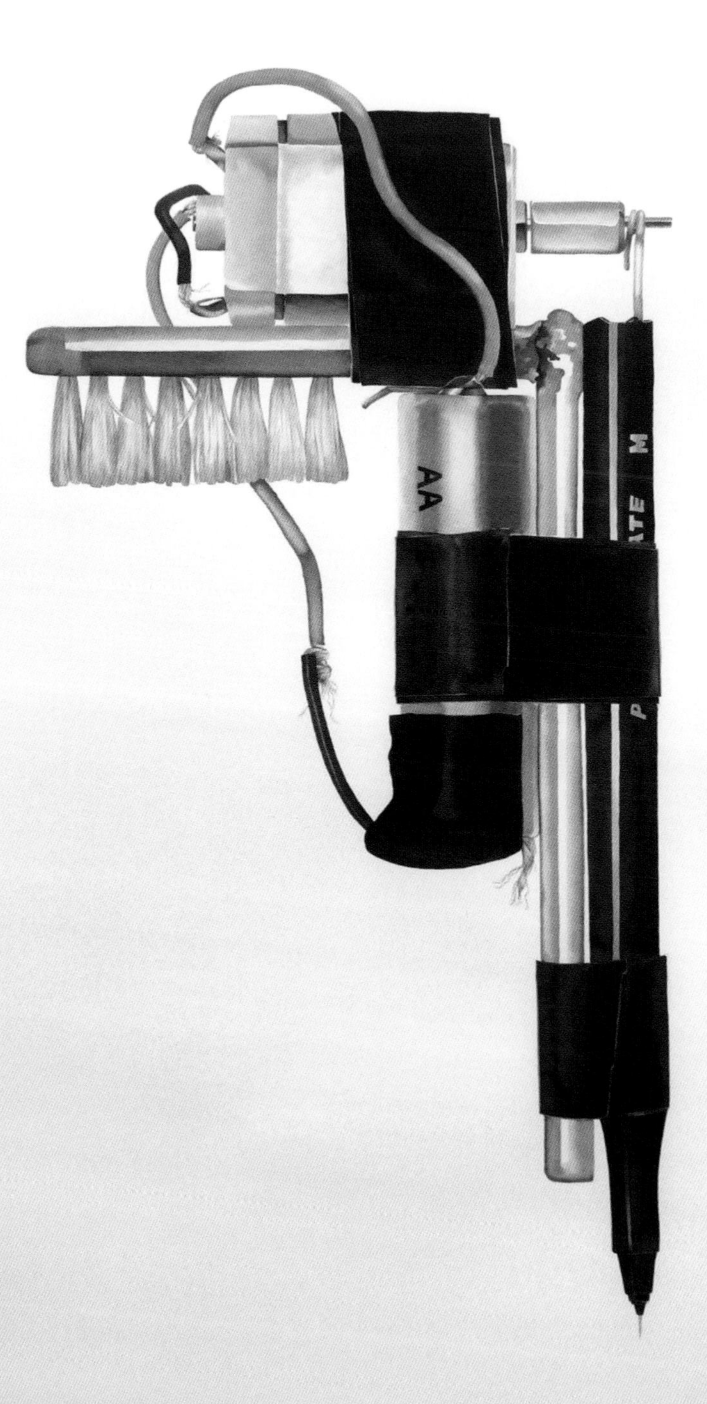
AA

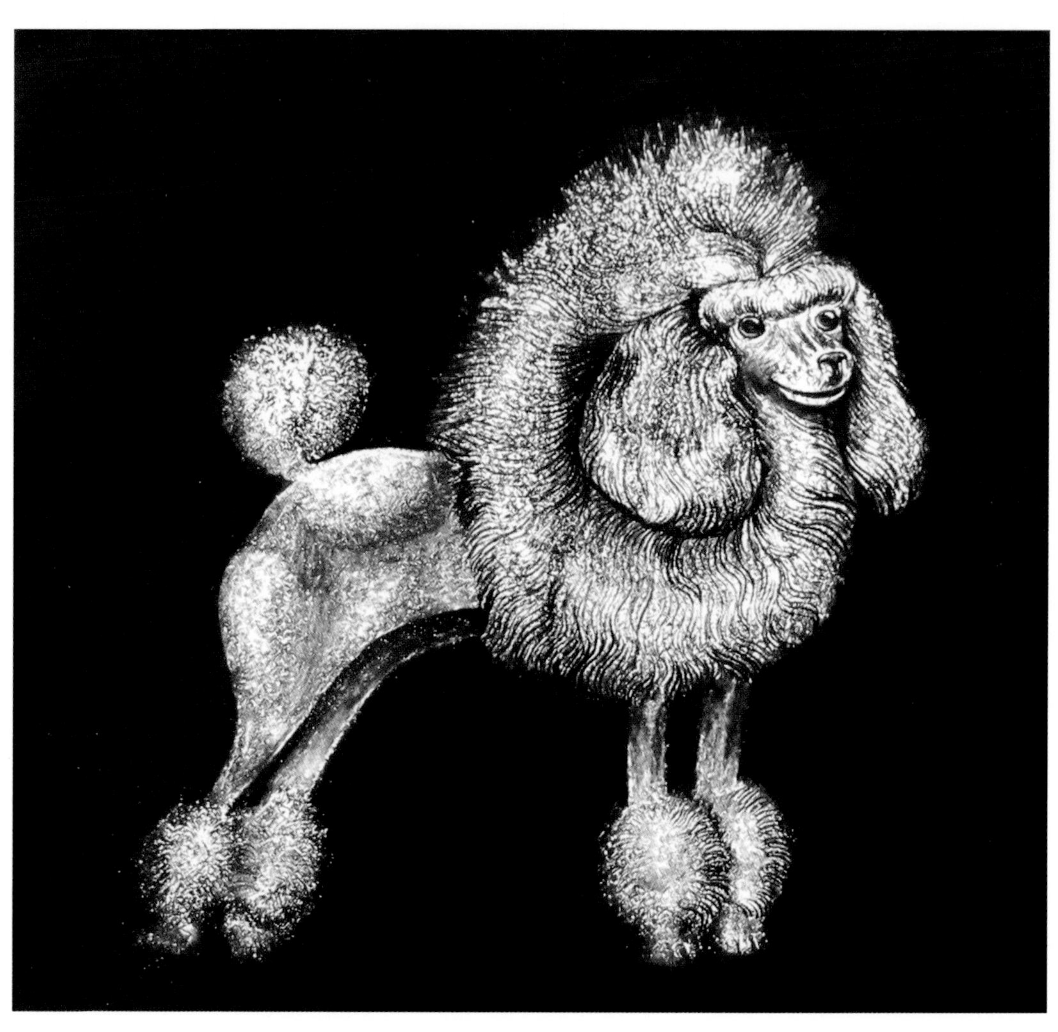

Scott Campbell, Poodle, 2010, cocaine on black velvet, 101.6 x 101.6cm

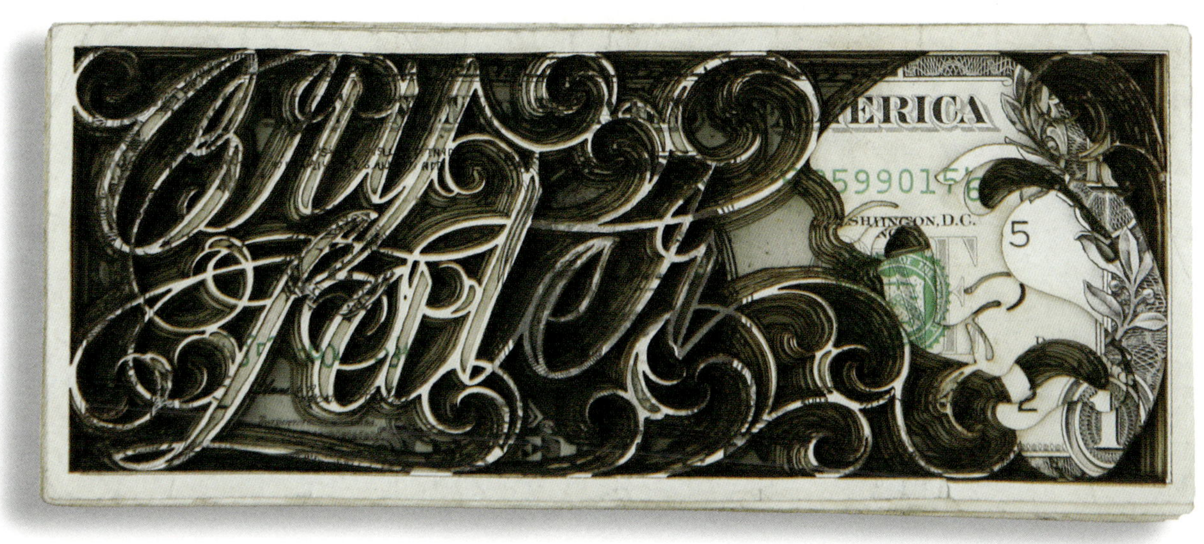

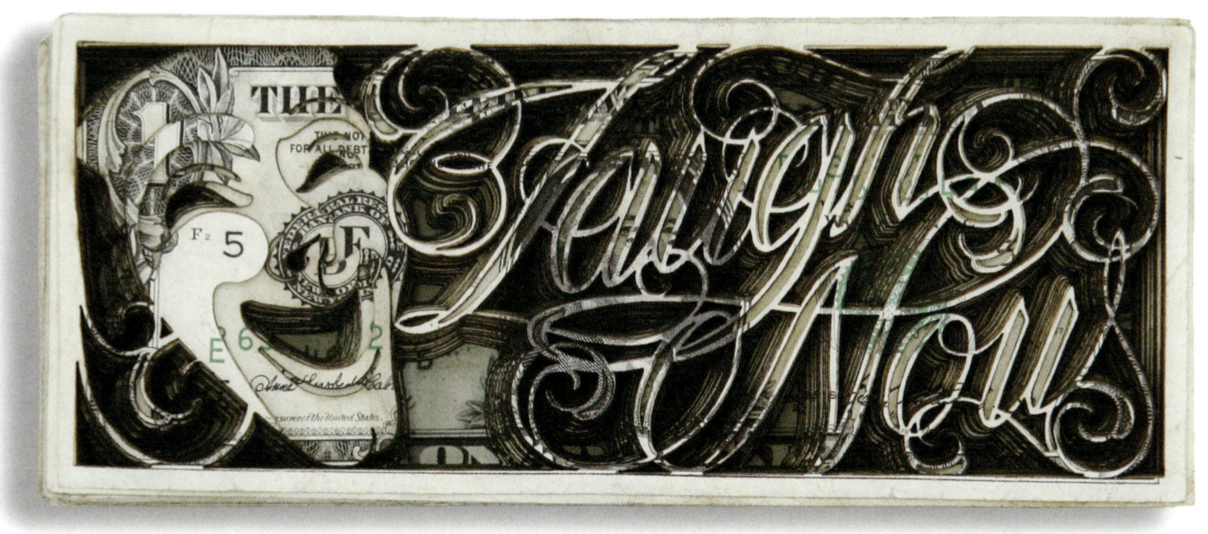

Scott Campbell, Laugh Now, Cry Later, 2009, cut US dollars, 7.6 x 15.2 x 5cm each

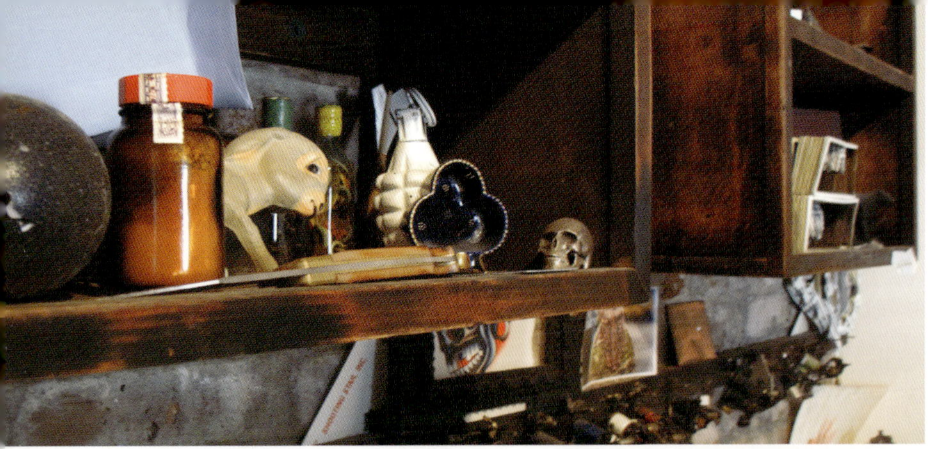
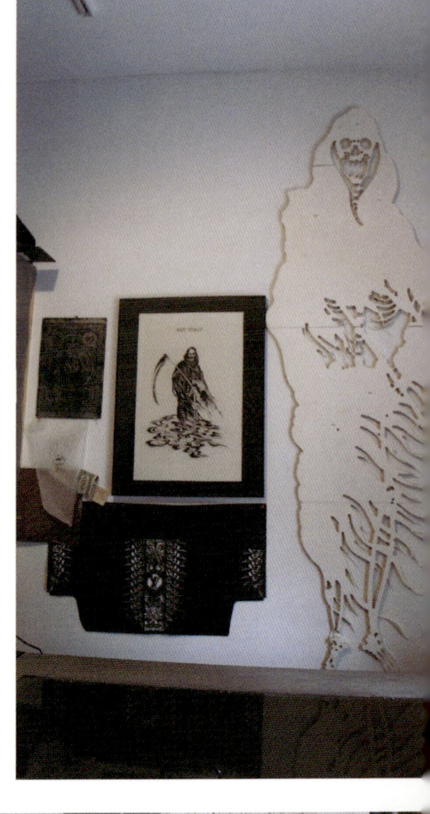
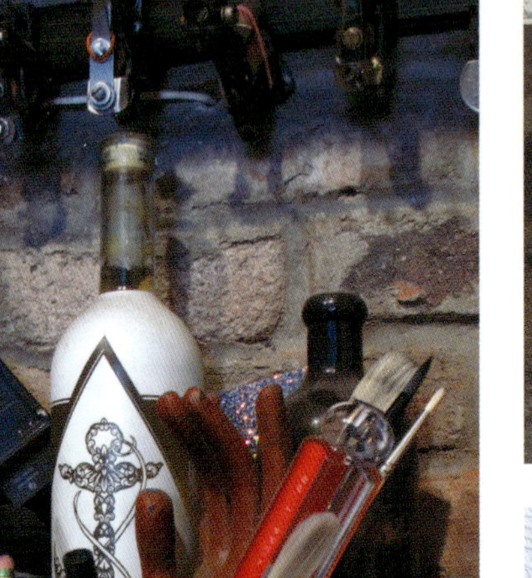
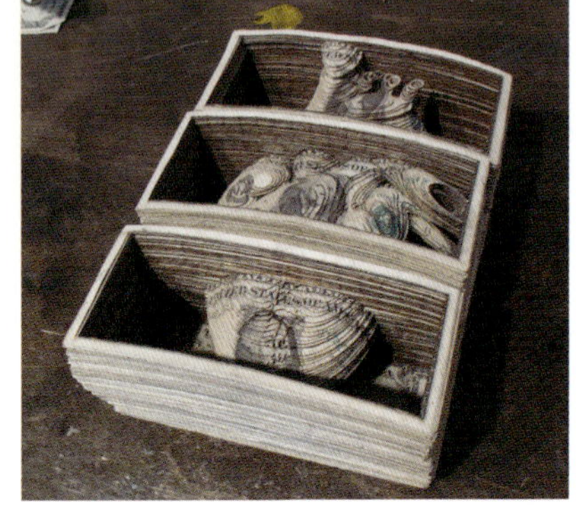
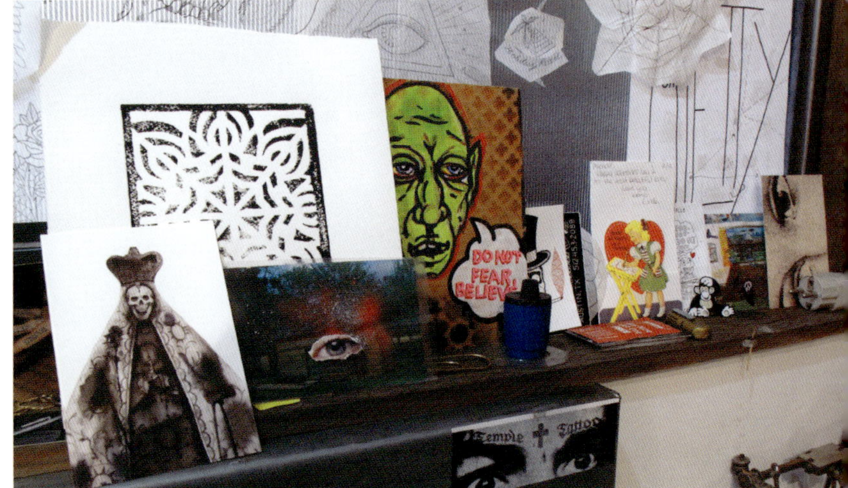
DO NOT FEAR BELIEVE!
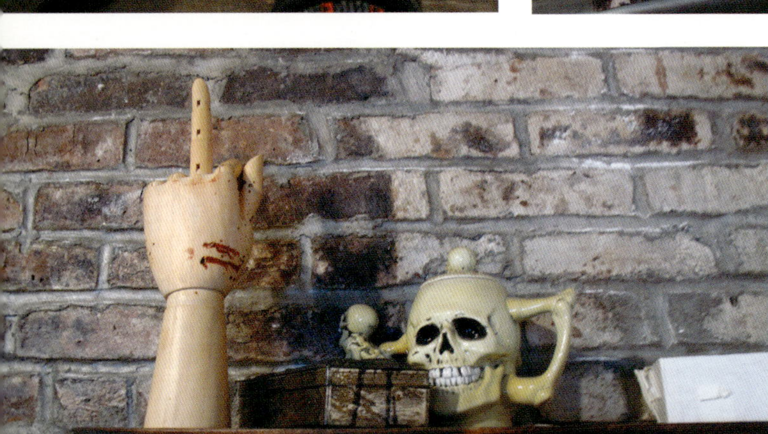
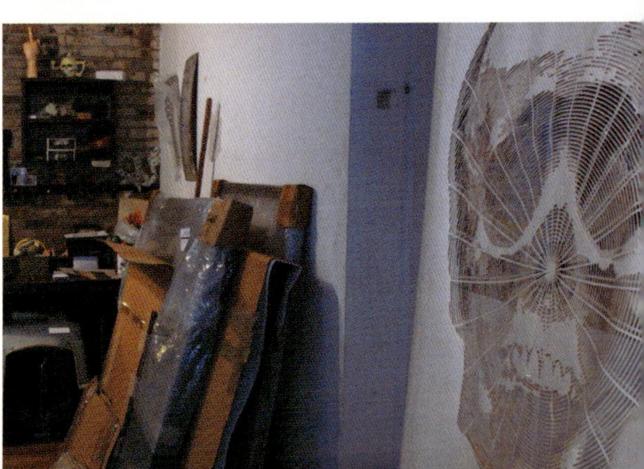

Scott Campbell Daddy was a Charmer, 2011, cut uncut US currency sheets, 53.3 x 63.5cm

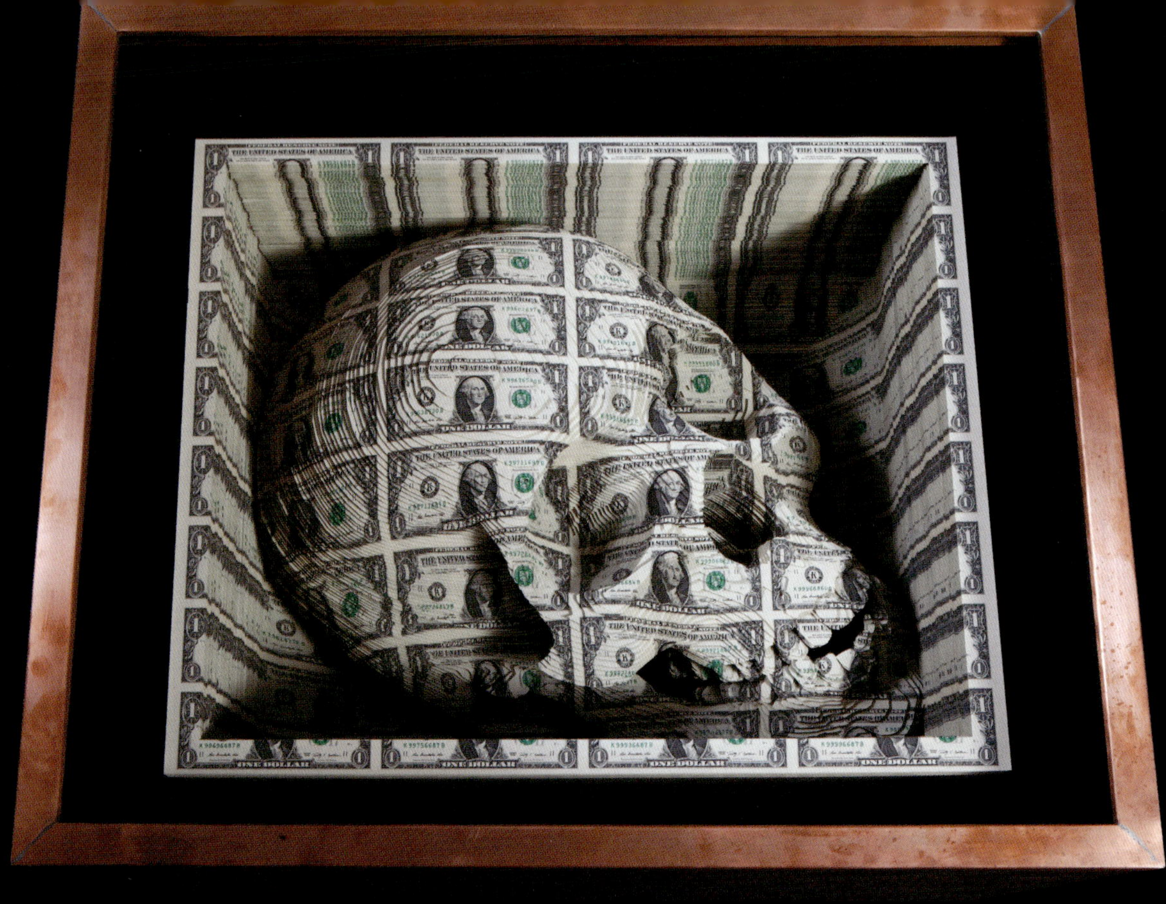

Scott Campbell Noblesse Oblige 2011 cut uncut US currency sheets copper box 53.3 x 63.5 x 47.6cm

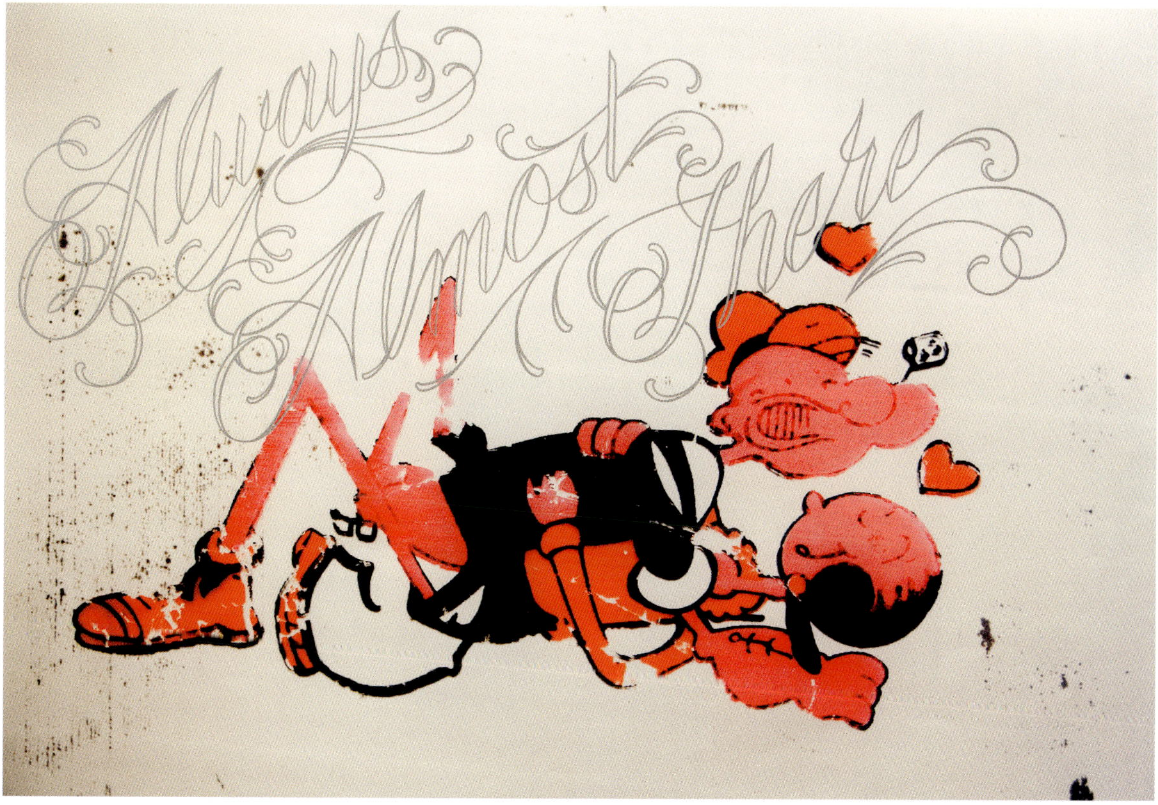

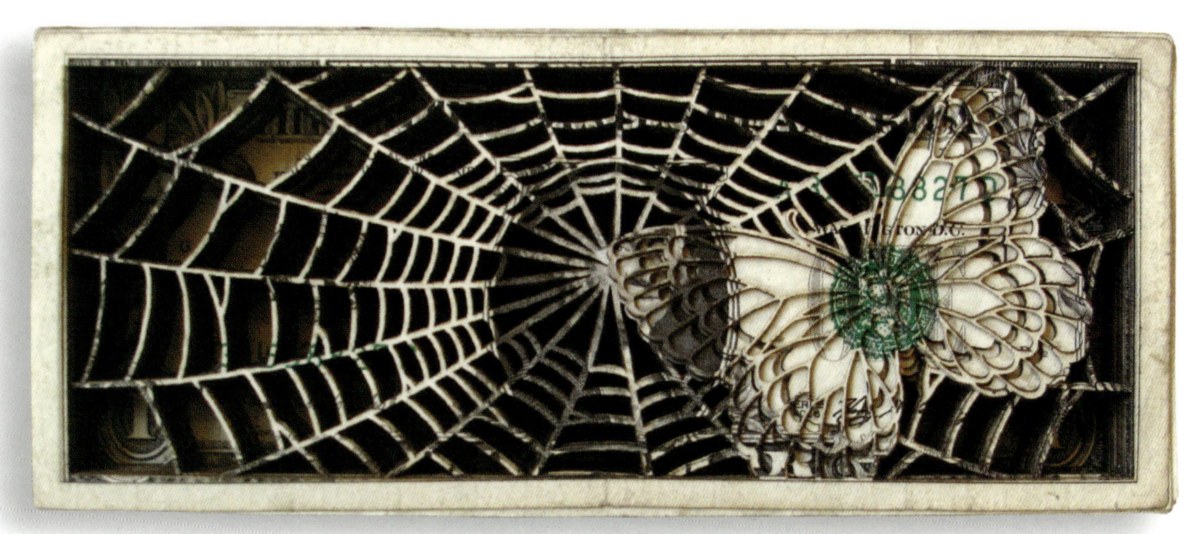

(top) **Scott Campbell**, Always Almost There, 2010, acrylic on giclee print, 71.1 x 104.1cm
(bottom) **Scott Campbell**, Butterfly Web, 2009, US cut dollar bills, 7.6 x 15.2 x 5cm

SHAWN BARBER

Born – 1970
Hometown – Cortland, New York
Study / Apprenticeship – AAS Cazenovia College, BFA Ringling College of Art. Apprenticeship with Mike Davis at Everlasting Tattoo in San Francisco, CA
Lives and Works – Los Angeles, California
Years as a tattooist – 3 years
Favourite medium – oil paint

For Shawn Barber, his creative impulse always comes back to the art. In tattooing and in painting his extremely sincere drive is a very personal journey of humble respect and dedicated work.

Barber paints the most abject, dark and horror-inspired renderings of dolls, but he is better known for documenting what he calls "the art of tattoo". His main body of work – large, fluid oil paintings of tattooed bodies – speak with an intimate magic of the strength of personality behind the skin.

As he says, his works are "not just portraits of randomly tattooed people. These are paintings of artists; very specific, contemporary, influential, controversial, pioneers and renegade artists."[1]

Barber paints with visceral and palpable energy in a way that makes his works ring with a brand of photorealism and simultaneously with moments of abstract expressionism. With a studied nod to classical painting, Barber's portraits are incredible documents of our own moment in history.

Based in Southern California, Barber paints every night of the week and currently tattoos three days a week at his private studio Memoir Tattoo, which he shares with his partner, Kim Saigh.

As an artist turned tattooist, his transition was one marked by hard yards, new ideas and a fresh slate. Despite his experience as an illustrator and painter with hard skills in drawing, anatomy, composition and art history, the craft of tattooing presented its own world of unique challenges.

"Art and craft go hand in hand. 'Anyone' can be an 'artist' – 'craft' shows how serious you are about your art. Tattooing is a very mechanical process with limitations and rules. Understanding and honouring this reality as the backbone of tattooing, (while) art can play freely within it's confines."

And what he has learnt from tattooing has fed directly back into his painting practice. "Tattooing is a deliberate medium. If you're not deliberate, the work is not going to last or look good. The more purposeful you are with the process, the more power and impact will show in the design and application. Tattooing has definitely influenced my drawing hand with painting."

From his first crude tattoo of a black Spiderman at 16, Barber's own body bares a collection of work by a multitude of artists; Kim Saigh, Bryan Bancroft, Henry Lewis, George Campise, Jason Kundell, Phil Holt, Paul Booth, Stanley Moskowitz, Mike Wilson, Carlos Torres, Nikko Hurtado – to name a few; and also a few fine artist's first tattoos: Coro Kaufmann, Michael Hussar, Kevin Llewellyn, Tara McPherson and Nate VanDyke.

"Everyone says it and it's an appropriate statement – 'Tattooing gives you what you put into it'. The harder you work with sincerity for progression, you will see the benefits. It's an obsessive way to live, and I love it."

1 "Forever and Ever: New Works by Shawn Barber" by Justin Giarlia (ed), 9mm Books, San Francisco, 2008, p.15

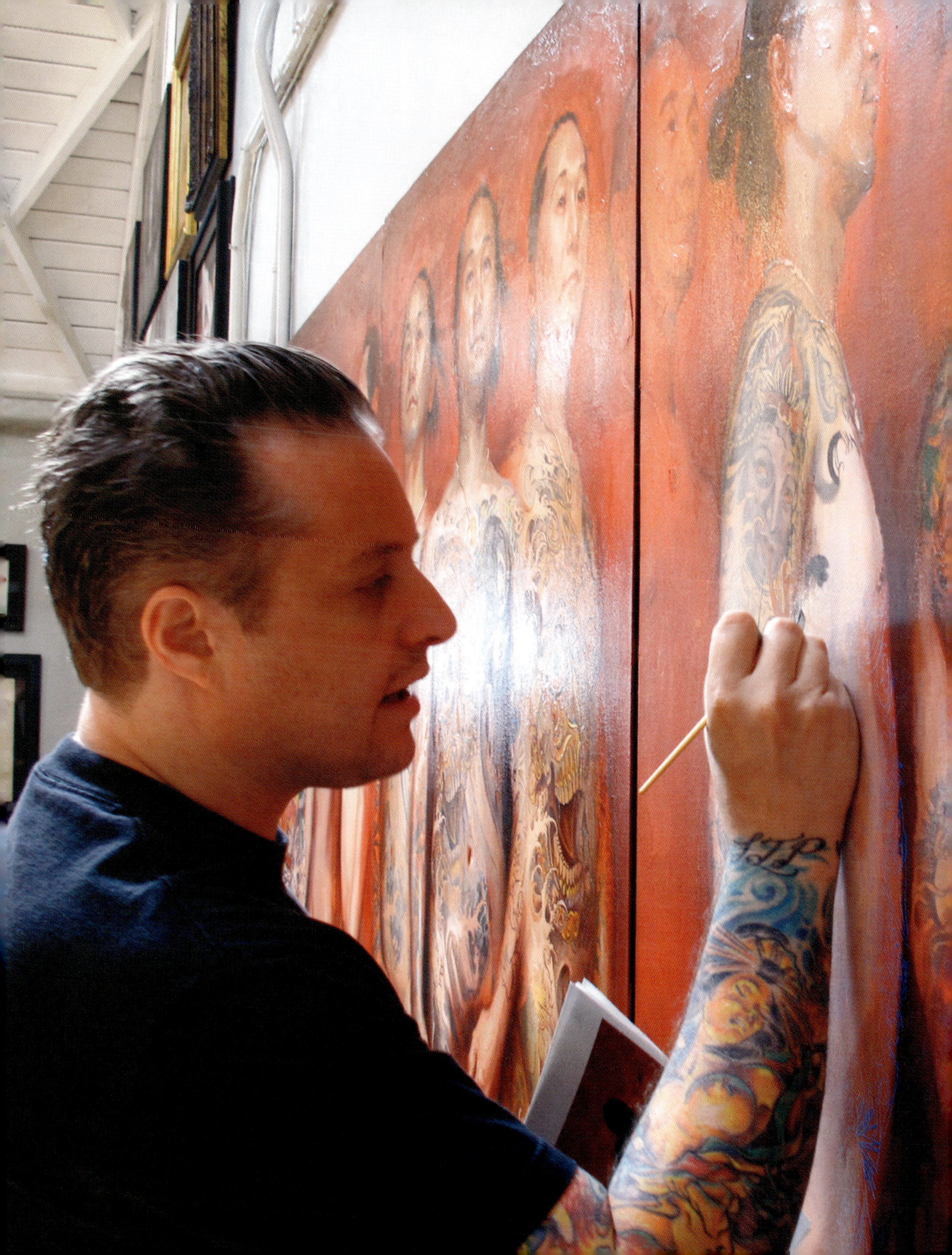

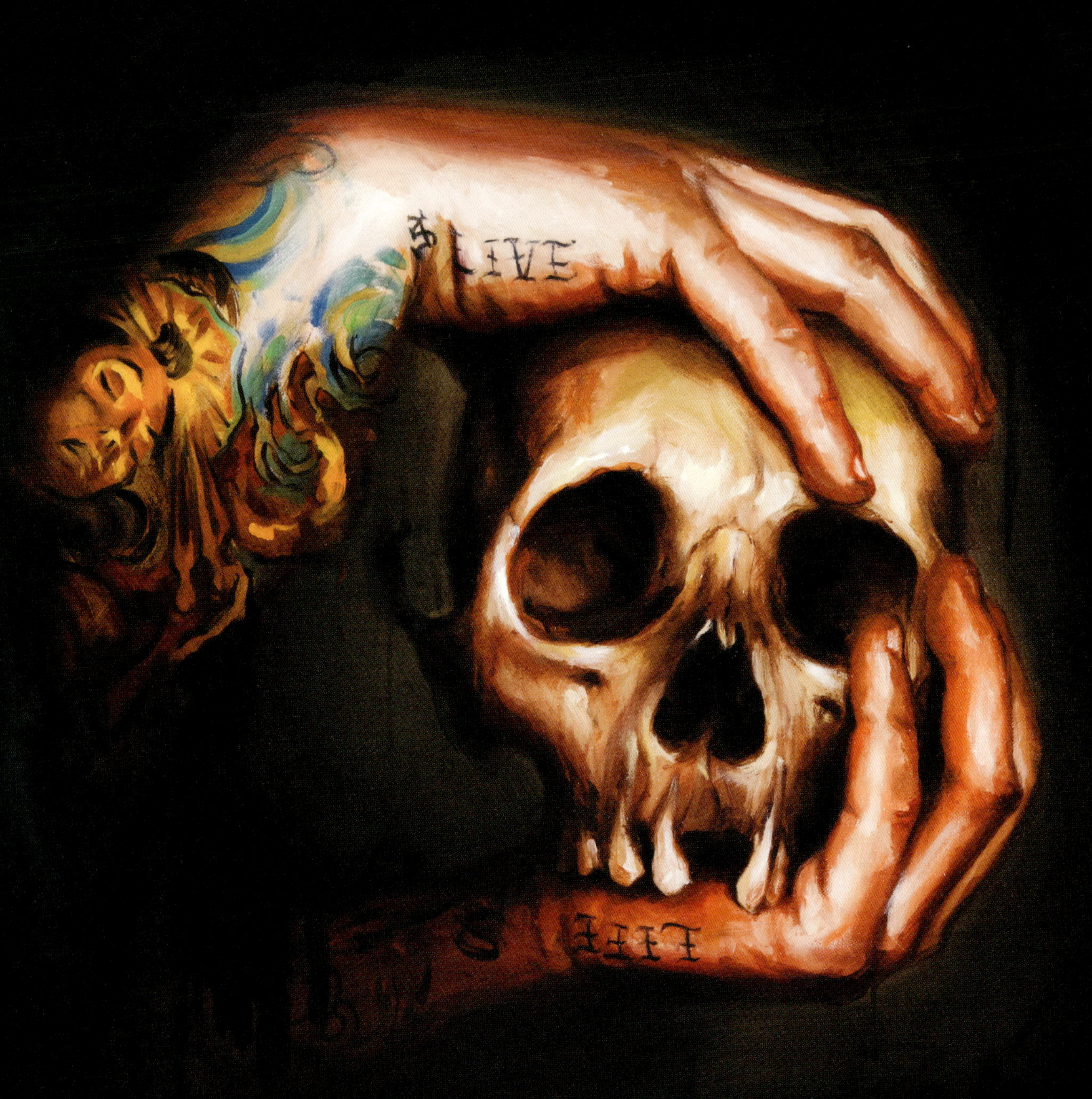
LIVE
LIFE

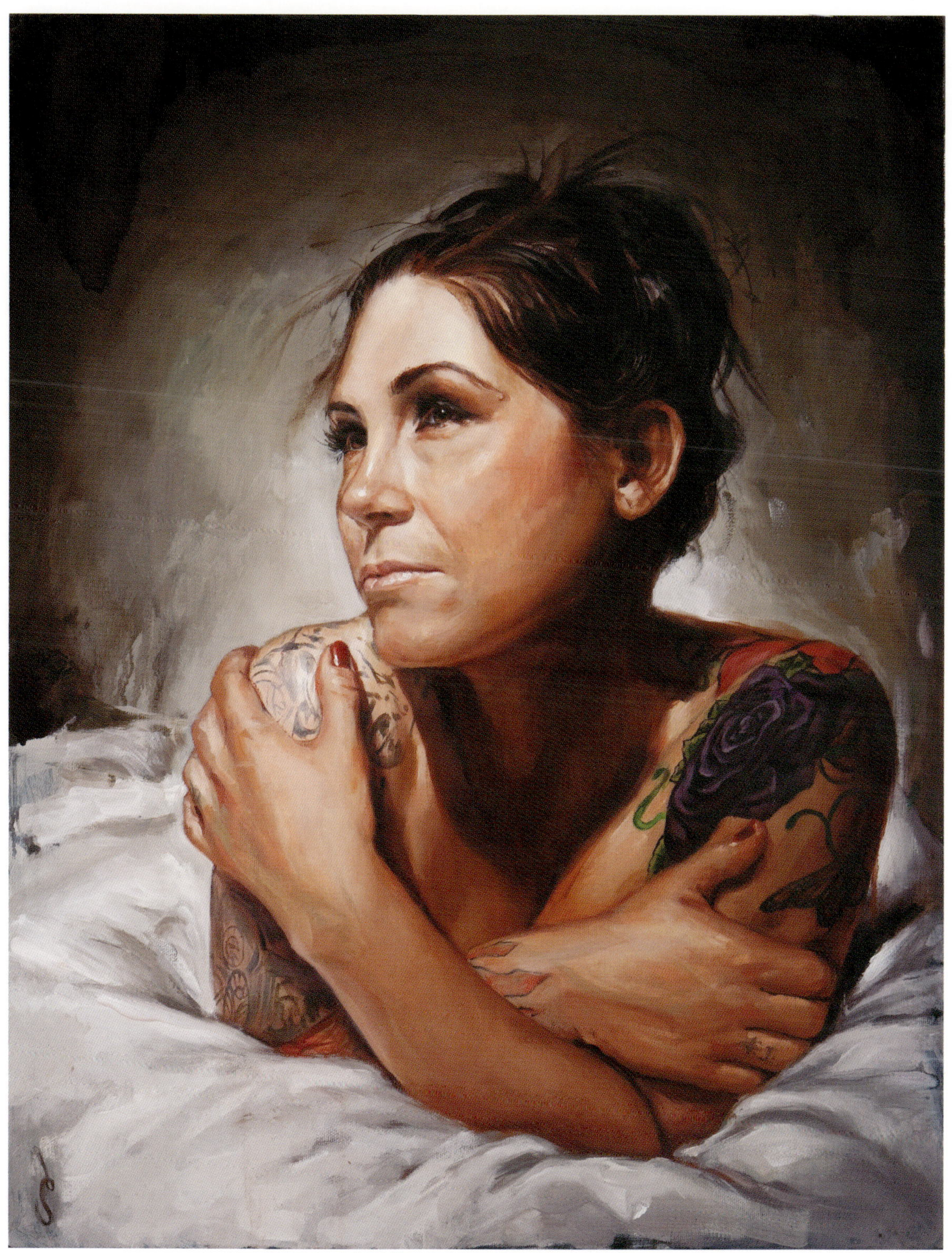

Shawn Barber, Portrait of the Artist, Kim Saigh, Head Study 1, 2009, oil on canvas, 60.9 x 45.7cm

(opposite) **Shawn Barber**, Live Life Skull, 2009, oil on canvas, 76.2 x 60.9cm

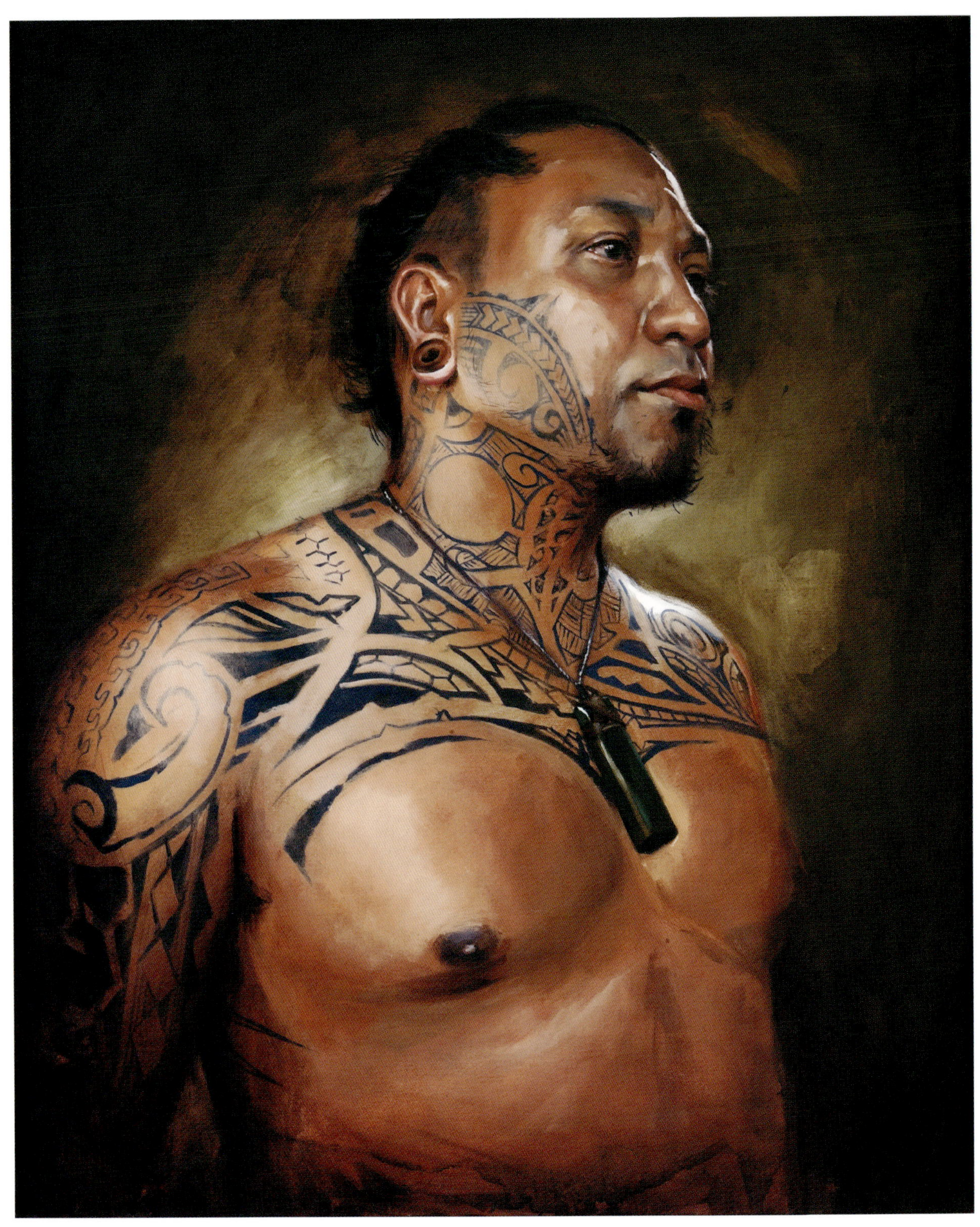

Shawn Barber, Portrait of the Artist, Aisea, 2009, oil on canvas, 76.2 x 60.9cm

(opposite) **Shawn Barber**, Mike Giant Forearm Study, 2007, oil on panel, 60.9 x 40.6cm

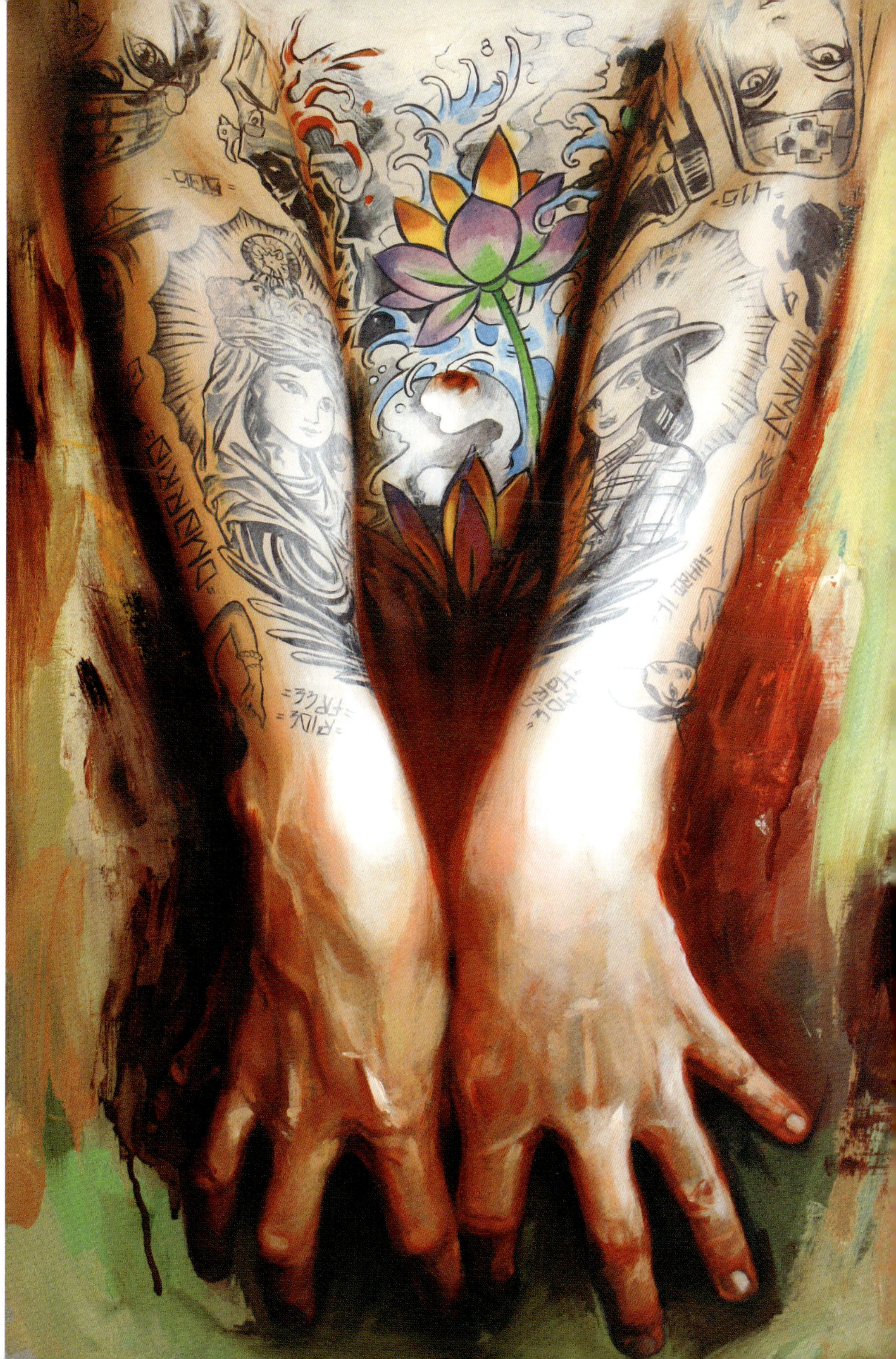

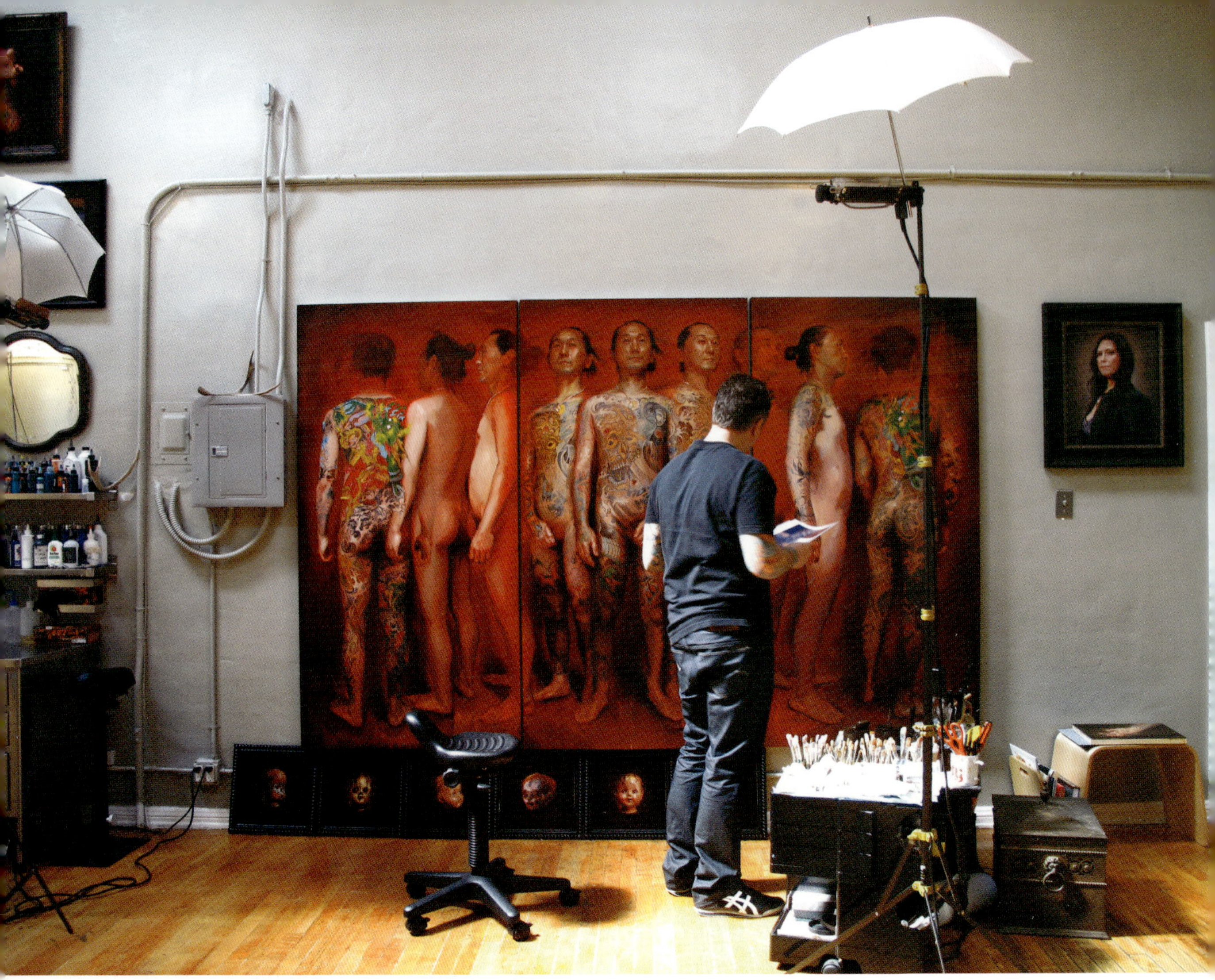

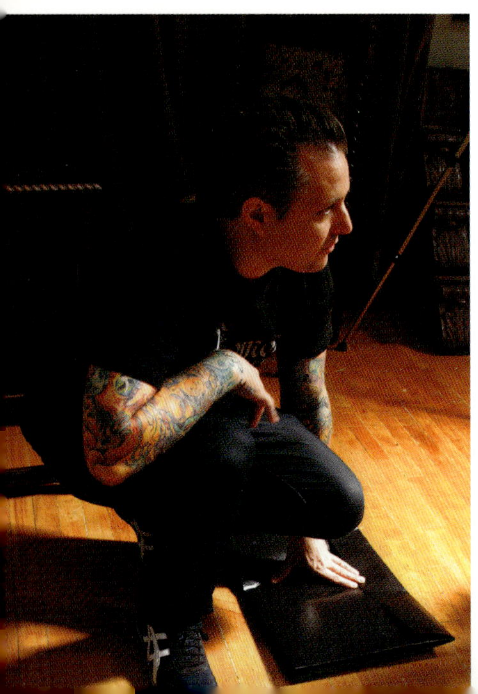

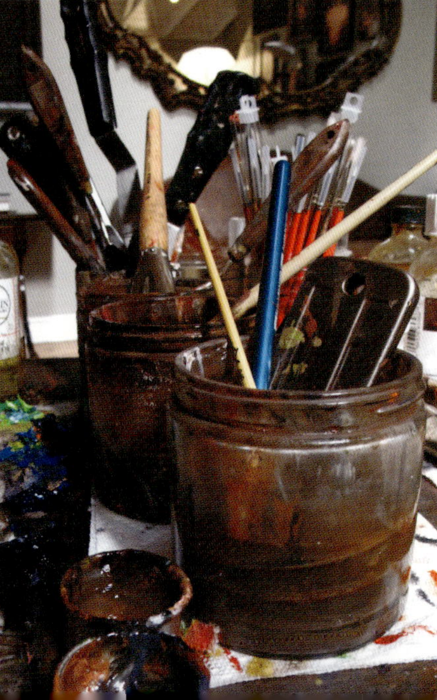

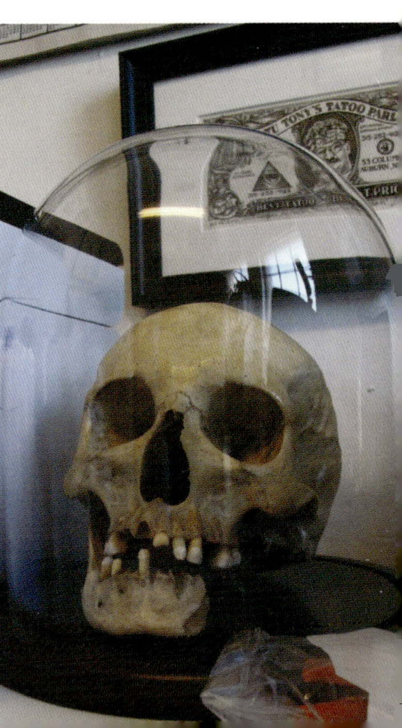

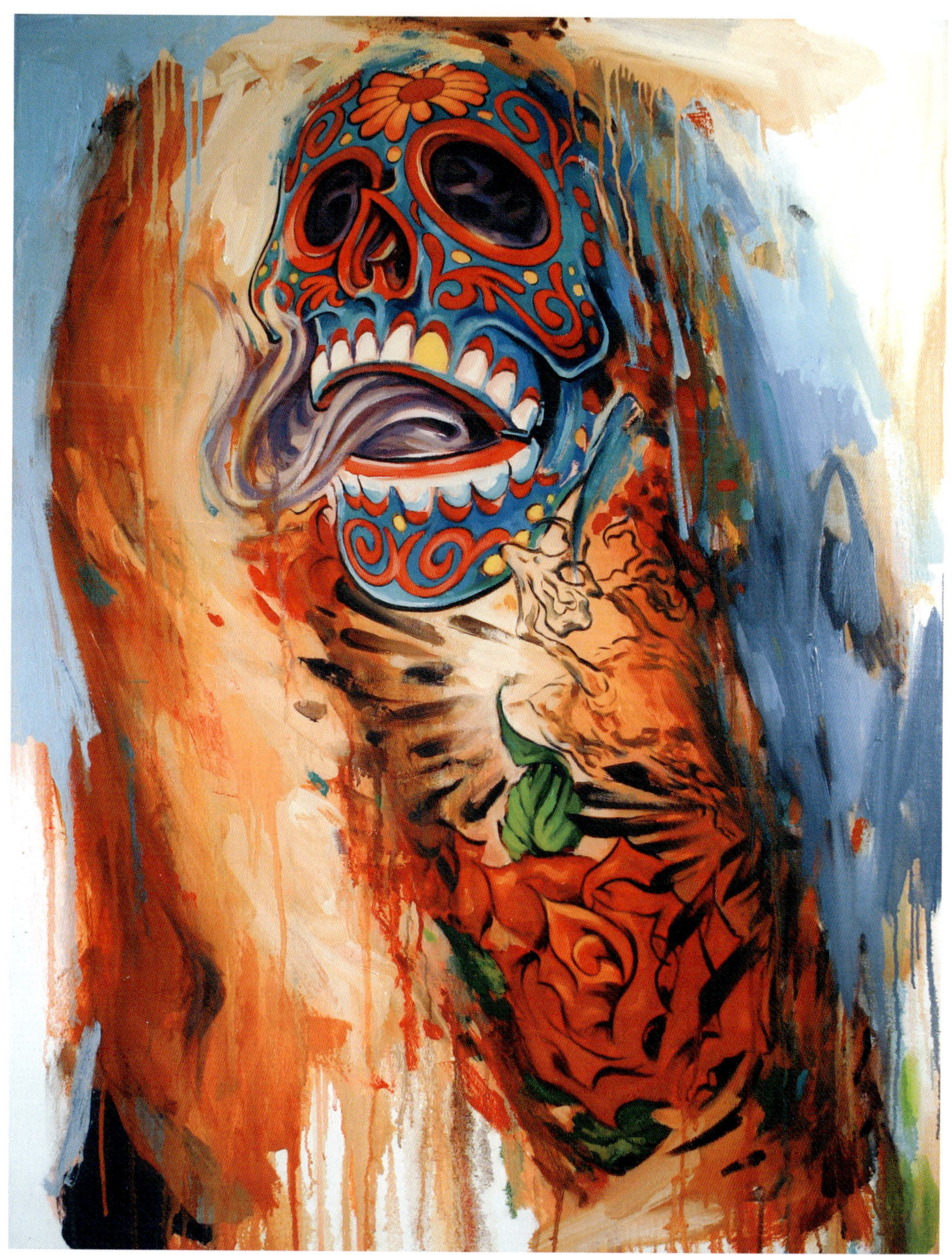

Shawn Barber, Portrait of the Artist, Greg Mocilnikar, 2005, oil on canvas, 101.6 x 76.2cm

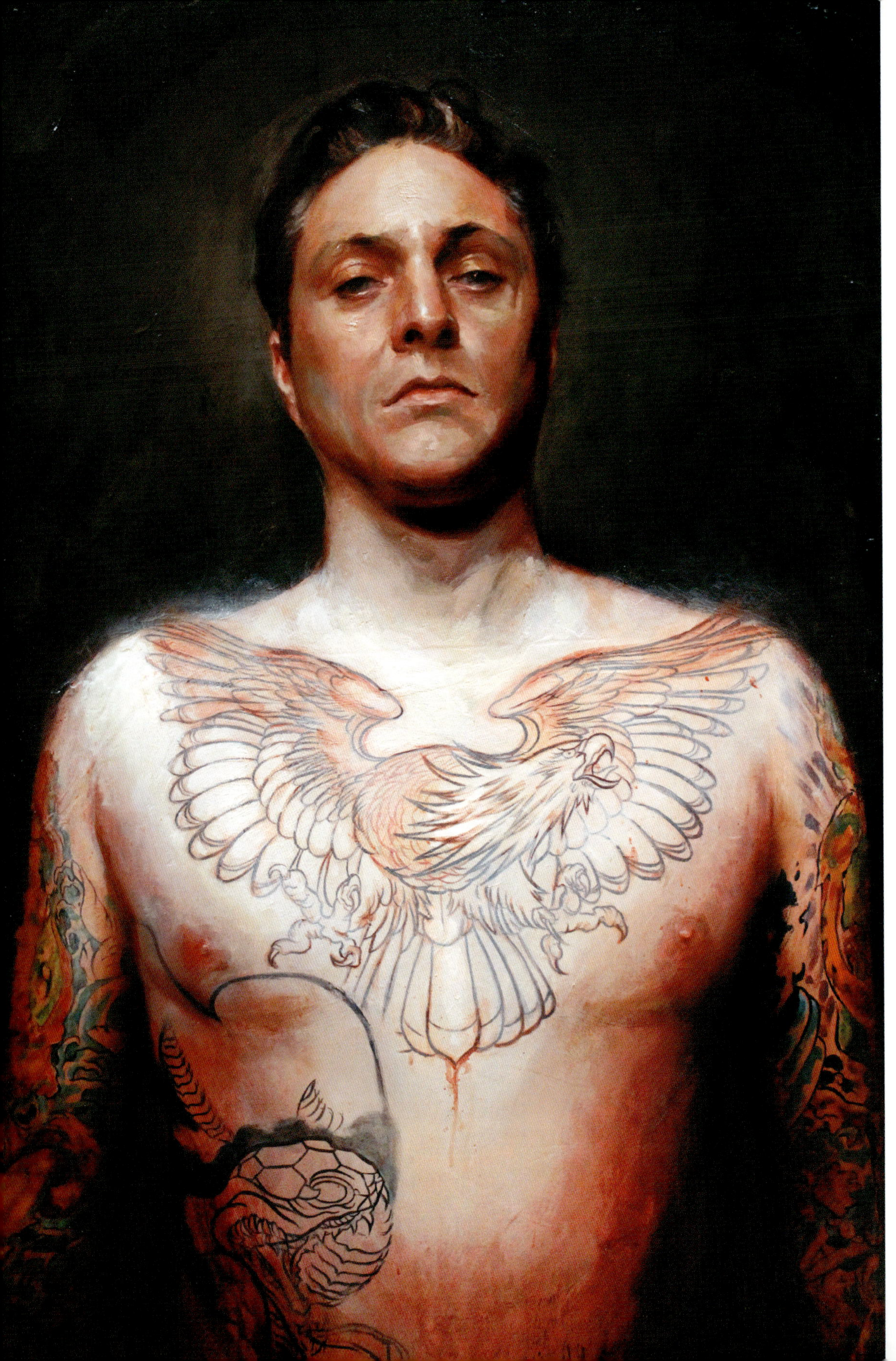

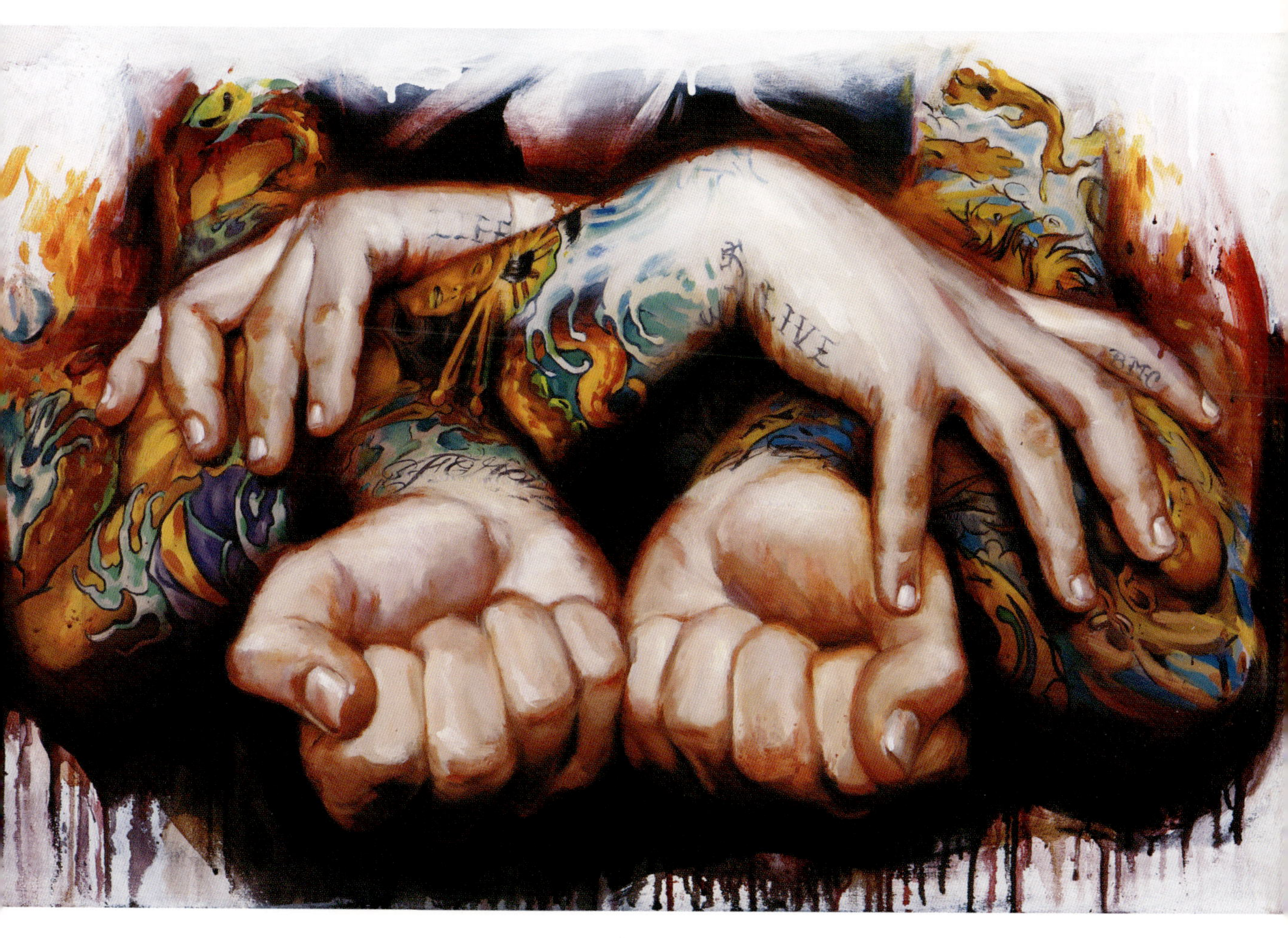

Shawn Barber, Tattooed Self Portrait IV, 2008, oil on canvas, 45.7 x 71.1cm

(opposite) **Shawn Barber**, Tattooed Self Portrait at 39, 2010, oil on canvas, 76.2 x 60.9cm

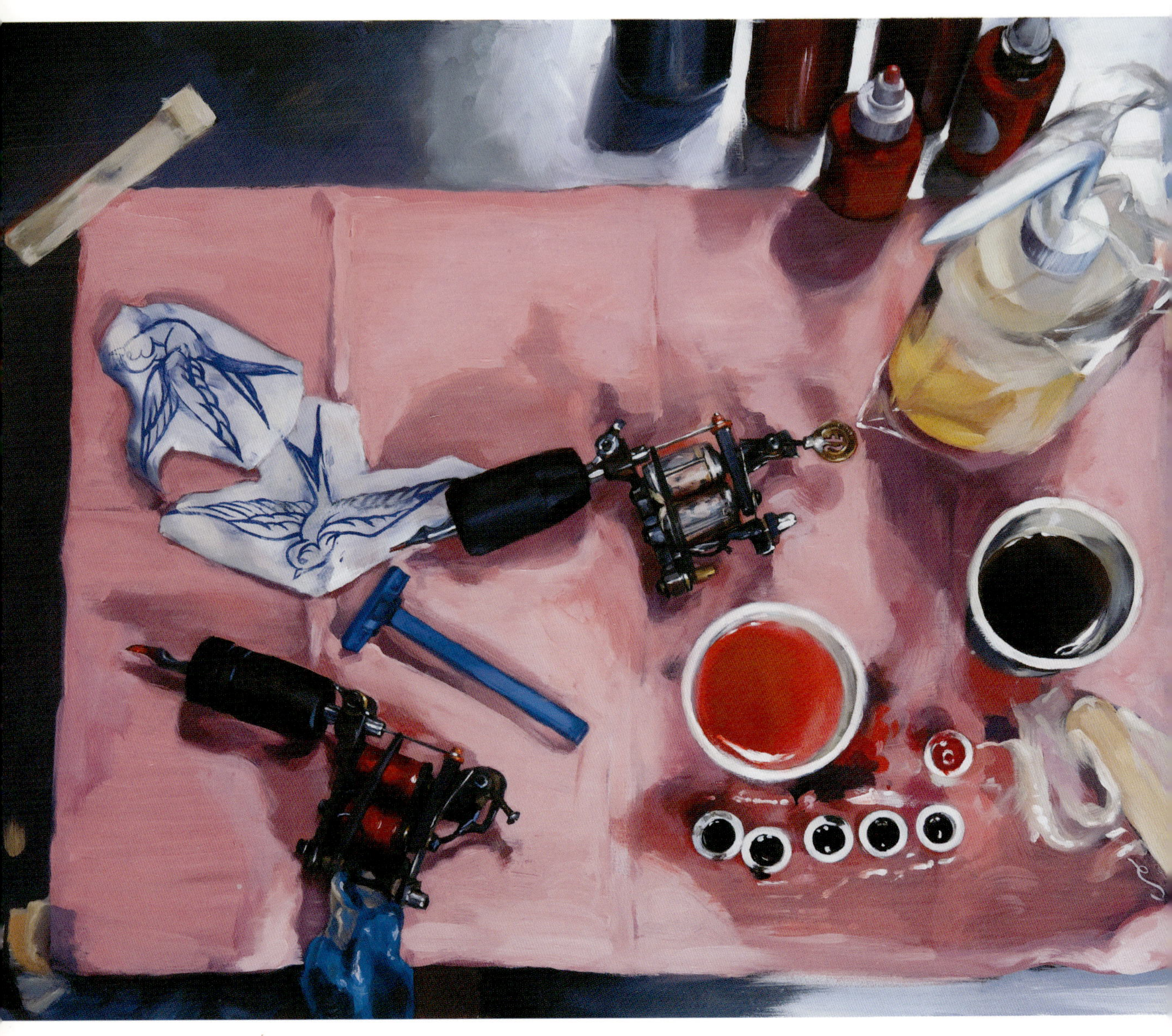

Shawn Barber, Traditional Still Life I, 2009, oil on panel, 40.6 x 50.8cm

(opposite) **Shawn Barber**, Last Gasp, 2011, oil on panel, 50.8 x 40.6cm

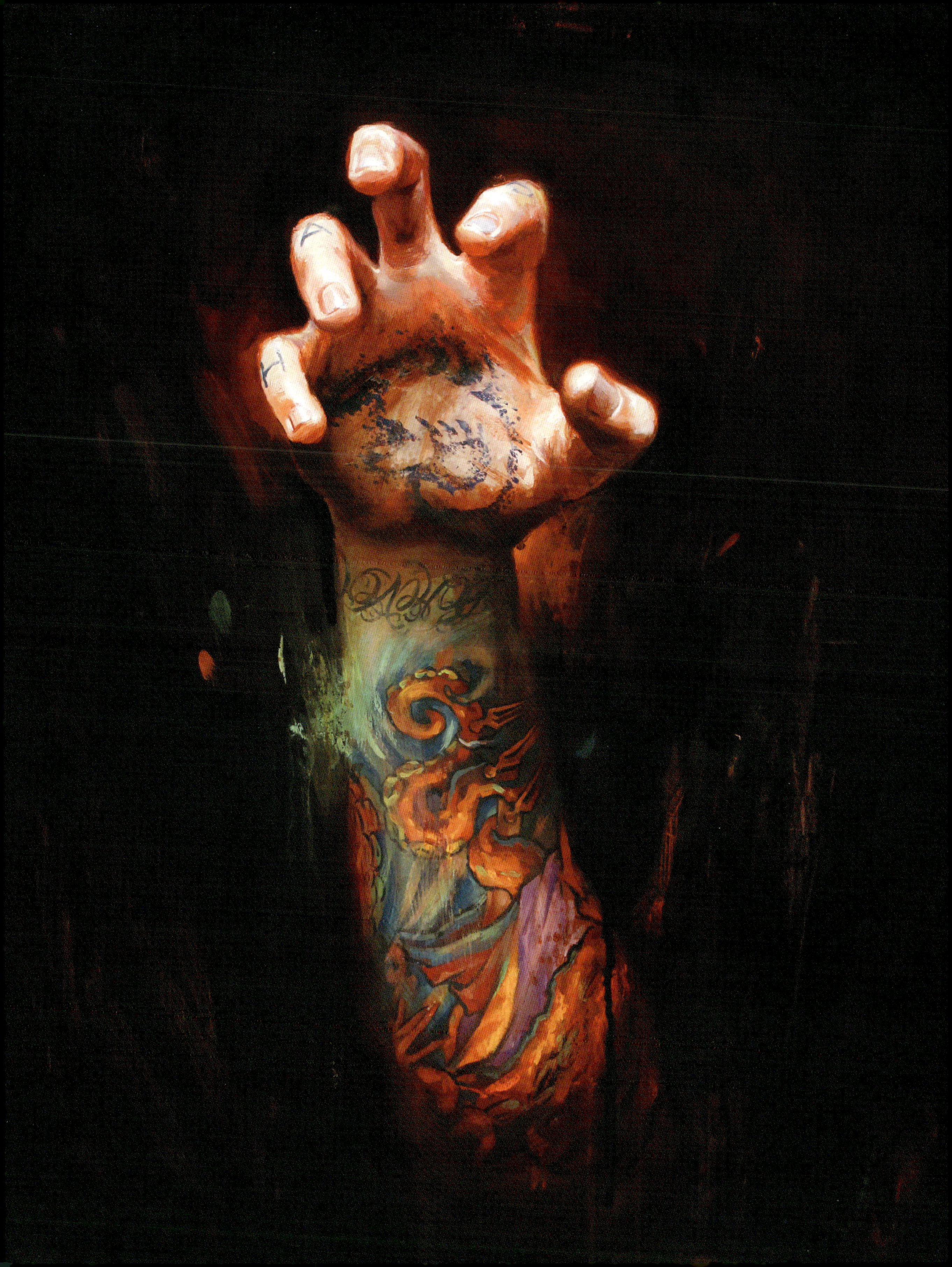

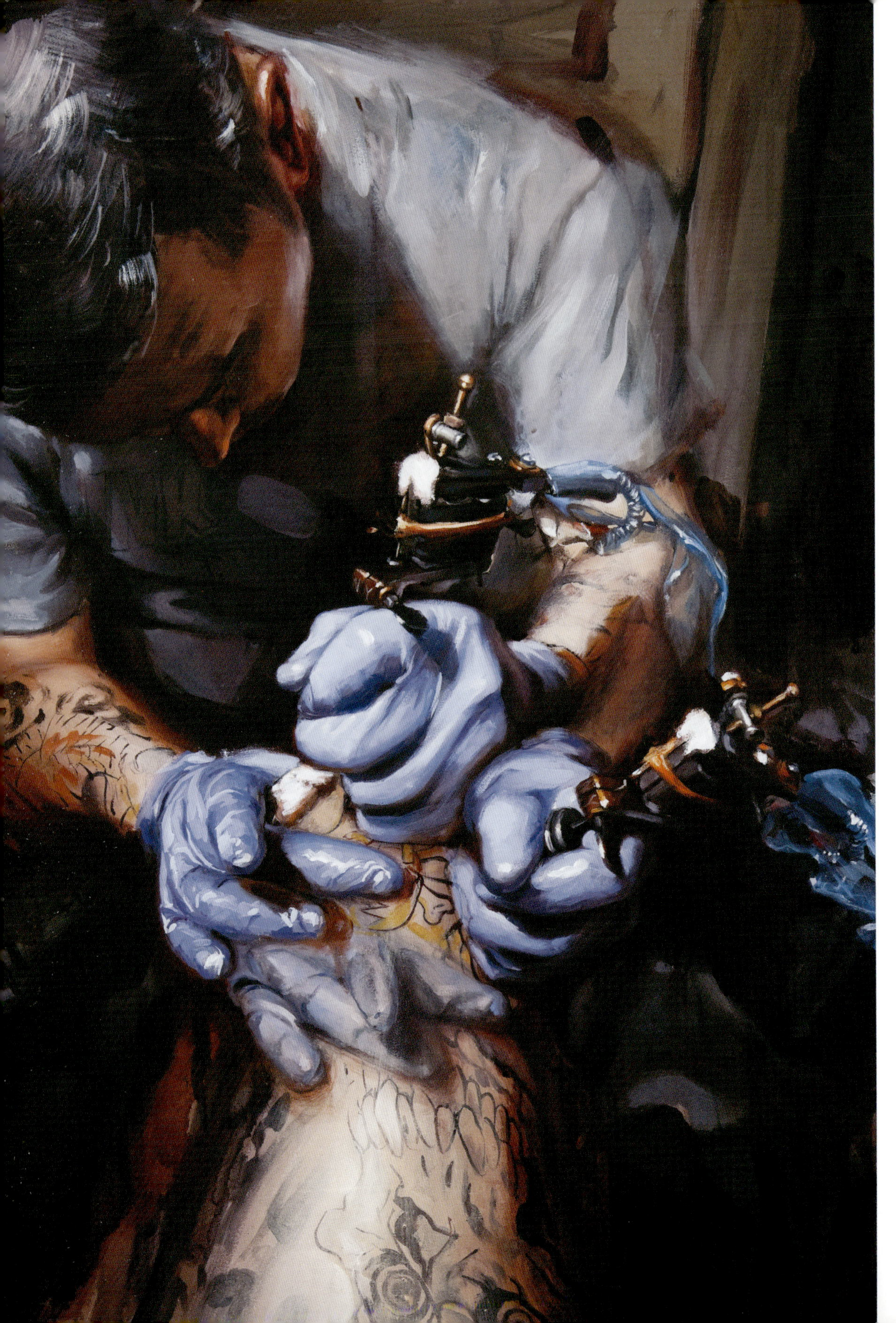

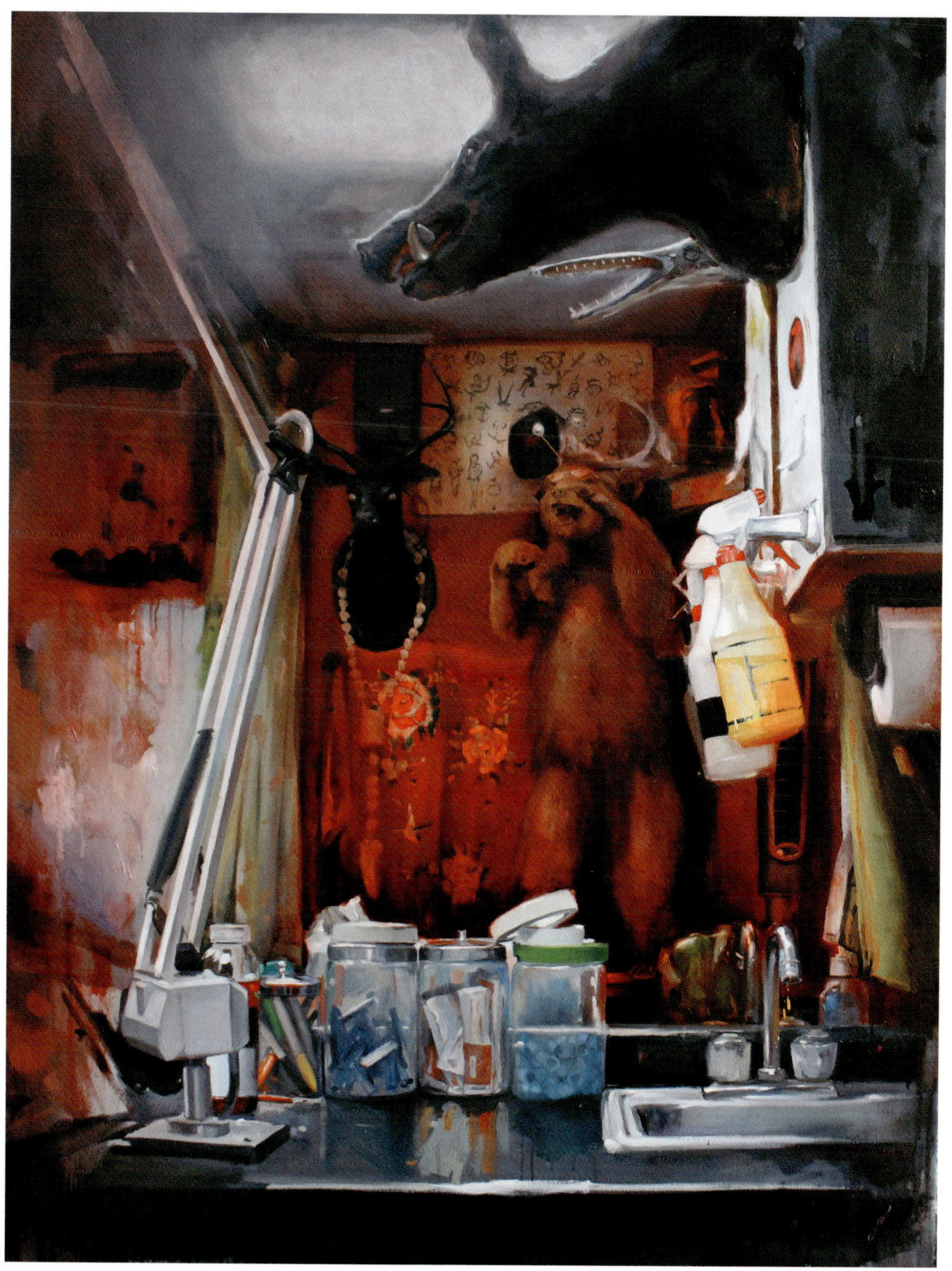

Shawn Barber, Civ's Spot, 2010, oil on canvas, 121.9 x 81.2cm

(opposite) **Shawn Barber**, Steve Boltz at Work, 2009, oil on canvas, 76.2 x 50.8cm

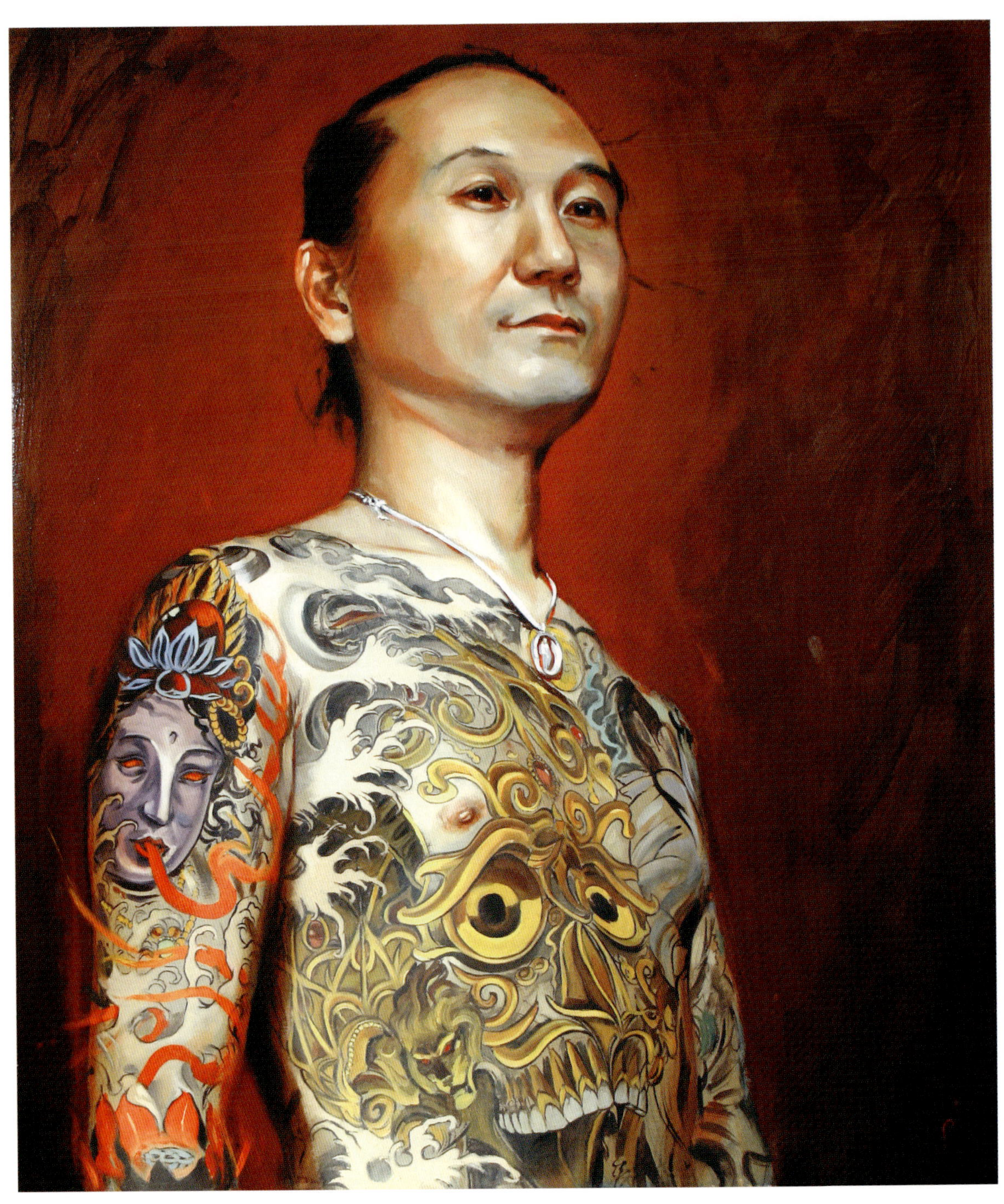

Shawn Barber, Portrait Study of the Artist, Shige, Study, 2007, oil on panel, 76.2 x 60.9cm

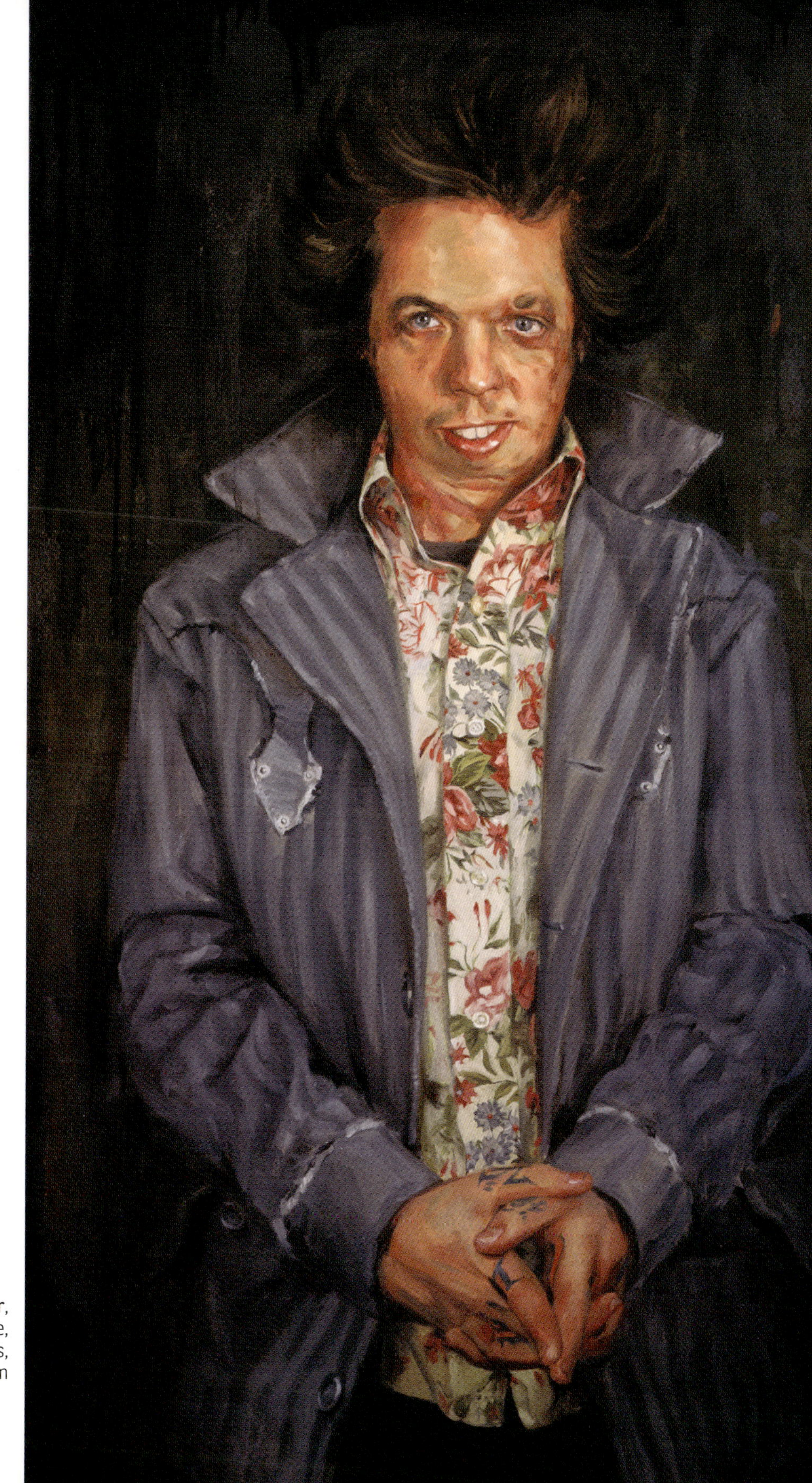

Shawn Barber,
Portrait of the Artist, Grime, 2006, oil on canvas, 106.6 x 60.9cm

THOMAS HOOPER

Born – 1979
Hometown – Hastings, East Sussex, UK
Study – BA Hons Drawing at The London Institute of Art & Design, Camberwell
Lives and Works – Brooklyn, New York
Years as a tattooist – Not Enough
Favourite medium – Ink

Thomas Hooper is the British tattoo artist and painter who has brought his own brand of intense darkness to New York, standing boldly against a backdrop of popular colour drenching in tattoos.

As a tattooist in great demand, his trademark work mixes complex pointillism, meditative patterning and line-work which draw from the traditions of sacred geometry. As he says, "I'm just obsessed by patterns and repetition."[1]

Thomas brings new life and contemporary warmth to historical, ancient and iconic spiritual symbolism. He digs deep to reference original source material such as European woodcuts and etchings from the 1500s through to the late 1800s, as well as Tibetan and Western occult symbolism. "I have a theory that if it looked good five hundred years ago, it will look good now. I'm not trying to reinvent the wheel with each tattoo. I just want to do good tattoos."[2]

His dark and sober language of tattooing is held together by his expert use of black and grey. He uses different shades of warm and cool greys and blacks to give depth to his work. Subtly executed with powerful impact.

For Thomas this blackness relates back to a simplicity that is at the core of who we are as human beings. "I just like black because it's carbon, it's what we are, it's inert with us... it's not going to react or do anything. It will age with your skin beautifully and it's just there."[3]

This recipe of darkness combined with a meditative mindset, transfers into his fine art practice which represents a freedom from the demands of everyday tattooing.

"I generally don't even think about tattooing when I am experimenting with other media... when I'm doing a painting I'm doing exactly what I want to do, so I'm not thinking how its going to look, or if someone's going to be happy with it, there's no pressure."[4] As opposed to the very precise and pre-meditated nature of his tattoo work, Thomas's paintings revel in chance, spontaneity, accidents and the kind of tactility that can not be replicated on skin. Large swaths of organic ink pools, media that reacts with each other in unpredictable ways. Works on paper which threaten to decay before your eyes. Overt abstraction mixed with precise renderings and patterns.

Skulls reappear in his both tattoos and fine art. He even published *The Book of Skulls*, an epic reference document of over 400 different human and animal skull photographs. He takes the symbolic power of the skull on a very sincere level.

"For me it contains a mysterious spirituality, symbolising death, rebirth and the element in between our life and nothingness... our minds are as vast as the universe, yet when we die that giant infinite mass disappears and we are left with this vessel – the skull."[5]

And amidst all the darkness and symbols of death, for Thomas his work is full of overt positivity. "The language I'm trying to use first off is not to say anything negative , always positive... just good, positive, strong symbols."[6]

1 "Gypsy Gentleman" episode 1, Marcus Kuhn (director), 2011. **2** "Thomas Hooper" by Robert Ryan, Tattoo Artist Magazine, #23, December 2010. **3** Kuhn, op. cit. **4** "Thomas Hooper Interview" by Chad Koeplinger, Total Tattoo, November 2010. **5** unpublished interview excerpt with Miki Vialetto, August 2009. **6** Ryan, op. cit.

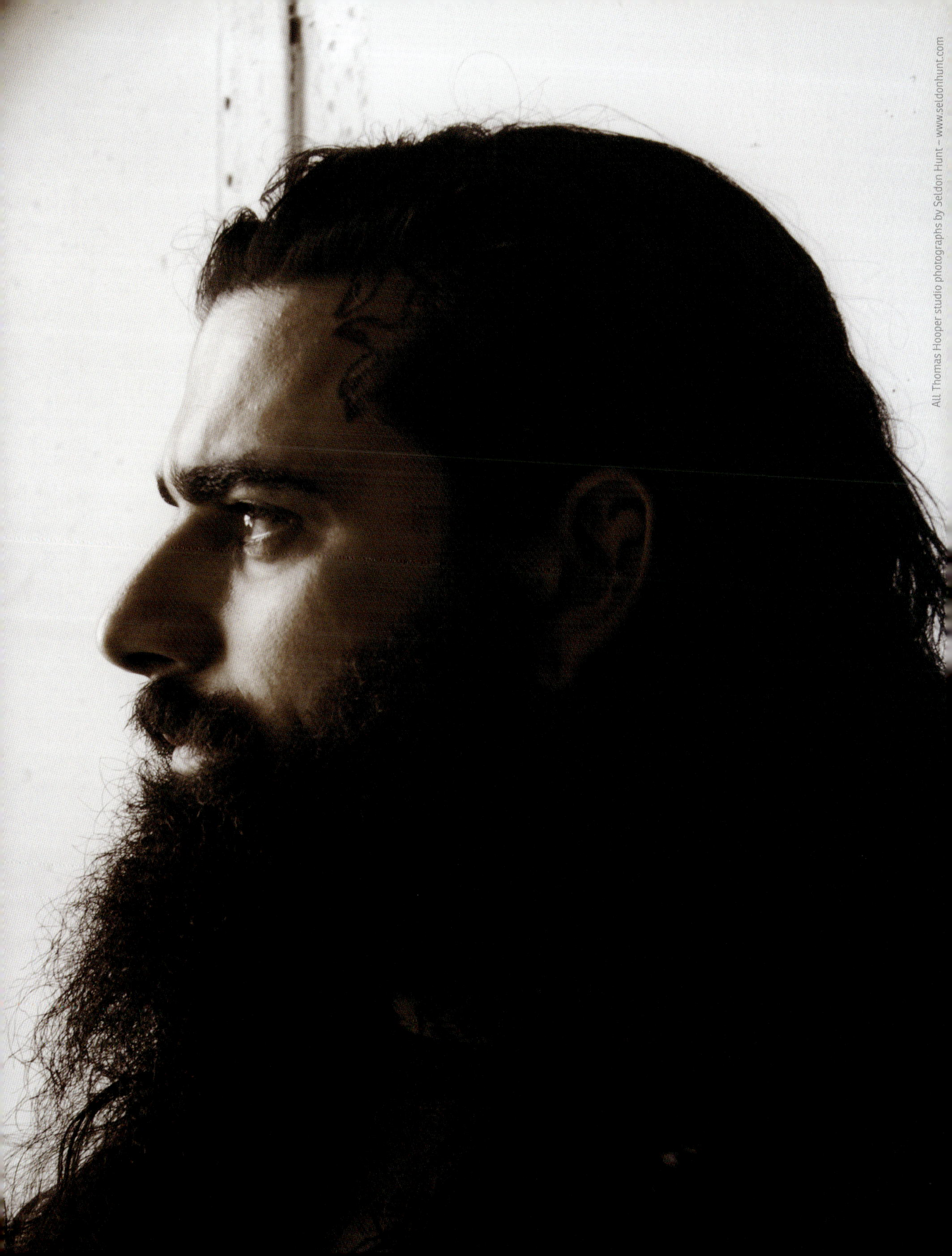

All Thomas Hooper studio photographs by Seldon Hunt – www.seldonhunt.com

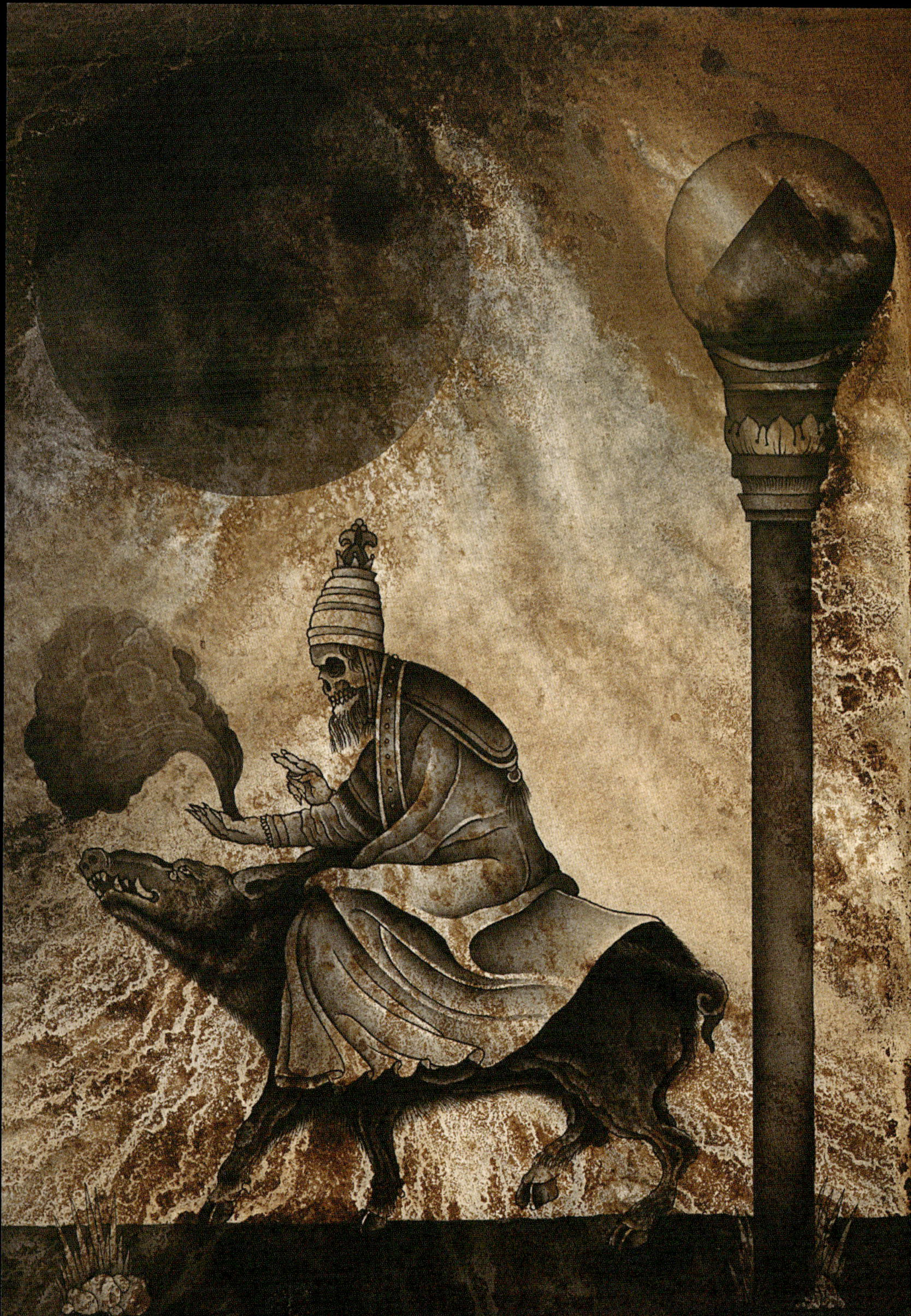

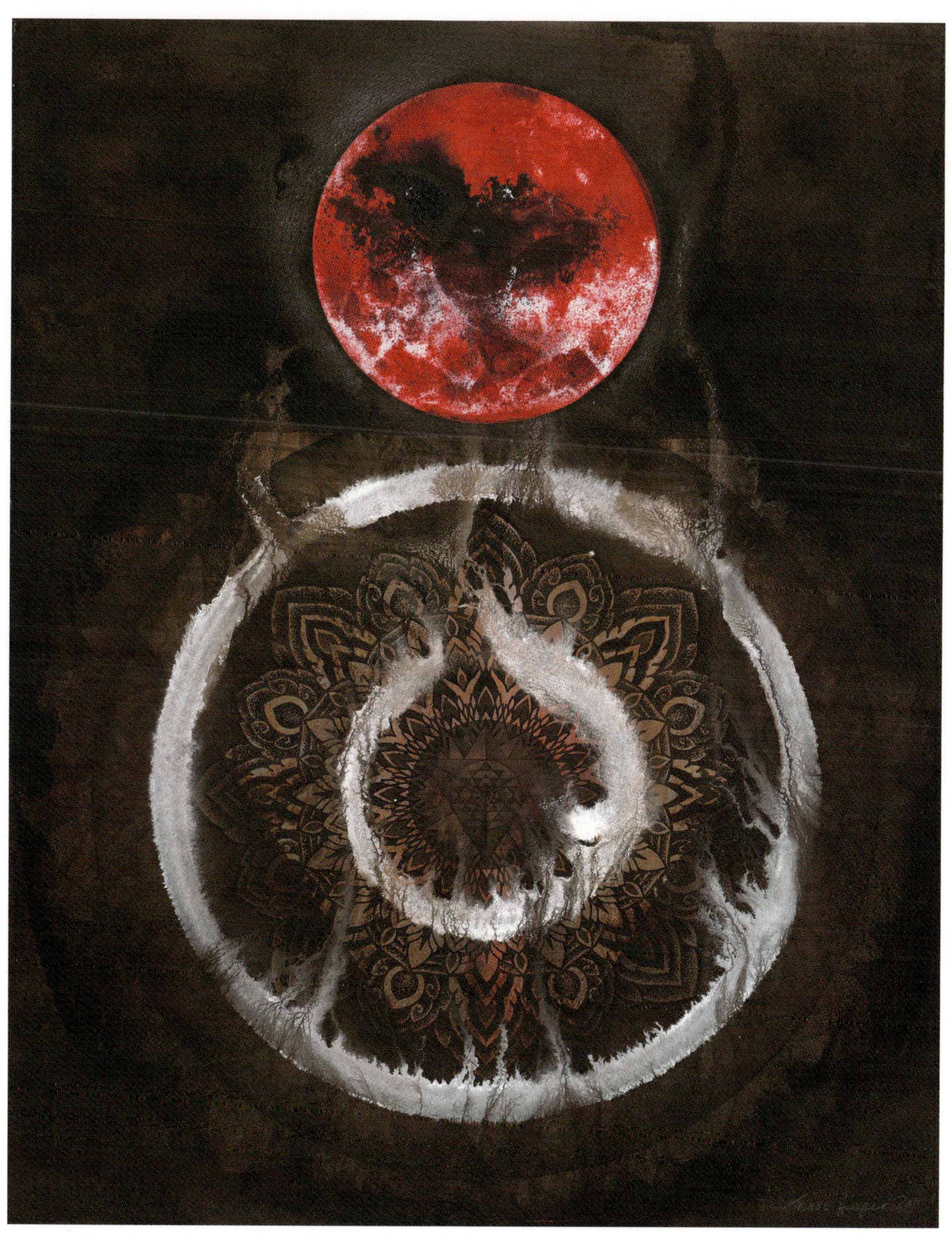

Thomas Hooper, Red Sun, 2010, ink, spaulding red and acrylic on paper, 76 x 56cm

(opposite) **Thomas Hooper**, Lazerus, 2010, ink on paper, 45.5 x 25.5cm

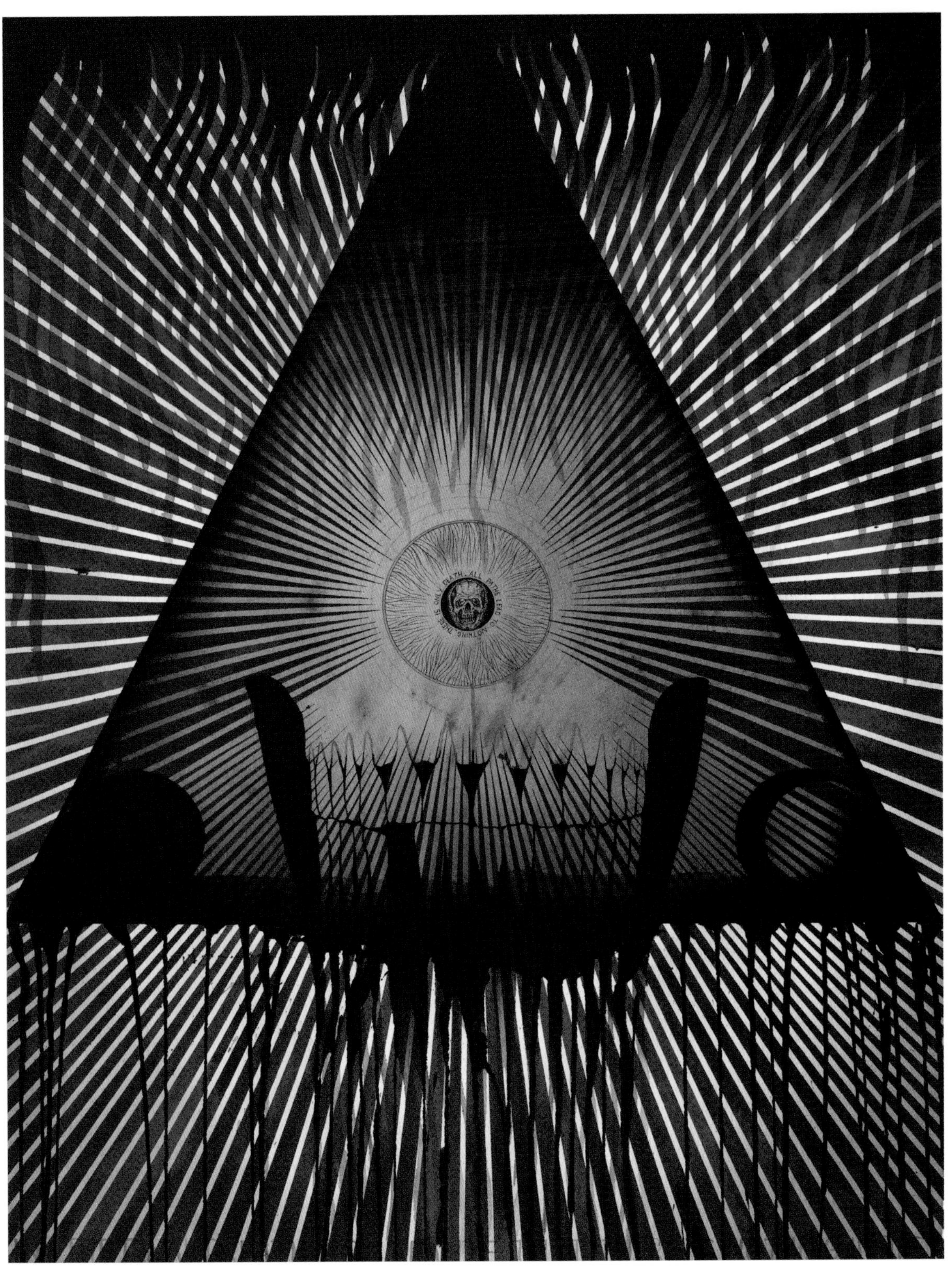

Thomas Hooper, Enter, 2008, ink on paper, 76 x 56cm

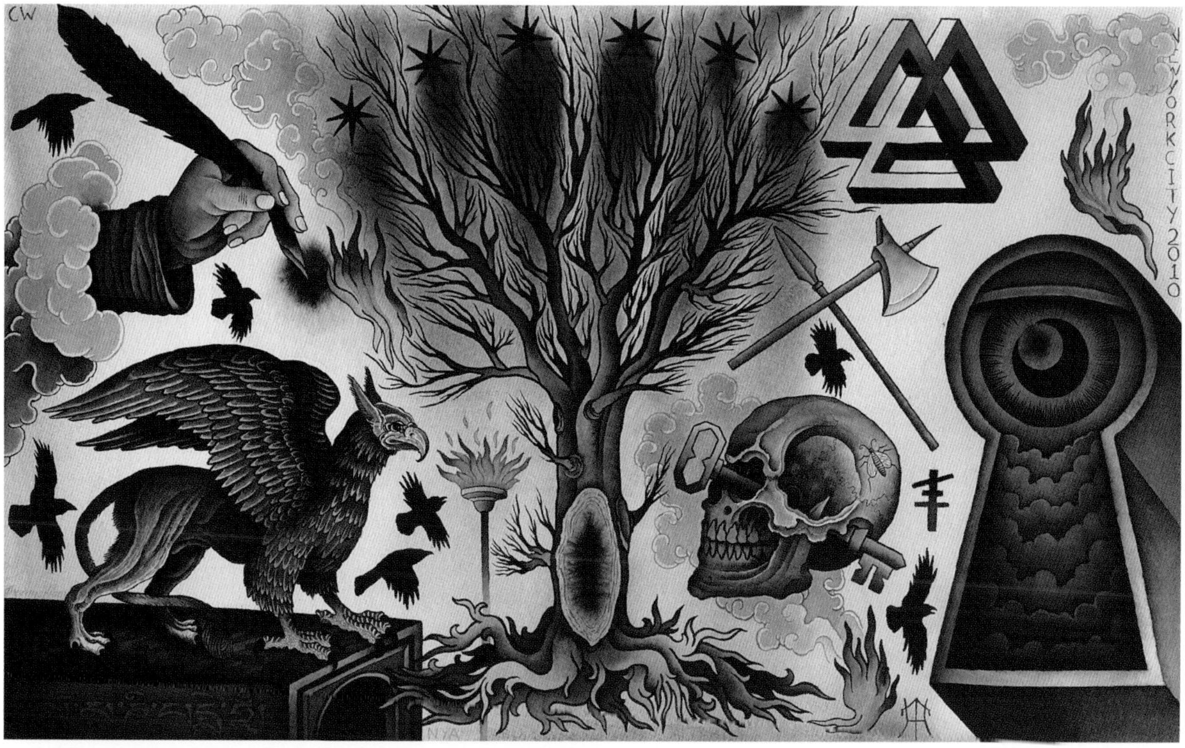

Thomas Hooper, Griffin Flash, 2010, ink on paper, 28 x 38cm

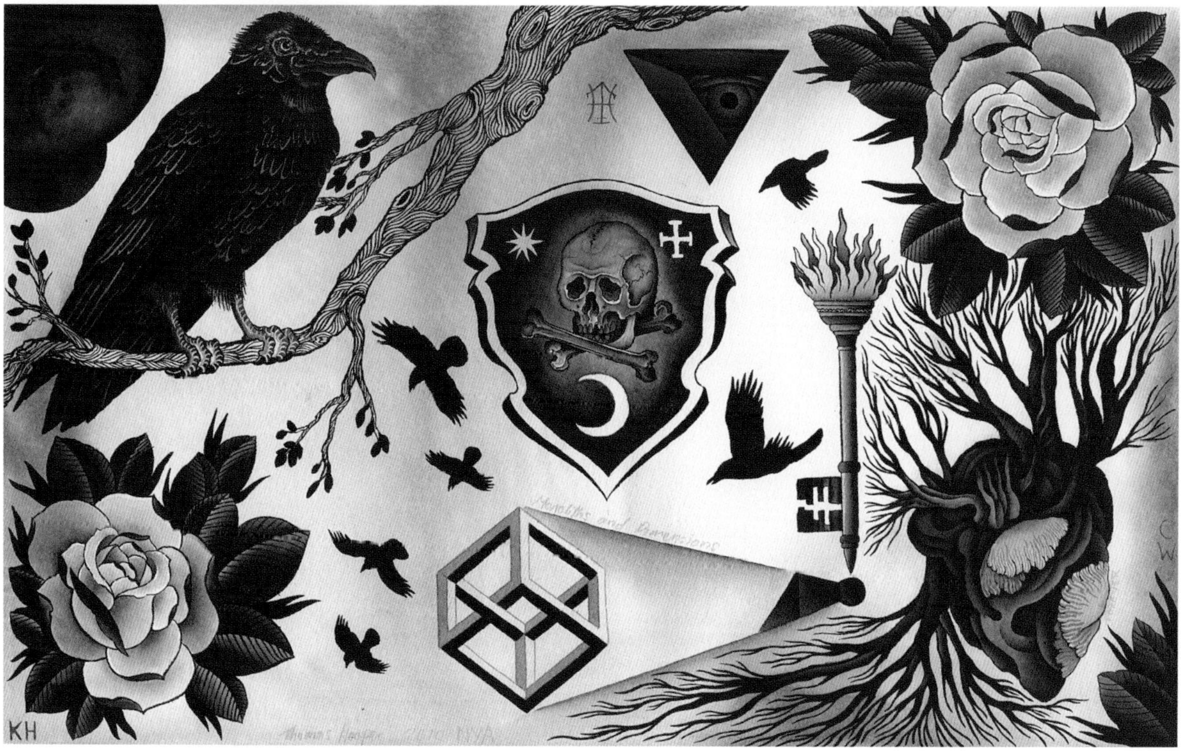

Thomas Hooper, Raven and Shield Flash, 2010, ink on paper, 28 x 38cm

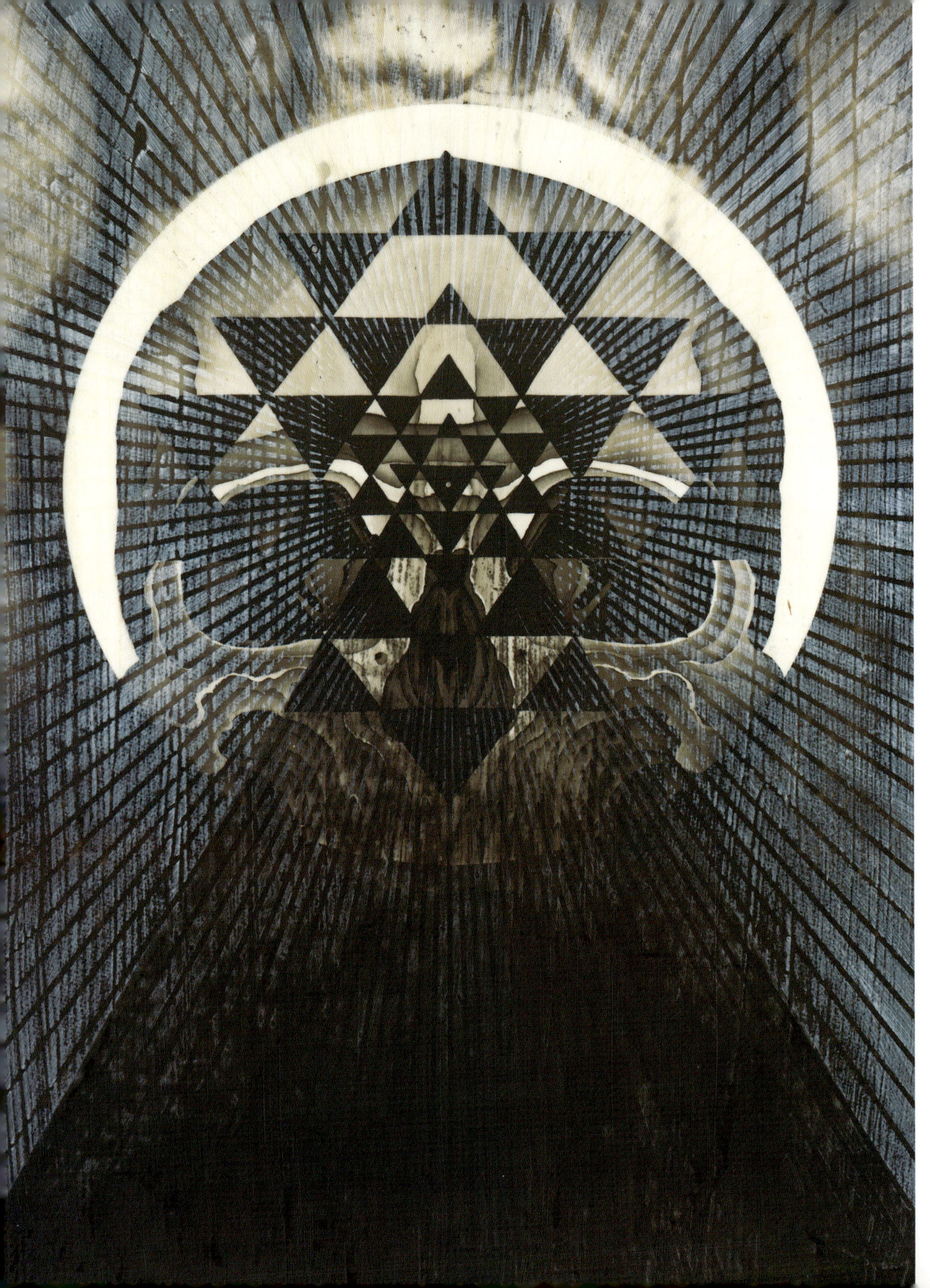

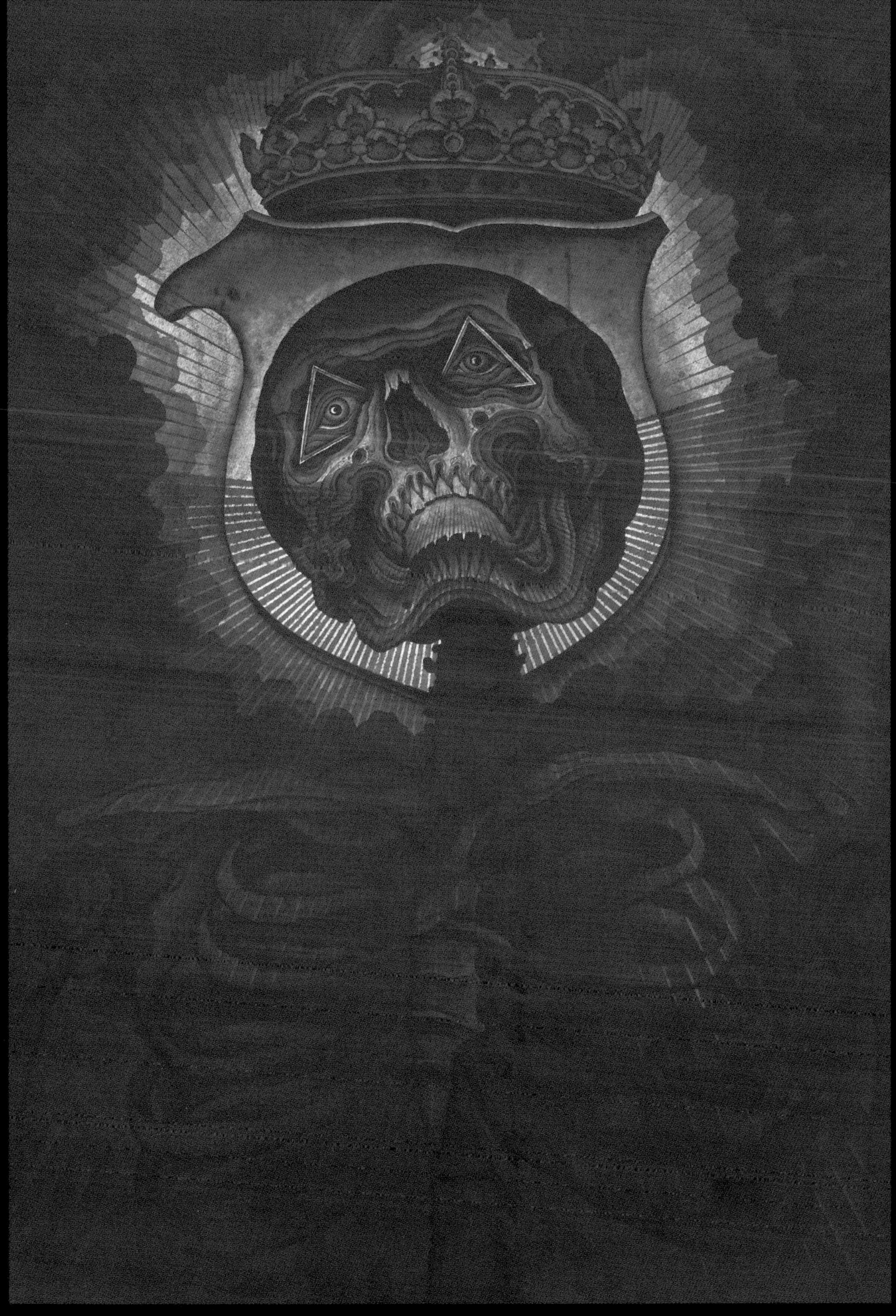

Thomas Hooper, Darkness Comes Alive, 2009, ink on paper, 147 x 96.5cm

(opposite) **Thomas Hooper**, Skull Pyramid, 2010, ink and acrylic on paper, 76 x 56cm

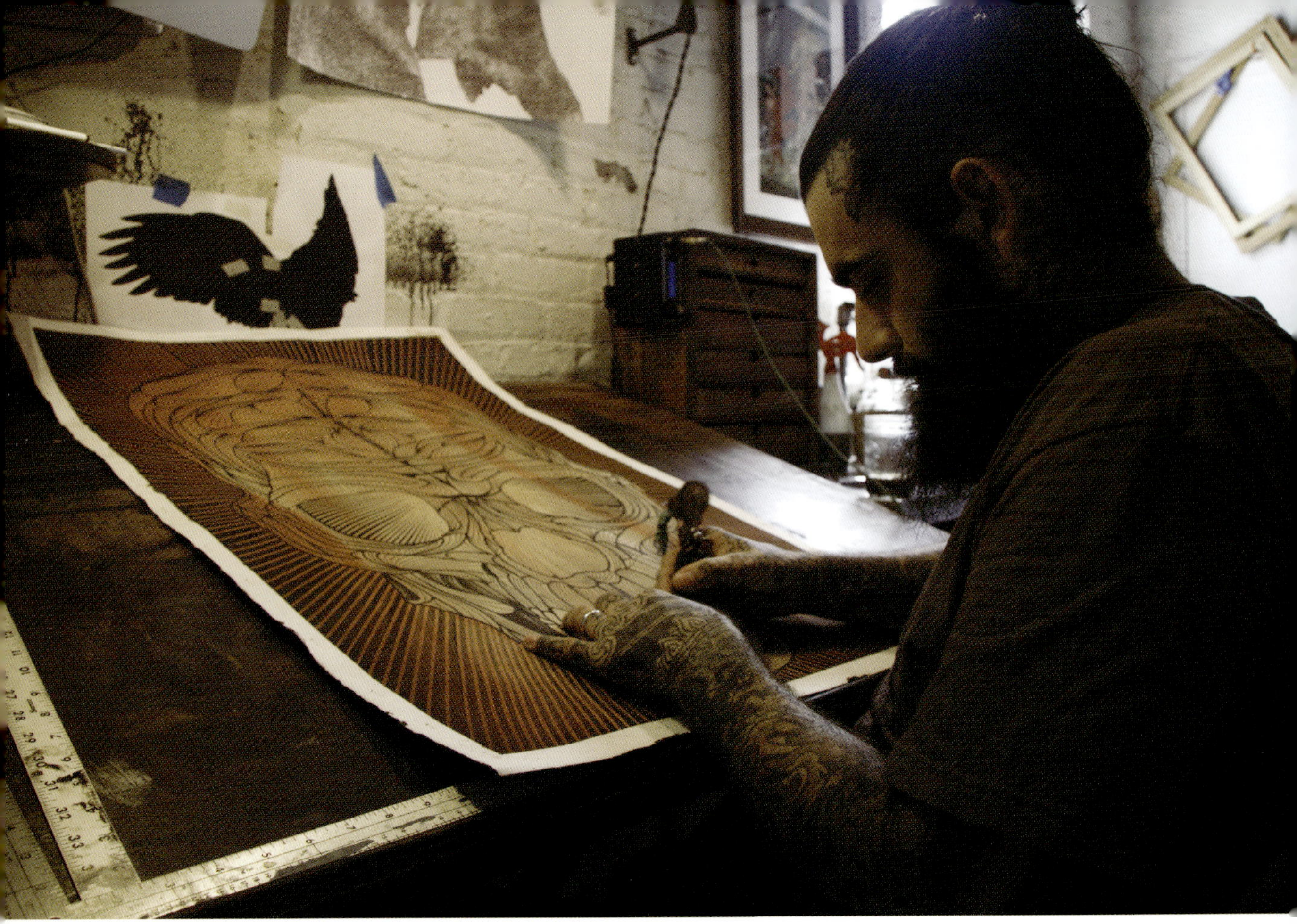

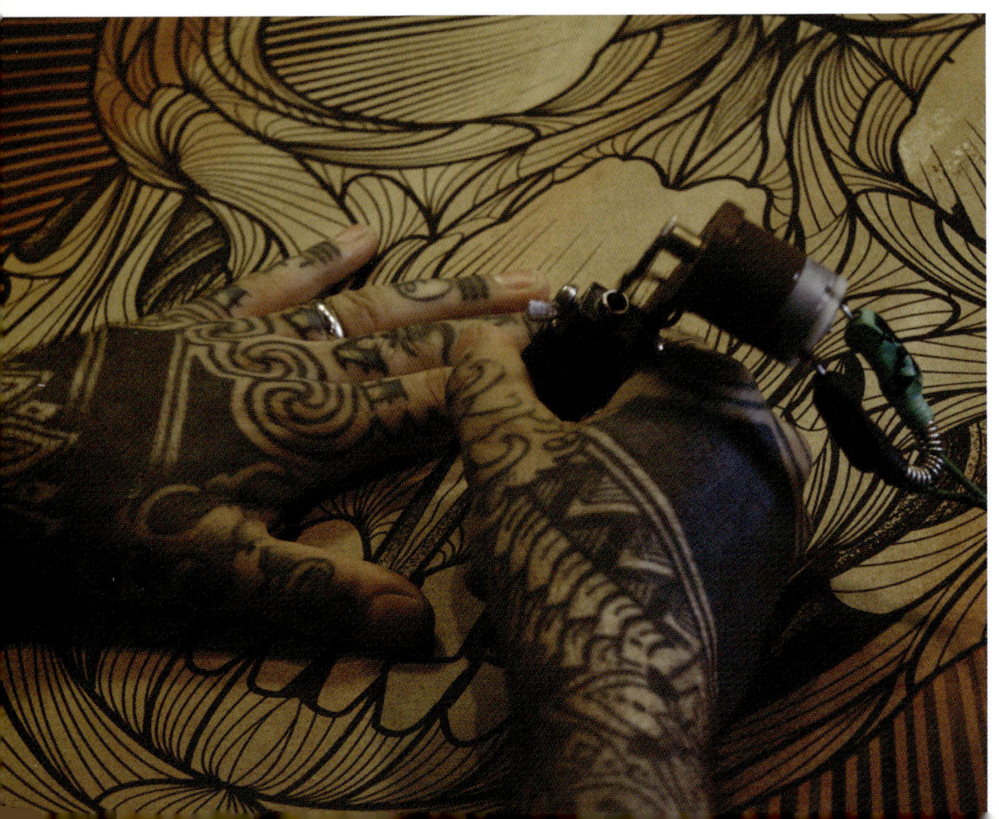

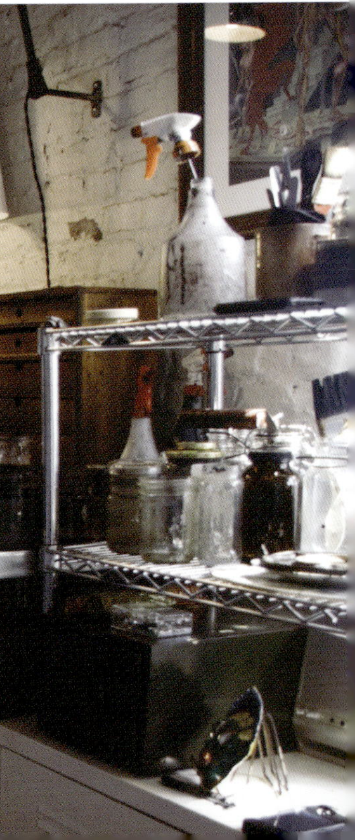

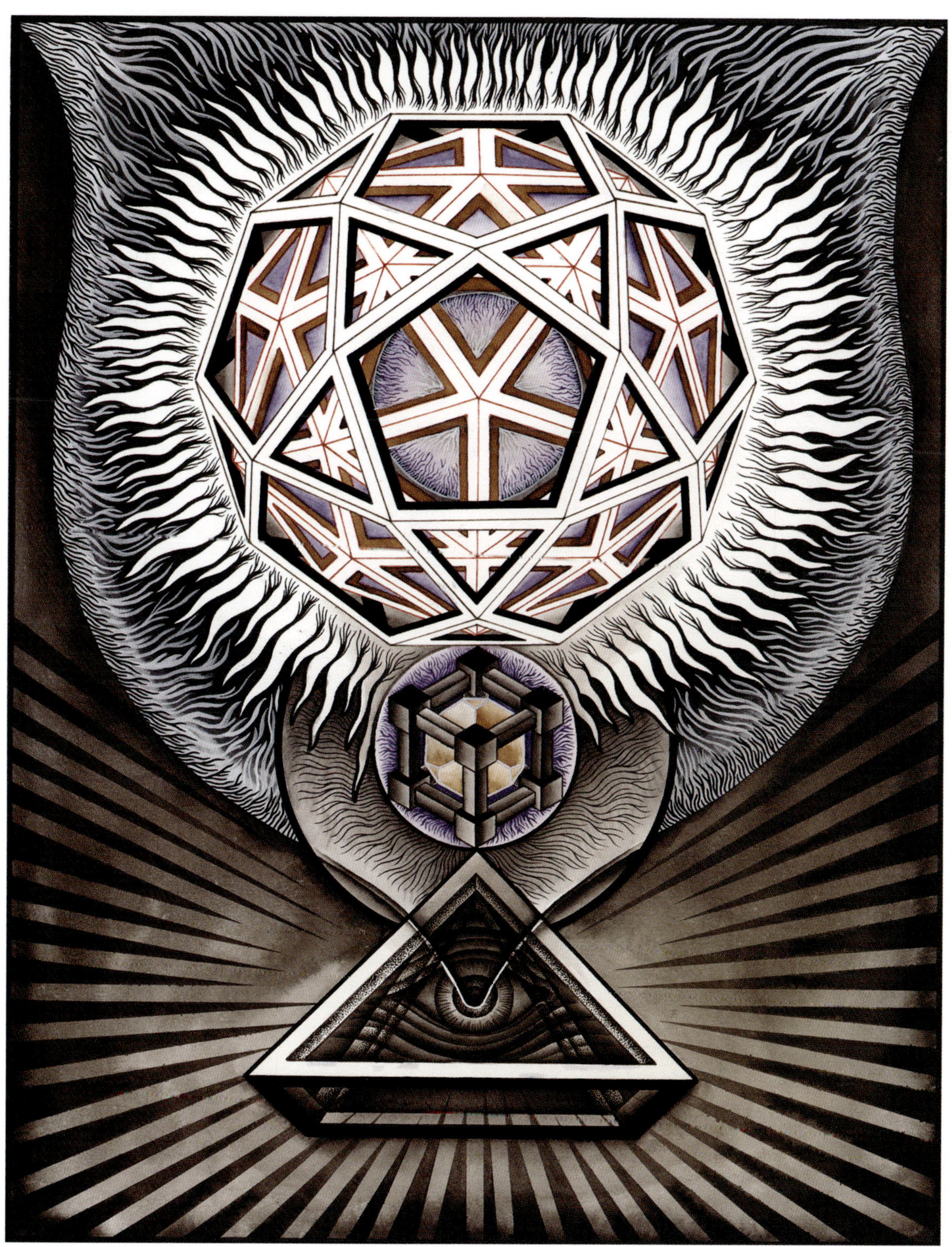

Thomas Hooper, Illumination, 2010, ink on paper, 38 x 30.5cm

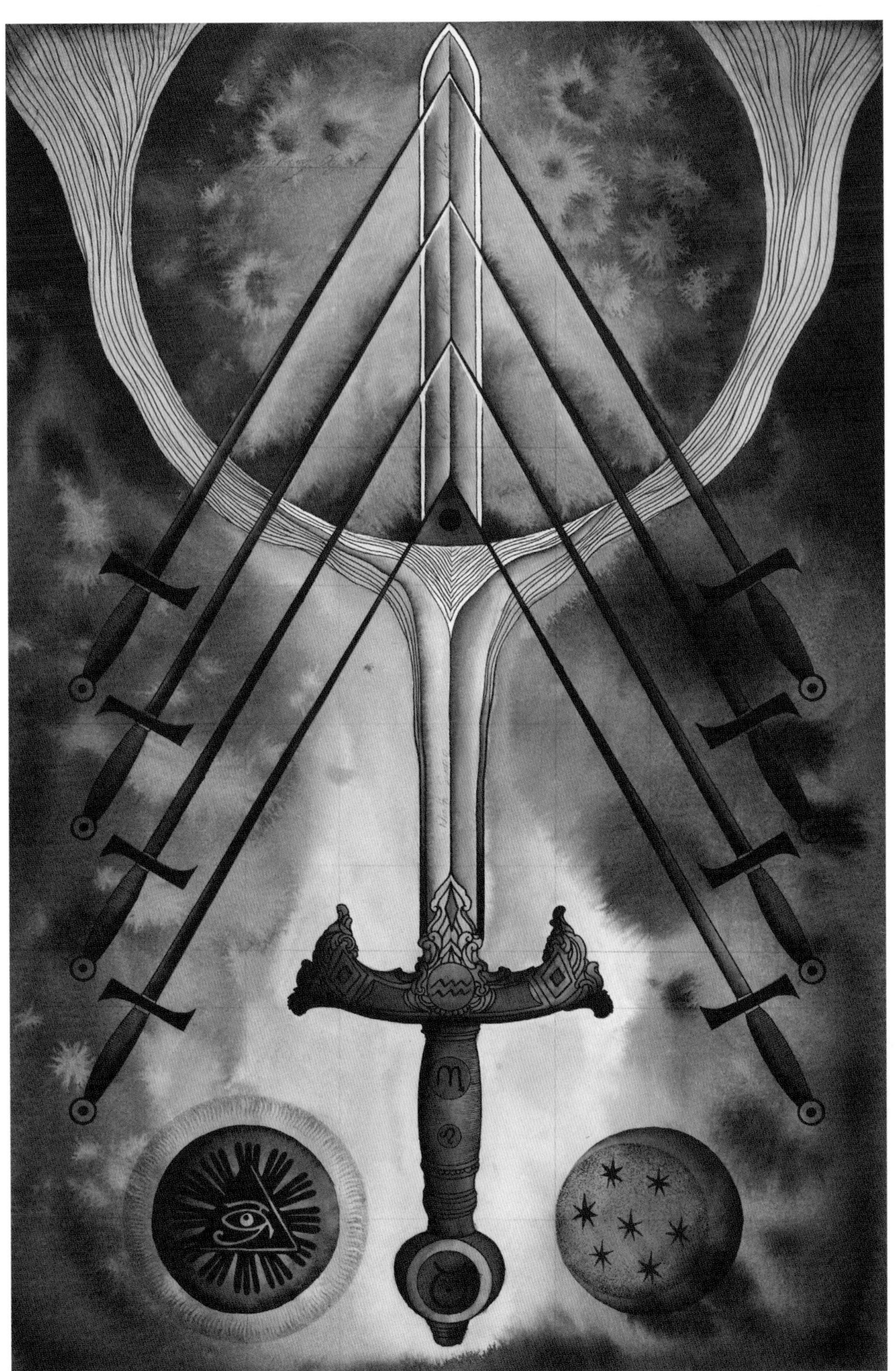

Thomas Hooper,
Tombs 5, 2011,
ink and graphite
on paper,
76 x 56cm

(opposite)
Thomas Hooper,
Wolf, 2009,
ink and acrylic
on paper,
76 x 56cm

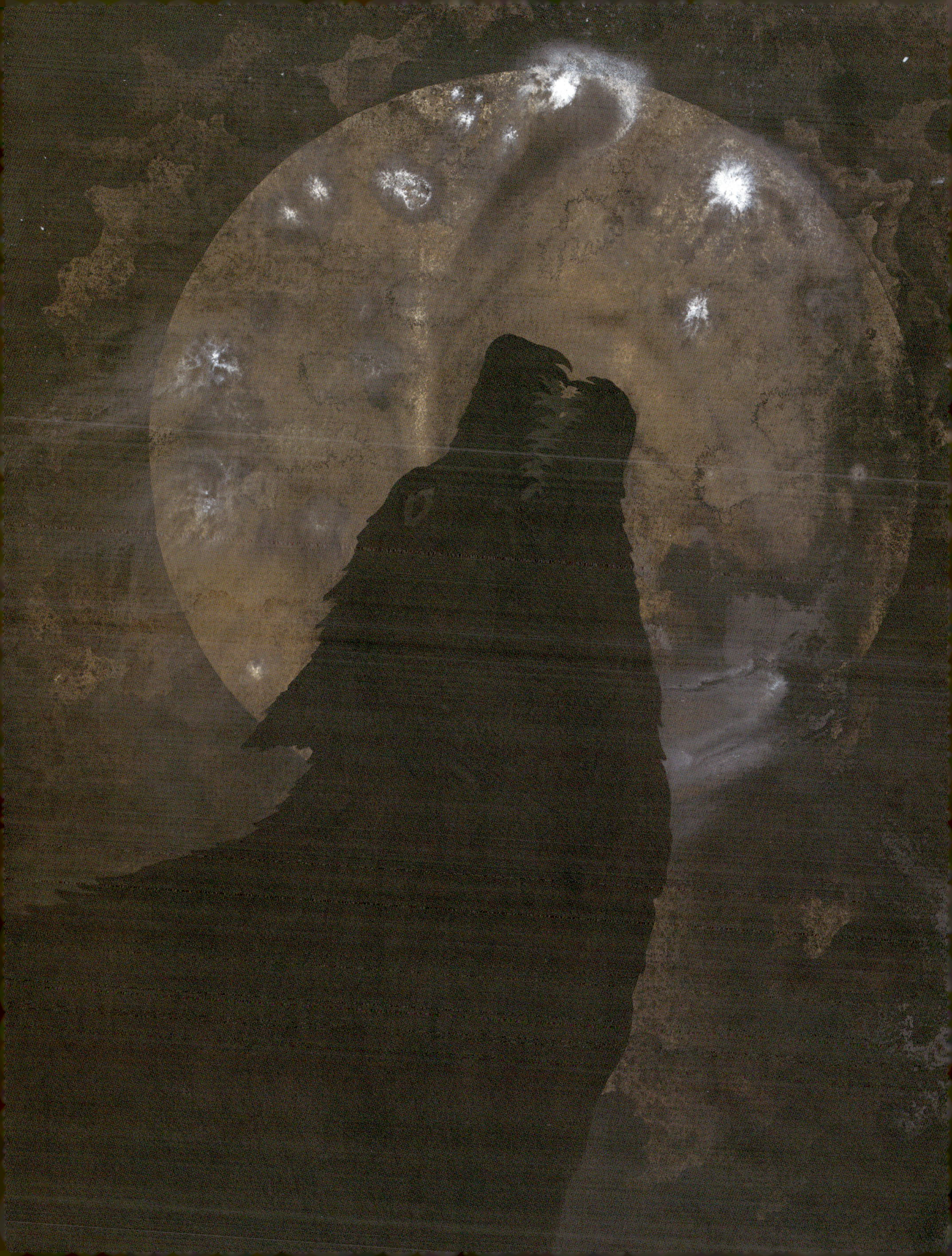

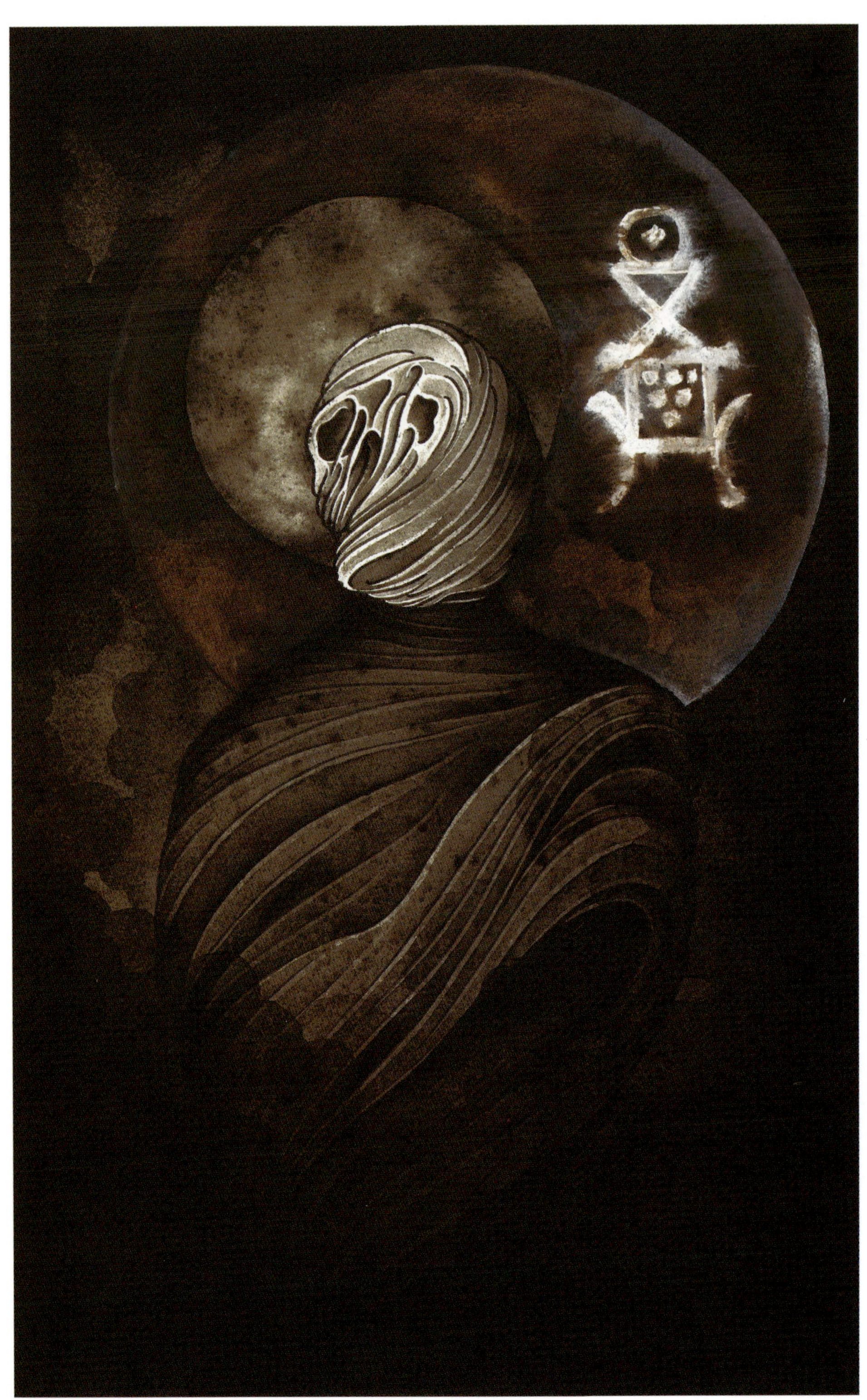

Thomas Hooper,
Shroud, 2009,
ink on paper,
23 x 16.5cm

(opposite top)
Thomas Hooper,
Surface to Air A,
2010, ink, acrylic and
gesso on paper,
56 x 76cm

(opposite bottom)
Thomas Hooper,
Surface to Air B,
2010, ink, acrylic and
gesso on paper,
56 x 76cm

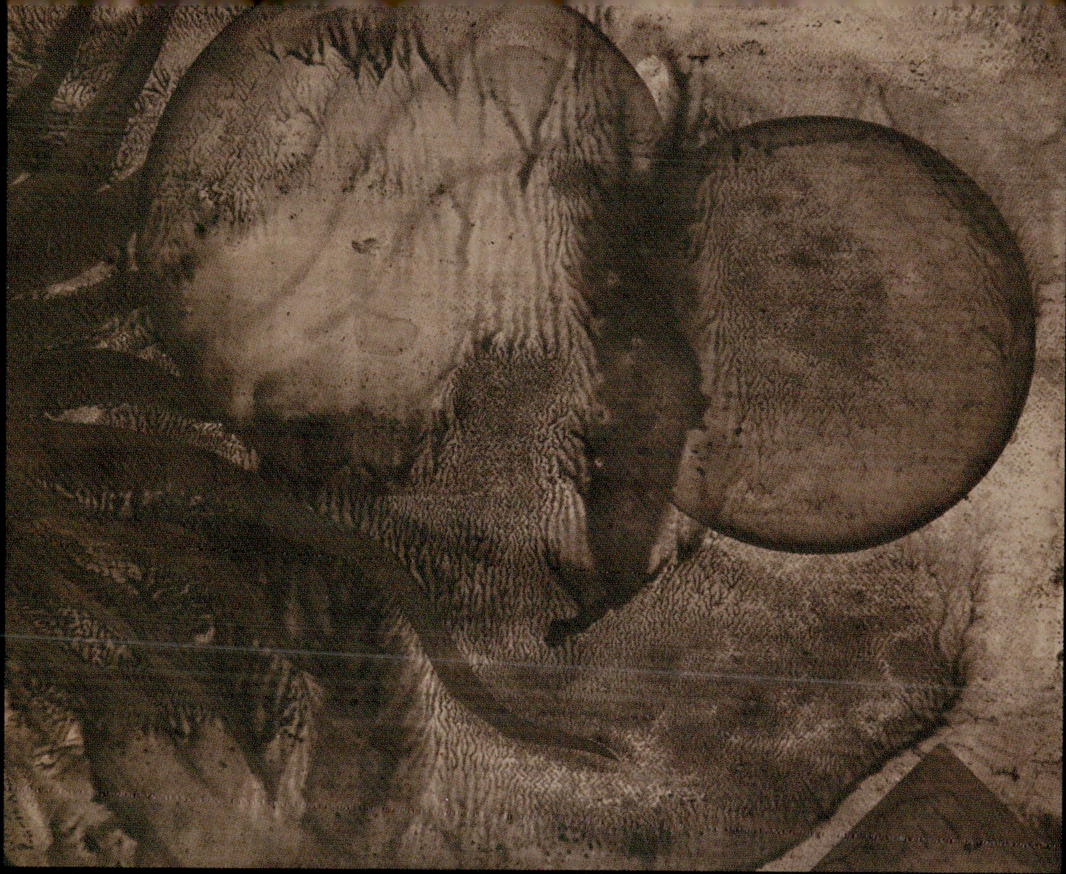

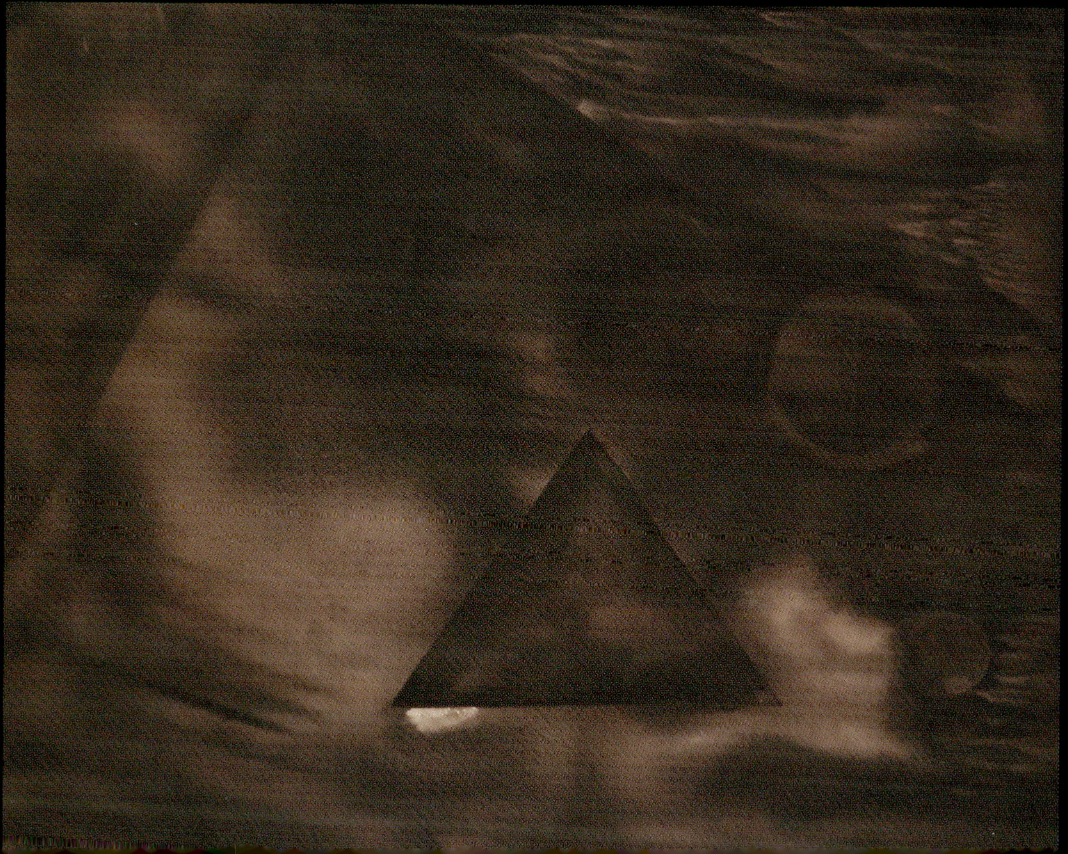

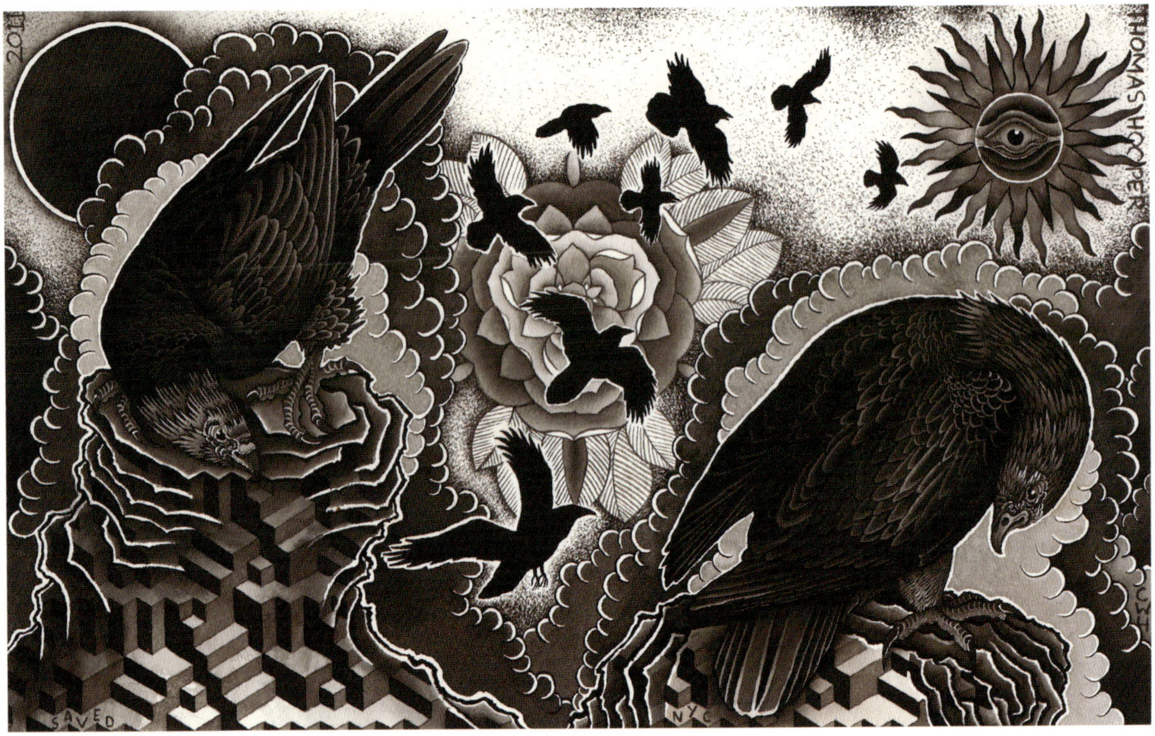

Thomas Hooper, Eagle and Raven Flash, 2011, ink on paper, 28 x 38cm

Outré Gallery and Publishing is a counter culture art salon, book merchant and store specializing in an array of alternative and underground artist goods from all over the world. Some call it lowbrow, others pop-surrealism – we like to think of our breadth as encompassing this but also going beyond.

We focus on limited edition prints, original artworks, hard-to-get curios and books – all with an edgy, off-centre feel.

With galleries in Melbourne, Sydney, and Perth (Australia), we specialize in mail order worldwide, feature exhibitions by international artists, publishing, specialist events and personalized service for new and experienced collectors.

Our publishing arm includes titles such as: *Tattoo Darling, Tattoo Mystique, Supersonic Swingers: New Works by Shag, Beatsville, Apartment Living is Great, Taboo: The Art of Tiki*, and forthcoming books including: *Night Flower – The Life and Art of Vali Myers, Thrift Store Art, Outré Journal*, and *The Art of Keith Weesner*.

OUTRÉ GALLERY PRESS

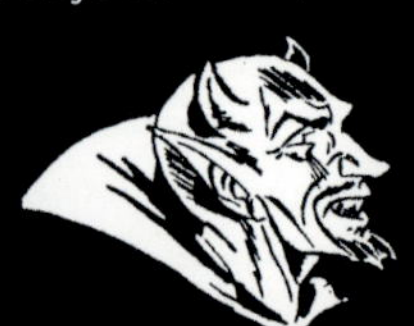

www.outregallery.com